Study Driven

Study Driven

A Framework for Planning Units of Study in the Writing Workshop

Katie Wood Ray

HEINEMANN • PORTSMOUTH, NH

Heinemann
A division of Reed Elsevier Inc.
361 Hanover Street
Portsmouth, NH 03801–3912
www.heinemann.com

Offices and agents throughout the world

The author and publisher wish to thank those who have generously given permission to reprint borrowed material:

"Real Trees: Where they come from. And where they came from." by Timothy Harper was originally published in Delta Airlines' *Sky* magazine (December 2004). Reprinted by permission of the author.

"Cheetah Chase" by Susan Yoder Ackerman. From *CLICK* magazine (July/August 2005, Vol. 8, No. 6), text copyright © 2005 by Susan Yoder Ackerman. Reprinted by permission of Carus Publishing Company.

"Backyard Camp Out" by Gerry Bishop. From the September 2004 issue of *Ranger Rick®* magazine. Copyright 2004 by the National Wildlife Federation®. Reprinted with the permission of the publisher, the National Wildlife Federation®.

(Credits continue on p. 290.)

Library of Congress Cataloging-in-Publication Data
Ray, Katie Wood, 1964–
   Study driven : a framework for planning units of study in the writing workshop / Katie Wood Ray.
     p. cm.
   Includes bibliographical references and index.
   ISBN 0-325-00750-0 (alk. paper)
   1. Creative writing (Elementary education). 2. English language—Composition and exercises—Study and teaching (Elementary). I. Title.

LB1576.R374 2006
372.62′3—dc22
                                               2006003258

Editor: Lois Bridges
Production: Elizabeth Valway
Cover design: Catherine Hawkes, Cat and Mouse
Interior design: Jenny Jensen Greenleaf
Composition: Publishers' Design and Production Services, Inc.
Manufacturing: Steve Bernier

Printed in the United States of America on acid-free paper
10 09 08 07 06 ML 1 2 3 4 5

To Shauna Jones

Contents

SECTION THREE Resource Sections 187

Acknowledgments

This book would not have been written if it weren't for the thinking I've been able to do with my current study group: Mark Hardy, Gaby Layden, and Isoke Titilayo Nia. They are three of the deepest thinkers I know, and I'm deeply indebted to each of them for stretching my thinking again and again in our twice-a-year retreats. When they read parts of this manuscript as I was writing it, they said it was *hard*, and coming from them, that's a good compliment. Thank you all three, and I look forward to lots more years thinking with you.

I first learned about genre study from Lucy Calkins and my colleagues at The Teachers College Reading and Writing Project, and everything I'm writing about now stands on the shoulders of what I learned while working at the project. Thank you to that group for all you have meant to my learning life and to the lives of so many others. Randy Bomer, especially, and the nonfiction study group he led while we worked together at the project, continue to influence my thinking in significant ways. You will see Randy's words quoted often throughout the book.

I'd also like to thank the three amazing teachers whose classroom studies directly informed the writing of this book. Emily Steffans, who took on the hardest study she could think of when she wanted to launch study in her writing workshop. Lisa Cleaveland, who's been my friend and colleague for years and who continues to push my thinking as I watch her engaged in deep study with her first graders. And Jenifer Smith, who took the idea of study and brought such richness to it in her fourth grade writing workshop. Thank you all three for so graciously sharing your teaching with me and for allowing me to share it with so many others.

A few friends have been especially helpful to me in the course of writing this book. Lester Laminack continues to be a true friend and inspiration, though I seem to see him mostly at the airport now! Thank you Lester for your continued collegiality long after we've both left the university. Mary Baldwin, Patricia Bricker, and Matt Glover have all offered encouragement along the way and been more than willing to help me think through some of the harder ideas as I've worked to make sense of them. Each of them has also helped in the sense that they've made the time spent writing far less lonely. A call or email in the middle of an eight- or nine-hour day in front of a computer screen is a very welcome diversion.

I'd also like to thank every school, school district, education coalition, summer institute gathering, and conference committee who have invited me into your midst these last few years. I deeply appreciate the opportunities you give me to come and meet such fine, fine teachers all across the country. And a special thank-you to those of you who've allowed me to come into your classrooms and teach your students. That aspect of my work means the world to me, and I want you to know how much I appreciate it.

In the past few years I've been privileged to work with many fine people at Heinemann, and I'd like to thank a few of them specifically. Tracy Heine has made my life infinitely less complicated by handling all the details of my consulting work for me. Thank you so much, Tracy, for all your help, and I wish you all the best in your new endeavors in life. Betsy Feldman and Angela Dion were fabulous to work with in getting my online courses up and running. Thank you both so much for all the work you did to make those courses a reality. And thank you to Vicki Boyd for the breadth of your vision when it comes to providing excellent professional development resources for teachers. It's been both a pleasure and an honor to work with you.

For this book specifically, I must send a big thank-you to Amy Rowe at Heinemann who worked so tirelessly to help secure all the permissions for reprinting whole texts in the book. Thank you, especially, Amy, for trying so hard to get people to lower their prices—I truly appreciate it! And Lois Bridges, my editor for the third time with Heinemann, thank you so much for all your support along the way. Thank you especially for being so accessible (and for answering emails almost immediately, even when I send them at 8:00 A.M. east coast time to you on the west coast). I've been honored to work with you.

My family, the Woods and the Rays, continues to be an endless source of support and encouragement to me. Thank you all, and especially thank you to my sister Shauna, to whom this book is dedicated. Now the secret is out—*I'm Shauna Jones' sister*.

And to my closest friend and companion, Jim Ray, once again, thank you . . . well, thank you just for everything, but especially for understanding how important it is to me to follow my convictions in my work. I promise I'll keep trying to have an idea like J. K. Rowling's, but until then, thanks for supporting me in writing about the ideas I do have.

Introduction

One of my favorite poets was doing a book signing at a recent conference I attended. As I approached her table, no one else was there so I decided to take the opportunity to tell her how much I loved her work. I explained that she was one of the few poets whose books I would order sight unseen. I told her that her anthologies of poems usually anchored any genre study of poetry I taught because I wanted children to see how she took a single topic and wrote a whole collection of poems about it. I told her how much the students I work with and I had learned from her about how to write poetry, particularly how to trust in the beauty and simplicity of images and words. I said that we loved her author's notes because they helped us understand how she found poetry in the world around her. I thanked her for all the many ways her poetry had enriched my teaching for years and said I couldn't wait for more and more wonderful books from her.

When I finally finished my somewhat effusive outburst, she asked me if I knew they had newly developed curriculum guides and lesson plans to go with many of the anthologies I'd just spoken of with such affection.

My heart sank just a little.

I tried not to show it and I said something like, "Oh, how wonderful." I didn't want to hurt her feelings and I knew she meant well, but curriculum guides and lesson plans were not what I wanted or needed. I mean, I'd just described in fairly specific detail how her books had been beside me, enriching my teaching for years! You see, what she didn't understand was that the teachers I work with, their students, and I anchor our *studies* of how to write poetry well in her anthologies of poems. If we had lessons, we wouldn't need study, and it's study that drives us.

We love study, and we love it for so many reasons. First, we love it in its full verb sense because it requires us—teachers and students—to be active in the pursuit of curriculum. Lock us in room full of this poet's books and let us have at them. Come back in a few days and we'll tell you more than you want to know about how to write poetry well, and, more importantly, we'll be writing some pretty good poetry of our own by then. We love to *study* things, and we know how to study things, and we love that there is nothing to the teaching unless we're there making it happen.

In contrast, lessons—even heady, interesting lessons—are already written and ask us to be sort of passive and just listen or do what they say. They would ask the same thing of the class next door, or the class across town. And though they may go by the name "study," we realize no one's really *studying* anything if the lessons are already written. We love engaging in work that asks more of us, as study does.

We love study because it allows us to ask very big questions about writing, questions that never feel finished, such as, "How do people write poetry really, really well? Where do they get their ideas? What's their process like, from ideas to finished poems?" Studies begin with questions like these, and then study itself, in the verb sense, leads us to answers. Lessons, on the other hand, begin with the answers already written. And sometimes, because they were written so far away from us, we're not even sure what the questions were to begin with.

We love study because it expands curricular possibilities. Who knows what we might learn in five days, locked in a room full of wonderful poetry? Lessons, necessarily, reduce curricular possibilities because someone must predetermine what they will be. That would be okay if we weren't dealing with such big questions in our studies. But to reduce a question like, "How does someone write poetry really, really well?" to a few manageable answers belies the complexity of the question itself, and we embrace its complexity.

Related to this, we love study because we are energized by the idea that we don't know exactly what we'll be talking about on, say, Thursday, but we know it will be good, because this poet's books are so good. We like knowing we have to contribute, we have to help build, the content that will lead us to Thursday. We find school much more interesting that way, when we play such an important role in shaping what happens there, and the expansionist stance of study makes it feel like anything is possible. When someone else has already done all that building and shaping for us, it's a little bit harder to get excited about it all.

We love study, and this book is about *study* as a driving force in the teaching of writing. I'm so excited to have finally written about it in such a way that I hope other teachers and students can get excited about it, too. I hope this book will give you both the confidence to engage in authentic study with your students (if you're not already doing that; I know lots of you are), and the practical know-how to fill your studies with rigor and challenge.

I've organized *Study Driven: A Framework for Planning Units of Study in the Writing Workshop* into three sections that move from grounded understandings to informed practice to supportive resources. I settled on this organization because it represents one of my most fundamental beliefs about teaching: that best practice is always *informed* practice. But I also believe we're at a critical juncture in our profession that calls on us to be even more than informed, it calls on us to be *grounded* in what we believe about teaching and learning.

As you look at the contents, you'll see that Chapters 1 through 7 are the "grounding chapters" and my hope is that they will build theoretical, foundational understandings about study as an instructional framework for the teaching of writing. Chapters 8 through 12 are the "informed practice" chapters and they explore each phase of an instructional framework for study in detail. In them, you'll find a suggested menu of possibilities for classroom work inside each phase. In Chapter 13, "The Tension of Time, the Promise of Depth," I've attempted to pull everything together and think about study as a realistic option in the time-pressed world of school where teachers and students live out their days.

In between each of these thirteen chapters, I have inserted twelve Craft Pauses, little time-outs to marvel at the wondrous words of writers. I've pulled the pauses from all walks of my reading life: children's literature, adult literature, poetry, journalism. The purpose of these pauses is twofold. First, they are celebratory. I love to celebrate wondrous words and take every opportunity I can to share them. I hope you enjoy them just for the sheer delight of writers writing well.

Second, the Craft Pauses are meant to demonstrate the kinds of things you and your students will learn about writing when you study it together. All of them I've pulled from my own years of looking closely at what writers are doing when they write well. I know that it may be hard to imagine what might come of study if you've never engaged in it, so in addition to what you will see in the regular chapters, I want the Craft Pauses to add another layer of demonstration of what's possible.

Finally, Section Three is the resource section and it begins with its own introduction that will help you understand how to use the resources. Following the introduction, I've included ideas for more than thirty different studies you might undertake in your writing workshop. Thirty ideas for studies are a lot of ideas, but actually my suggestions are in no way exhaustive. My hope is that as you read through them, some of them will appeal to you and you'll think, "I'd like to study this with my students," and others will give you ideas for studies you'd like to try that I haven't suggested as possibilities. After all, the beauty of knowing how to engage in study with your students is that you can study *anything* in basically the same way.

Grounded
Understandings

Two Snapshots of Studies in Action

Fifth Graders in a Genre Study of Commentary

On a Saturday afternoon in January, Emily Steffans went to the library and began searching through the archives of familiar newspapers and magazines. Emily was getting ready to launch a study of commentary in her fifth-grade writing workshop, and she wanted to find some good examples of this kind of writing for the study. She was looking for op-ed pieces by columnists who explore topics she thought might interest her ten- and eleven-year-old students, no small challenge for sure. The daily offering of opinions about what's happening in the world is found in these columns, often published with the writer's photograph beside them so readers can see the "voice" behind the writing. Randy Bomer (1995) has said of this type of writing that it is where "our society entertains its most important conversations" (185). The writing in op-ed columns ranges from reflective commentary—sometimes poignant, sometimes humorous, sometimes both—to the clear, staunch positioning more characteristic of editorials.

At the end of her search, Emily had six op-ed columns she felt could anchor her study and two writers (see Figure 1.1) who would become mentors for her students: Leonard Pitts of *The Miami Herald* (winner of the 2004 Pulitzer prize for commentary) and Rick Reilly of *Sports Illustrated* (voted "National Sportswriter of the Year" ten times). The topics of the columns she selected ranged from Reilly's thoughts on whether fourteen-year-old Freddy Adu is ready for a professional soccer career, to Pitts' boisterous commentary on how absurd he finds PJ Squares, ready made layers for peanut butter and jelly sandwiches, which ends with this thought: "If you're too busy to make a peanut butter and jelly sandwich, you're too busy." Emily photocopied the texts she selected and made each of her fifth graders a packet with their own copies for study.

FIGURE 1.1 *Texts Emily Selected to Anchor Her Study of Commentary*

"Ready-made Sandwich Just Too Convenient" by Leonard Pitts.
   The Miami Herald, November 17, 2003, www.miamiherald.com.
   Explores the issues of a time-pressed society and how people can take
   time-saving conveniences to ridiculous extremes.

"Ready Freddy" by Rick Reilly. *Sports Illustrated*, December 1, 2003.
   Considers whether fourteen-year-old soccer phenom Freddy Adu is ready
   to play in a professional soccer league.

"Worth the Wait" by Rick Reilly. *Sports Illustrated*, October 20, 2003.
   The story of a sixteen year old with cerebral palsy who runs track for his
   high school team with reflections on what this story says about life.

"A Year in the Life of Broken-Down Technology" by Leonard Pitts. *The Miami
   Herald*, December 1, 2003, www.miamiherald.com.
   Commentary on the high price we sometimes pay for the conveniences of
   technology in our lives.

"Expert Testimony" by Rick Reilly. *Sports Illustrated*, October 13, 2003.
   One of a number of Reilly's columns on the ongoing problems between
   Kobe Bryant and Shaquille O'Neil of the LA Lakers.

"The Fat of the Land" by Rick Reilly. *Sports Illustrated*, September 16, 2003.
   Reilly's thoughts on the sedentary lifestyles of many young people and the
   connection lifestyles have to obesity problems.

During their writing workshop time, Emily and her students immersed themselves in reading and rereading these texts along with other pieces of commentary
the students found and added to their packets. They used sticky notes and highlighters and empty margins to mark what they noticed about how the articles
were written. As they came together each day, the students charted their noticings (Figure 1.2) and used talk to deepen their understandings about how commentary is crafted effectively. Along the way they found specific lines of inquiry
they wanted to follow, such as why questions are so common and the role of
humor in this kind of writing. Emily often modeled with her own writing how
she might try the various techniques they found. Sometimes she invited the children to try things out with her in their writers' notebooks.

As the whole-class study progressed, students were also developing self-
selected topics for the pieces of commentary they would write near the end of the
study. Much of this idea building happened in their writers' notebooks, but it

FIGURE I.2 *Chart of Noticings from the Inquiry*

Commentary might . . .

✦ ask questions to introduce a topic—start with a lot then use the op-ed piece to answer them
✦ use repeating lines
✦ shorten topic sentences into one word (more appealing to the reader)
✦ use one-word questions for first sentence
✦ exaggerate to make a point or add humor
✦ compare the topic to something else (doesn't use the actual word to describe)
✦ use sarcasm when appropriate
✦ use lists of adjectives to describe
✦ use an interview related to topic or use quotes from others
✦ "pull out" a quote and make it bigger
✦ give solutions if the topic presents a problem
✦ insert small paragraphs of comments/opinion in between longer paragraphs
✦ use plain humor
✦ wait to introduce the topic until the middle so the reader doesn't stop reading because of the topic
✦ admit when the writer doesn't know the topic
✦ end with a personal comment/opinion/idea
✦ point fingers at people/things that are causes of the problem—but indirectly
✦ use a title that grabs interest, but doesn't give the topic
✦ use shocking facts
✦ use bullets to call attention to ideas
✦ change point of view if the goal was to make you think
✦ use personal comparisons
✦ give facts both pro and con

also included lots of talk about their topics, and some research and gathering of information they thought they might need for their writing. Studying the pieces of commentary Emily had gathered gave the students a feel for what kind of information they would need, such as quotes, statistics, and so on.

At the beginning of her study, Emily could not have named the specific content her students would uncover over the course of the next few weeks. But this didn't mean that Emily wasn't incredibly purposeful about what she wanted to come from the study. First, she had very specific, guiding questions she wanted the study to address:

- What kinds of topics are appropriate for commentary?
- How do writers of commentary develop their topics?
- How is commentary *crafted* in ways that makes it compelling for readers?

From experience, Emily knew a blank chart would always fill up with students' noticings. She's learned to turn these noticings into content-specific understandings, strategies, and techniques that address her guiding questions and that her students can use to gain increasing competence as writers. Because of this, Emily was comfortable to wait and see what would emerge as important content in the study.

Finally, while it may seem at odds with this wait-and-see stance to content development, Emily was also very planful about the course the study would take. She engaged in what Dorothy Watson called "planning to plan" (Watson, Burke, and Harste 1989). Knowing that studies of this kind aim for depth, not coverage, Emily determined in advance approximately how much time she would devote to each phase of the inquiry, and she developed short assessments to help her students pace themselves through the work of the study and to help her keep a handle on their progress. Figure 1.3 shows the three assessments she used during the study.

Because Emily's students knew they were expected to write something that was similar to what they had been reading, something that could take its place in their packet of commentary, their inquiry had that wonderful sense of urgency that writers who are expecting to write something know so well. When I visited her workshop midway through the study and conferred with some of her students, there was an almost tangible feeling of *living toward something* in the room, reminiscent of the feeling a class has when they are going on a trip or putting on a play. And because Emily had chosen such amazing writers to mentor her students, there seemed also to be a feeling among her students that what they would eventually write was going to be *good*.

After lots of study and conferring and time spent fine-tuning their drafts as best they could, Emily's fifth graders celebrated writing their very first commentaries, a kind of writing new to most of them only a few weeks before. They had written about the dangers of low carb diets, the risks of Internet chat rooms, the controversies of program funding in their local school district, and a rich variety of other self-selected topics. Because of the natural range of development in the room, there was certainly a range of quality in the writing, but Emily simply let each of her students write a piece of commentary as well as he or she could,

FIGURE 1.3 *Assessments to Guide the Study*

FIRST ASSESSMENT—EARLY IN THE STUDY

✦ Describe the topic you have chosen for your commentary. Explain it in detail and tell why you have chosen it.

✦ What material do you already have in your notebook related to your topic? When you finish these questions, put this sheet in your notebook where your topic is.

✦ Write about the plans for notebook work you want to do to support you in writing your commentary.

SECOND ASSESSMENT—AS STUDENTS ARE DRAFTING

✦ What techniques did you use in your commentary? Why did you choose them? Was there an op-ed piece we read that you found particularly helpful to you as a writer?

✦ Take me to the places in your draft where you tried specific techniques. Put a number by each spot. Walk me through your thinking about using them. Pay special attention here to helping me see how you used what we learned in the study to help you as you drafted.

✦ What revision have you started already? Did you find yourself changing parts as you wrote them? Have you read it aloud to yourself or to someone else? If you have not done any revising yet, what strategies do you think you'll use?

THIRD ASSESSMENT—AS STUDENTS ARE REVISING AND EDITING

✦ You should have read your draft aloud. Tell me what you found out about your draft as you did this. Be specific.

✦ Take me to the places where you revised. Put a number by each spot. Walk me through your thinking about the changes you made and why you made them.

✦ As you edited, what types of mistakes did you notice? Was there one type of mistake you noticed more than another? Why do think that's so?

and in doing so, made the task achievable for all of them. Figures 1.4 and 1.5 show two of her students' columns, selected because they represent a range of development.

Reflecting on the work the class did as a whole, Emily told me that what she loved most was that the op-ed columns really looked like fifth graders wrote them, but they also "just sounded so editorial-y."

FIGURE 1.4 *Student Commentary About Walmart*

What Will We Do?

I was just thinking about all the things going on in Columbia. It's sort of like what's going on in the country Columbia, with all the drug wars. But thankfully in our city it isn't drugs, but the 4th or 5th Walmart, all the construction and all the crazy bike lanes. You know: city stuff.

But why Walmart just about a mile from another one? Is it for the Laurie's and Kronke's view or convenience? Our Low's is so small compared to St. Louis, who probably has the same amount of Walmarts as us. Think about that Walmart.

But then again what's the big deal? Yes, it's a stupid idea, but think about it: It's a WALMART!!!!!! There's no stopping Walmart. Nobody revolted to putting bike lanes in crazy places. Nobody revolted to building those huge apartments behind Smithton! Since when did the smiling yellow guy become everybody's enemy?

Oh, and did you know that Sam Walton once said that if people wanted Walmart out of there, then they would get out of there? Bye, bye Sam, bye bye rollback dude, bye bye Walmart.

Guess what? Forget about that because they're still building it. Soon our town is going to be in the Guiness Book of World Records for most Walmarts per person! Yep, West Broadway is officially a non-smiley face free zone. Sign and all. But it could still be that somebody revolts or something happens. That'll be the day for the people who have a sign that looks like this: Walmart on West Broadway ☺ instead of this: No Walmart on West Broadway ☺.

Yes, they are even selling signs for about 5$ that protest against Walmart.

What will it be like in the future? How many of "Sam Walton's Paradises" will we have in Columbia? Hopefully not many more.

FIGURE 1.5 *Student Commentary About Shaquille O'Neal*

Should We Look Up to Him?

Why do people look up to Shaq. Why doesn't shaqs teammates respect him.

Shaq doesn't get along with he's teammates. Why I don't really know. But I know why he doesn't get alone with kobe. Because when kobe was injured kobe was talking a lot about shaq but shaq was not going for thet so he was sending bad messages back to kobe.

Why do you think Shaq would lose he's job. Well I think that shaq would lose his job because of arguing and threaning his teammates. I think his coach would not put up with it. And he would just throw him out of the game.

Why do you think that shaq does not play well. To give you an example he does more of arguing then playing. But don't get me wrong he can put on a show for you.

I think that shaq shouldn't be on tv because of he's temper problem. You would never know if the camera guy messes up and he start yelling at him.

Why do you think kids look up to him? Only why I look up to him is because he is a good player. But he can be a bad in flues for kids.

First Graders in a Study of How Writers Use Punctuation in Interesting Ways to Craft Their Texts

On a Thursday morning in November, the first graders in Lisa Cleaveland's writing workshop are having a conversation with their teacher about the work a particular mark of punctuation, an ellipsis, can do for a writer. The following is an excerpt of that conversation. As you read, notice how the talk moves seamlessly from the children's thinking to their writing to their reading, and eventually to a metaphor that captures the spirit of the work this mark can do in a text.

LISA: Before I write down all your explanations, let's just talk. What are you thinking about an ellipsis? Give me some reasons to use it—how you would use it as a writer.

CHASE: It could be used like if you're doing a surprise.

LISA: "Like if you're doing a surprise." Could you give me an example?

CHASE: Like, "Happy Birthday!" and then you open the present and it has a clown inside it.

LISA: Okay, so like you've got on the page, "Happy Birthday" and then an ellipsis, turn the page [does a page turning motion with her hand], and then there's the giant clown coming out.

CHASE: [Nods yes.]

LISA: And that's a place where you've used it with the text, and then as you turn the page, if there aren't even any words, you've used it to kind of leave the reader hanging until you see the illustration. That works. You could do that. You could totally use it like that. So kind of a surprise element is what you're thinking about. You know, turn the page and there's a surprise after you've used it. [A pause while everyone is thinking.]

CAROLINA: You could use it like a surprise party. Like you're hiding under a table and then you put a little ellipsis and you say, "Surprise!"

LISA: Okay, so what would your words be before the ellipsis? What would you be saying?

CAROLINA: Like, "One . . . two . . . three . . . " [her voices rises after each number indicating the placement of the ellipsis].

LISA: Oh and I hear it! Did you hear it in her voice? "One . . . two . . . three . . . " and then we turn the page and what do you have?

EVERYONE: SURPRISE!

LISA: And that would be the text? Surprise?

CAROLINA: [Nods yes.]

LISA: What about, have any of you ever used the ellipsis just at the end of something and just kind of left it? [There's a pause as everyone's thinking.] Umm, kind of like Caleb. Let's think about your book. How did it go with the roller coaster? What did you say on that page with the ellipsis?

CALEB: "But . . . I threw up."

LISA: Yea, it said something like, "We had fun on the roller coaster," and the next page said, "But . . . " and the next page said, "I threw up." So you kind of left us hanging when you said, "But. . . ." You know, we *thought* you were going to say, "But . . . it wasn't that fast" or "I'm so cool it didn't scare me." But instead you were like, "But . . . I threw up!" [Laughter in the room.]

ANNA: It's like a guy hanging off a cliff.

LISA: "It's like a guy hanging off a cliff." I like that. Explain that. Tell us more.

ANNA: It's like a guy hanging off a cliff and then everything freezes.

LISA: Because that ellipsis is kind of leaving you hanging there, like, "What's going to come next?"

ANNA: Yeah. Like he's thinking, "Am I going to fall or stay on the cliff?"

LISA: It's kind of got you in the middle, right? Like you're thinking it could go either way. Can you see that? Like what she said? You don't where it's going to go—where the text is going to go? I like that Anna.

[Another long pause as everyone is thinking.]

LISA: Umm, Carolina, do you remember when you read *The Whales* today, do you remember in there a place, or did you read where there was an ellipsis in that book?

CAROLINA: No, there wasn't any ellipsis but they showed what different kinds of whales there were.

LISA: At the end they did, but there is a place in there that has an ellipsis and I think that it's just leaving you hanging like that, she puts it at the end of that sentence, or she uses it just to leave you thinking. We'll look back into that in a little bit and I'll let you get that and read it to the class.

This conversation took place in the middle of a study of how writers use punctuation in interesting ways to craft their texts, and the goal of the study was to help these very young writers do just that. Lisa wanted her students to bring thoughtful intention to their work with punctuation, and to understand it as a powerful crafting tool available to them as writers.

Days before this conversation took place, Lisa had gathered a basket of picture books in a variety of genres with one thing in common: the writers had used punctuation in interesting ways to craft their texts. Her basket included several books, but here are a few of the titles:

Click, Clack, Moo, Cows That Type	Doreen Cronin
Diary of a Wombat	Jackie French
Eaglet's World	Evelyn Minshull
Hoptoad	Jane Yolen
Psssst! It's Me . . . the Bogeyman	Barbara Park
Puddles	Jonathan London
Roller Coaster	Marla Frazee
The Great Gracie Chase	Cynthia Rylant
The Wonderful Happens	Cynthia Rylant
Yo! Yes?	Chris Raschka

The children knew some of these books before the study even started, and some of them they were encountering for the first time. On one of the first few days of the study, Lisa sent the children out in groups of twos and threes with a book or two from the basket and a supply of sticky notes. Their work that day was to mark and make notes on pages where they saw punctuation being used in what they thought were interesting ways. Many of the children could not read all the words in the books independently, but that didn't stop them from being able to study the punctuation. Figures 1.6 through 1.10 show samples of children's notes from books.

FIGURE 1.6 *"I noticed it has an ellipsis and a period." From* Scarecrow *(1998) by Cynthia Rylant*

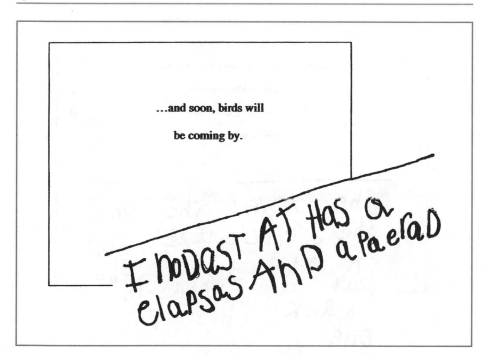

His wings pressed against hard roundness. His beak clicked.

Click-click. Click-click-click.

FIGURE 1.8 *"She used the word* she *intentionally and on the title she put an exclamation mark. This is one!"* From The Great Gracie Chase (2001) by Cynthia Rylant

Once there was a little round dog named

Gracie Rose. She was a very good dog.

She helped the bigger dog watch the house.

She kept the kitty company.

She even sang to the fish

When it was lonely.

FIGURE 1.9 *"(s)he writes commas" From* Hoptoad (2003) *by Jane Yolen*

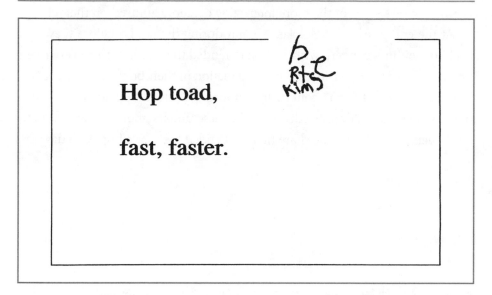

FIGURE 1.10 *Not clear what the note says, but the noticing led to lots of talk about a colon and the work it can do in a text. From* The Wonderful Happens (2000) *by Cynthia Rylant*

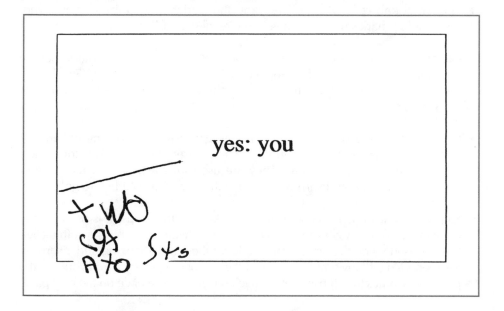

Over the course of the next few weeks in writing workshop, Lisa read aloud from the various books and she and her students studied the punctuation on the pages the children had marked. Using exploratory talk (Barnes 1992), they worked together to name the different kinds of work they saw various punctuation marks doing in the texts. As they encountered each new understanding about punctuation, Lisa helped them imagine using the marks in similar ways in their own writing. After lots of looking at texts and talking and imagining, they charted what they had learned about the potentials of different marks. Figure 1.11 shows some of the more interesting content captured on their chart.

At the end of each whole-class session during the study, before they went back to their independent writing, Lisa reminded the children to be very intentional as they made decisions about punctuation in their books. In writing conferences, she asked them about their decisions, and she differentiated the kinds of help different children needed to make these understandings about punctuation their own. During the share time that ended the workshop each day, Lisa

FIGURE 1.11 *Highlight of the Punctuation Chart from the First-Grade Study*

✦ You would not use a period in a title.

✦ The writer knows how she or he wants the reader to read the writing. Every punctuation mark says something to the reader—it tells you how to read it.

✦ Exclamation mark. Use it at the end of a sentence. Exclamation marks can be used for anger! Happiness! Crying! Fear! Telling someone to stop (Stop! No!). Joy! Loud! Big and bold! Screaming! Anything you want to be read with lots of expression.

✦ Comma. It is used when you want a little pause in your writing (when you think the reader will need a pause). It may be used when you say someone's name (Lauren, how are you?). They are used in a list: dogs, cats, clothes, Gameboy, jewelry, and surprises! Or like this: Yes, I would like to go!

✦ Ellipsis. Use it to pause (stop a little bit). A "thinking ellipsis" is used for the reader to think about what the writer has said. A "wait, something is coming" ellipsis is used when the writer wants to leave the reader hanging and a surprise idea is coming. Many times it is used at the end of the sentence and you turn the page. Sometimes the ellipsis is at the beginning of the sentence on the next page.

✦ Colon. Use it when you have a list coming or if you are getting ready to say something important (quotation or explanation). A list colon: "On the farm there are many animals: horses, cows, pigs, sheep, and dogs." A quotation colon when something important is said: "My mom was so mad she said: Get your clothes off the floor!"

✦ Parentheses. Used to go around a remark or words said to the side. A little more information is given to what is being talked about. "And soon the whole town was watching (or running in) the Great Gracie Chase!"

had children explain the different punctuation decisions they were making (that's how they knew about Caleb's "throwing up" page with the ellipsis on it).

Eventually the study of how writers use punctuation in interesting ways had to end, but the thinking about it didn't stop. Talk about punctuation extended across the year and became just one more way the children looked at published texts and thought about their own work as writers. Figures 1.12 through 1.14 show some interesting ways the children used punctuation to craft their texts across the year.

FIGURE 1.12 *Hyphens are used to stretch out the word* long—*making the way it's written match the word's meaning. "Four giraffes with their l-o-n-g, l-o-n-g necks eating leaves."*

FIGURE 1.13

We went to Fun Depot

I went to the batting cage.

Laser Tag

I went to the roller coaster.

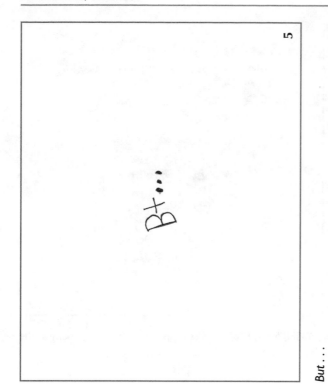

But . . .

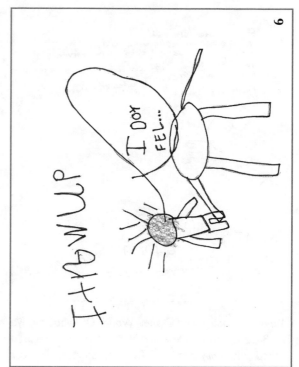

I threw up. I don't feel . . . .

FIGURE 1.14

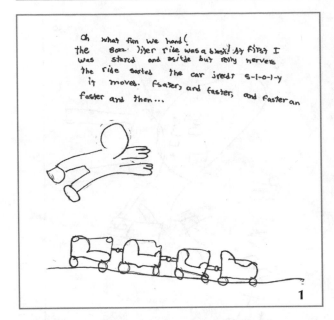

From Anna's memoir about Disney World: Oh what fun we had! The Buzz Lightyear ride was a blast! At first I was scared and excited but really nervous. The ride started. The car jerked. S-l-o-w-l-y it moved. Faster, and faster, and faster and faster and then . . .

WOSH! It went so, fast like a flash of lightening, jerking in the sky.

Oh what fun we had! Eating the cotton candy was so, yummy, I could not stop eating (And oh I was a mess). Oh what fun we had!

Immersion and Inquiry in the Teaching of Writing

Study Driven is a book about the instructional framework both Emily and Lisa used to carry out this teaching in their writing workshops. Perhaps you noticed this framework embedded in the stories you just read. Lifted from the particulars of these teaching stories, the framework looks like this:

Gathering Texts	The teacher, sometimes along with students, gathers examples of the kind of writing students will do.
Setting the Stage	Students are told they will be expected to finish a piece(s) of writing that shows the influence of the study.
Immersion	During immersion (Cambourne 1988) the teacher and students spend time reading and getting to know the texts they'll study. They make notes of things they notice about how the texts are written. They think about the *process* writers use to craft texts like the ones they are studying.
Close Study	The class revisits the texts and frames their talk with the question, "What did we notice about how these texts are written?" The teacher and students work together to use specific language to say what they know about writing from this close study, developing curriculum as they go. The teacher, through modeling, takes a strong lead in helping students envision using what they are learning in their own writing.
Writing Under the Influence	Students (and often the teacher) finish pieces of writing that show (in specific ways) the influence of the study.

Framing instruction as study represents an essential stance to teaching and learning, an *inquiry stance*, characterized by repositioning curriculum as the outcome of instruction rather than the starting point. In this particular set of practices, the students' noticing and questioning around the gathered texts determine what will become important content in the study (the teacher doesn't determine this in advance), and depth rather than coverage is the driving force in the development of this content.

The idea of "uncovering curriculum" through inquiry certainly is not new (Harste 1992; Short and Harste 1996; Short, Schroeder, Laird, Kauffman, Ferguson, and Crawford 1996; Whitin and Whitin 1997) but it seems to have taken hold more as a teaching stance in integrated, content-area studies. In these studies, writing is used as a tool for learning and as a means to communicate that learning, but in the instructional framework just outlined, an inquiry stance is used to uncover curriculum *about writing itself*.

This book is about how to do this kind of inquiry work with your students, and I'd like to suggest that whether you teach kindergarten or college, using inquiry to generate at least some writing curriculum during the year is a sensible thing to do. I understand this is a bold claim, and in the next chapter, I'll explain the thinking behind it. My hope is that the snapshots from Emily's and Lisa's classrooms have given you an image of this work that you can return to again and again as you read forward in the book.

Craft Pause

NOTICE

In one of her "Talk of the Town" columns for *The New Yorker* about a party to celebrate the publication of Merv Griffin's autobiography, Jamaica Kincaid uses the word *great* (or some form of *great*) twenty-three times in the span of the approximately 700-word piece. Almost every sentence uses the word at least once. Here's a little excerpt with three *greats* in it (notice the rich comma work too):

> [the] chess set was great, and it had a real marble board; Bobby Short, the great saloon singer and pianist, was there, and he looked great; Edwin Newman, that St. George of the English Language, was there, and a lot of people were willing to swear that his presence alone was great.
>
> —From the collection *Talk Stories* (2001, 196–98)

From the opening lines of a vignette in Kathi Appelt's memoir *My Father's Summers—A Daughter's Memoir* (2004, 114) titled "Films in P.E.":

> We had to get permission slips signed by our parents in order to see the films in P.E. Every seventh-grader lived for the end of the spring semester when we would finally get to see the films in P.E. Legend had it that each year someone fainted while watching the films in P.E. and often a teacher would have to assist a student who broke down while experiencing the films in P.E. Even teachers were known to swoon, so gripping were the films in P.E.

In his commentary from 3/5/2000 published in *The Independent* (an international newspaper based in London), Salman Rushdie uses the word *mistake* nine times in six sentences totaling 140 words. He's writing about the verdict in the Amadou Diallo case where the jury acquitted all four police officers of any wrongdoing in the shooting, saying it resulted from a tragic *mistake*. Here's an excerpt:

> These mistakes were themselves the consequences of earlier mistakes. The policemen saw a black man on his own doorstep and made the mistake of thinking he was a criminal. They thought he reminded them of a sketch they'd seen of a rapist but, er, they were mistaken.

INSIGHTS ABOUT CRAFT

When a word or phrase is deliberately overused in a text, it draws significant attention to that word. Writers might choose to do this for a number of reasons. The overuse can convey a sardonic, mocking tone, as if the writer is saying, "This is what everyone else is saying, but don't believe a word (or perhaps *the word*) of it." Overusing a word or phrase can also convey a sense that the words themselves, and the saying of them, have taken on almost legendary significance.

2

Making a Case for Study

"Let's just talk. What are you thinking about an ellipsis?"

In the previous chapter, Lisa Cleaveland began a conversation about punctuation one morning with her first-grade students when she asked them this question, and there was no content to her teaching until the children started talking.

In many ways, this simple question—and the conversation that came about because it was asked—holds so much meaning about the work I am writing about in *Study Driven*. That's why I've chosen to return to it here. I introduced you to Lisa, and to a fifth-grade teacher, Emily Steffans, in the last chapter and showed you how they used the same instructional framework for study to develop curriculum through inquiry in their writing workshops. The purpose of this chapter is to explain why inquiry makes sense as a stance in the teaching of writing. But first, a little about the significance of Lisa's question.

In Peter Johnston's provocative book, *Choice Words: How Our Language Affects Children's Learning* (2004), he talks about "loaded invitations" that "construct particular identities" (17). "What are you thinking about an ellipsis?" I believe, is one such loaded invitation. In the simple act of asking this question, Lisa is teaching her students to think of themselves as people who *would* be thinking about an ellipsis. She is helping construct this particular identity in them, and their responses communicate she's doing a good job. They seem to believe they are the kinds of people who would, indeed, be thinking about an ellipsis.

Having studied her teaching for years, I know that Lisa fills her classroom with loaded invitations. Off and on all day, across content areas, she invites her students to tell her: "What are you thinking? What did you notice? Tell me more. Can you give me an example?" And certainly more important even than her offering these invitations, is what she does with the children's responses. She *makes* something of them. She uses them to develop important content that they can see hanging on the charts in the room. Her students' responses aren't just fillers to engage them for a moment before she gets on to the important stuff she wants to say; their responses *are* the important stuff.

Which leads me to the second thing that is so meaningful about the question, "What are you thinking about an ellipsis?" As I said before, there is no content until the children start talking. In their teaching, Lisa and Emily both make student responses the "important stuff" from which their writing curriculum is made. To state the obvious, there is no study without the students. And this is a decision these two teachers are making, a stance they are deliberately taking. There certainly could be content without students. There are definitions of an *ellipsis* and lots of other marks in any dictionary, writer's guide, or language arts textbook, and lessons could be planned using these definitions as content whether there were students there or not. But to have a *study* of punctuation—or commentary or anything else for that matter—you have to have students. As I pointed out in the introduction, the word *study* is both a noun and a verb, and that gives it a two-sided potential. For there to be a study in the noun sense, there has to be someone there to enact it in the verb sense, and that someone is students.

My challenge in this chapter is to make a case for choosing *study* rather than *content* as a point of departure in the teaching of writing. The intended outcome is exactly the same: sound, rich writing curriculum, it is how you get there that is different. And I have to make this case carefully because it runs counter to what seems to be the prevailing notion that standardized curriculum (*studies* only in the noun sense—predetermined series of lessons on a topic) is somehow more rigorous curriculum. I don't believe this, of course. I've never come across any standardized curriculum for first graders that suggests they might articulate the subtle, nuanced differences in the ways an ellipsis can be used. I also know that the only way to have standardized curriculum is to develop it far away from the students who'll be expected to use it as writers.

Let me explain now the rationale for taking an inquiry stance in the teaching of writing and why I believe "writing as study" is the most sensible point of departure. As I move through this explanation, I'll return often to the snapshots of Emily's and Lisa's studies to illustrate the thinking. I'll begin with what I believe are the teaching alternatives to an inquiry stance.

Other Possible Teaching Stances

One alternative teaching stance is not to connect the teaching to the study of any real-world (as opposed to school-world) examples of writing at all. If Emily decided to teach this way, quite likely her teaching would go something like this: First, she'd give her students a generic definition of the kind of writing they would be doing, say something like *persuasive* writing, defined as "trying to convince a reader of your point of view on an issue." Next, she'd give them some sort of graphic organizer or outline to use to organize their writing, and then as an example, she'd model writing a piece this way herself or lead the class in writing one together. Then, she'd ask her students to write their own.

If Lisa had taken this stance with her first graders and their study of punctuation, her teaching probably would go something like this: She'd teach them about one mark at a time over a series of days, writing example sentences to show each mark being used in the way she was teaching about it. Following this, she would give the students practice sentences and ask them to figure out where the marks should go.

Another alternative to inquiry is to use quality, real-world examples of writing, but instead of studying the texts with students, Emily and Lisa would point out the features they wanted students to attend to in the texts. In this case, they'd determine ahead of time which aspects of the writing they'd be teaching each day and would have selected their examples carefully to show these predetermined features. This teaching, which often also includes teacher modeling, usually happens in a series of directed lessons often called a "unit of study," but not involving any real study at all. With this alternative, it is possible to plan out the lessons ahead of time, and even for the lessons to be put together so they can be used in other classrooms.

I suppose there is also the alternative many of us experienced in school: no teaching at all. When this is the stance, students are simply given assignments for writing, they complete them, turn them in to the teacher, and then get them back with a grade on them. But since this a book about the *teaching* of writing, I don't need to spend any more time on this alternative.

And then there's inquiry that grows from studying well-written texts with students. The reality is, of course, that teaching often overlaps all of these alternative stances at different times in different ways. What matters most is what the basic stance to the teaching will be. Emily's and Lisa's basic stance was to generate the curriculum through inquiry with their students. Without a doubt, taking an inquiry stance in teaching takes more time than the alternative stances, so the investment of time needs to be worth making.

Let me explain now the reasons I think this is such a critical teaching decision, and as we go along I'll be careful to align my explanation with other professional literature so it's situated in a broader context.

Reading Like Writers

When teachers immerse students in reading and studying the kind of writing they want them to do, they are actually teaching at two levels. They teach students about the particular genre or writing issue that is the focus of the study, but they also teach students to use a habit of mind experienced writers use all the time. They teach them how to *read like writers* (Ray 1999; Smith 1988), noticing as an insider how things are written. Students learn to look at texts the way a mechanic looks at cars or a musician listens to music, to use the particular knowledge system of a writer (Harste 1992). Over time they learn to notice things about writing that other people (who don't write) don't notice, and all along the way this noticing helps them develop a vision for the writing they will do. If Emily and Lisa had done all the noticing for their students, pointing out the features they wanted them to see in the gathered texts, their students would have had no reason to learn to notice text features themselves. This is particularly critical to genre study.

That writers—even experienced writers—would read the kind of thing they are getting ready to write (genre study) is a lifelong habit. In the past two years I've had to read in this very specific way on three different occasions: twice because I was planning to write in a new genre for me (a foreword and an abstract), and once because I was writing for a journal I don't normally read. In this case, the genre—a professional article—was familiar, but genre is more than just form, it's also a "social category" (Kress 1999). I wasn't a part of the "society" that reads this journal, so I read back issues to get a feel for it. I was reading to get a clear vision for the kind of thing I wanted to write, and it's the kind of reading Emily was teaching her fifth graders to do with their genre study inquiry.

When I think about an inquiry stance, I always feel like this reason alone—*inquiry teaches students to read like writers*—is reason enough to teach from this stance as often as possible. Why? Because so many professional writers give the same advice when asked what a person should do to become a writer: *you have to read,* they say. It is discipline-based inquiry (Berghoff, Borgmann, and Parr 2003) that puts reading at the forefront of the teaching and lets students develop a knowledge base about good writing in the same way professional writers develop theirs.

Grounded Teaching

Of studies in school, John Dewey has said, "Anything which can be called a study, whether arithmetic, history, geography, or one of the natural sciences, must be derived from materials which at the outset fall within the scope of ordinary life-experience" (Dewey 1938, 73). While Dewey doesn't include writing in his list, I believe he could have, and his claim points to the significance of gathering real-world texts for inquiry. The kind of writing Emily wanted to study certainly exists "within the scope of ordinary life experience." Every newspaper, every day, has an op-ed page with examples of commentary on it, so there was no need to look outside that "scope of ordinary life experience" for material. And certainly there was no need to study punctuation outside of how it is used in actual texts. After all, their study wasn't about marks; it was about how writers *use* marks, and that's very different. Good writing is filled with evidence of writers' decision making about how punctuation should go.

When the first move in teaching is to gather real-world texts, this move provides some insurance that the teaching will be grounded and, for lack of a better word, *true*. Inevitably, when teachers teach writing without any real-world writing attached to it, they end up teaching things that just aren't true, or at least they aren't true all the time. Edgar Schuster (2004) calls theses things "mythrules." Anyone who has moved from a lesson-delivery stance to an inquiry stance has stories to tell about having to reconsider the content of his or her teaching.

Take, for example, the rule of thumb so many of us learned about the type of writing Emily asked her students to do: state the main idea in the first paragraph, and then give the reasons for holding that idea in subsequent paragraphs. But if you actually look at writing of this kind, most of it isn't written this way at all. Writers sometimes don't state their main idea until the very end, and sometimes they state it right in the middle as a turning point in the text.

There are so many examples like this, and particularly in the realm of usage issues. The *truth* is, writers of commentary (and many other kinds of writing) often purposefully exploit usage at so many turns as a way of, particularly, creating voice (Fletcher 1993; Romano 2004) in their texts. For example, that's exactly what Leonard Pitts (2003) is doing in this excerpt from a column about the now infamous Shaquille O'Neal–Kobe Bryant feud over whose team the Lakers is:

> Sometimes, I think you forget that. You and all the other millionaires who show up at games driving dream cars and leave them trailing dream women. Sometimes, I think you forget what it means when I allow you the privilege of coming into my home. The privilege of my support.

Pitts makes his sentences work together, sharing understood connections, giving the writing the sound of someone sort of holding forth on an issue, adding a little more "punch" to a point as an afterthought. He and other writers of commentary do this kind of language work all the time. When teachers teach writing with no writing attached to it, they rarely (if ever) teach *that* about it, and yet it's such a big part of what people who do this kind of writing know well.

With an inquiry stance, teachers let the writing itself shape and define what the content will be, and they are willing to accept the gray area that comes with that. "Inquiry does not narrow our perspective; it gives us more understandings, questions, and possibilities than when we started" (Short, Schroeder, Laird, Kauffman, Ferguson, and Crawford 1996, 8). There isn't just one way to write commentary, and there aren't just a few simple things to know about this kind of writing. By nature the content is expansive, nuanced, and full of alternatives. And if teachers try to change it into something simpler because the students are, after all, just ten- and eleven-year-olds doing this kind of writing for the first time, they end up teaching something that just doesn't ring true.

I understand that when teaching is simplified, when children are given a graphic organizer and a few simple guidelines to follow, they sometimes produce tighter, more polished-looking products than the writing I typically see students write out of inquiry. But when this happens, the very nature of what is being taught has fundamentally changed because writing doesn't exist like that in the world outside school. Edgar Schuster says he's been looking for a five-paragraphed theme in published materials since he started teaching in 1958 and has yet to find *a single one* (2004).

Related to this, if teachers eliminate the gray areas and give students a simple way to write something, not only is the teaching not true to the product, it isn't true to the process either. Outside of school, when faced with tasks that require composition, writers have to figure out how to write things. No one gives them a graphic organizer, and the struggle to organize and make everything work together is there anew every time they set out to write. This struggle is an essential part of the writing process, and if it's taken away, students develop a very false sense of how real writing gets done. In other words, what begins as an instructional decision, to have students use graphic organizers, becomes a curricular problem. Students learn something about process that just isn't true.

In an inquiry stance, teachers help children explore different alternatives for how to write something, and then they let them do what writers really have to do and make decisions about how their pieces will go. Does this make it harder on students? Perhaps. But when teachers simply ask them do it as well as they can and understand it will take lots of experience for them to get really good at it, it makes it achievable. Then, while students are getting that experience, what they are learning is grounded in the realities of real-world writing, both product and process.

Expanding Knowledge Base

In a conference with one of Lisa's first graders one morning, I asked Carolina to tell me about why she had decided to use a colon in the sentence you see in Figure 2.1.

FIGURE 2.1 *A Page from Caroline's Book About Daschaunds*

After she explained it was because of the list that followed, she lowered her voice in a conspiratorial whisper and told me, "Mrs. Cleaveland didn't even know what a colon was until she was in fifth grade."

Lisa had honestly shared with the children how much more sophisticated their understandings about punctuation were than the ones she'd learned in school—even in high school. Since I've been alongside Lisa so much the last few years, she and I have often commented that we've learned as much as the children have in many of the studies, and in the punctuation study especially. When we were in school, we just never really looked at how punctuation was actually used by very skilled writers, and we certainly never spent much time on some of the marks that do some of the most interesting work, marks like parentheses, ellipses, and colons. We spent so long trying to memorize all those comma "rules" that we never got around to these other marks.

Similarly, as Emily reflected on her study of commentary, she felt she had learned as much, if not more, than her students. I believe it's a good thing for teachers to feel like they're learning as much as their students during inquiry. If a teacher begins a study in writing by planning out what she wants to teach from her existing knowledge base, the study is necessarily limited to what that teacher knows. And I've learned from my own experience that often I don't even realize how limited my knowledge base is until I engage in inquiry with students.

As Kathy Short and Carolyn Burke (1991) point out, "For any curricular framework to be useful and generative, it must support all learners in the community (adults and children) in inquiry" (68). And teachers of writing, especially, *need* inquiry because to be content experts in every single genre of writing, on every aspect of craft and every writing process issue that arises is a tall order. But recognizing that you don't have the content expertise you'd like to have in writing doesn't have to limit your teaching or your students' learning. You can have *instructional* expertise instead. Instructional frameworks like the one Emily and Lisa used help teachers plan and implement generative inquiries that can be used to study any aspect of writing. The stack of texts changes, but the way the inquiry happens stays basically the same.

Now, over time, content expertise is certainly a by-product of instructional expertise. Emily knows a lot more about writing commentary than she did before this inquiry, and from future studies, she'll learn even more. Lisa's understandings about the workings of punctuation are extensive and nuanced after all her study with children through the years. As a matter of fact, both these excellent teachers could just as easily deliver a heady, interesting series of lessons on how to write commentary or use punctuation in interesting ways, attach them all to real-world text examples, and not engage in any inquiry with their students at all. But they're not likely to do this.

In their wonderful book *Understanding by Design* (2001), Grant Wiggins and Jay McTighe say, "If students are to understand what is known, they need to simulate or recreate some of the inquiry by which the knowledge was created" (33). Removing the inquiry from the teaching would diminish students' need to read and think like writers for themselves, and as Wiggins and McTighe point out, would most likely diminish the students' understanding as well. Students would think of their writing instruction as "business as usual" and simply wait for their teachers to tell them what they know, never understanding how that knowledge came to be.

The content expertise teachers acquire as they engage in inquiry over time with students is not wasted, however. Conferring, the one-on-one teaching of individual writers in a workshop, is greatly enhanced as the teacher's knowledge base grows (Anderson 2000; Ray 2001). Quite simply, the more teachers know, the better they confer and the more they have to offer in terms of differentiated instruction. Content expertise also helps teachers develop lessons that support the work students do as they move out of inquiry and into writing. Most teachers use the time when students are drafting and revising to teach whole-class lessons on writing issues that might help students write well but, for whatever reason, weren't significant issues in the close study of inquiry.

Perhaps most importantly, a growing knowledge base gives teachers "new eyes" to see what students are trying to do in their writing. In the student's commentary about Shaq and Kobe in Chapter 1, for example, Emily understood and appreciated what the student was trying to do as he framed the piece with questions and answers. This was a crafting technique they had learned was used in lots of commentary, and this young writer was quite intentional in his efforts to use the technique in his own writing. If Emily hadn't recognized this, she might have been struck more by what he didn't do in his piece than by what he did. I am moved by the profound implications of this for the writing lives of children, what it could mean to them if their teachers developed the eyes to see and appreciate what they are trying to do as writers instead of—or at least in addition to—what they haven't done.

Before Revision, Vision

Emily understood how important it was that she chose good examples for her study because whatever ended up in her stack of texts would form the vision toward which her students would draft. Once they were immersed in reading these texts, this vision would take shape and would be critical to the whole of the process, but particularly to the drafting and revising the students would eventually do. Emily knew that it would be difficult for her students to *revise* if they didn't have a vision to start with. Similarly, Lisa knew that a focus on *marks* rather than a focus on *texts* (where marks are used in interesting ways) would leave her students without the breadth of vision for why those marks matter to them as writers. Elliott Eisner (2003) says, "The writer starts with vision and ends with words" (342).

Sometimes I think teachers get frustrated with students because they don't seem to know what to do with revision, but I think it's worth asking, "Have I done enough to help my students develop a strong vision for the writing I'd like them to do?" Writers write well, often even in first drafts, when they have a clear vision of the kind of writing they will do. The immersion stage of inquiry is absolutely critical to the development of this vision, and its absence in the other stances to the teaching of writing is problematic.

Even when a series of lessons is tied directly to quality, real-world text examples, if there isn't a period of *just reading* from a range of texts, I don't believe students get the fullness of vision that comes from reading immersion. Lessons like these are designed to draw students' attention to specific qualities in the writing before they have had a chance to just read and get a feel—in a much larger, more visionary sense—for what this kind of writing is like in the world. Lessons like these also narrow the possibilities for what features of texts students might attend to in their reading, forcing students "to operate within the teacher's assumptive bounds" (Harste, Woodward, and Burke 1984, 14) instead of exploring other possibilities they might find on their own.

Related to this, the predictable move in inquiry from reading immersion, to close study, to writing, makes this clearly a whole-part-whole framework for instruction. Beginning with a stack of examples, the vision of either the text as a whole (commentary) or the writing issue under study as a whole (punctuation) is the point of departure in the teaching, and then the work to name the specifics of what makes it *good* writing, follows after that. If the point of departure in the teaching is, instead, with these specifics (as predetermined by the teacher or a set of curriculum materials), students are left with a part-to-whole understanding of writing that I fear never adds up.

Realistically, I believe part-to-whole is still the most prevalent curriculum orientation in the teaching of writing, and my theory about why is because with this orientation, curriculum feels more manageable. As teachers we like to know the "what" of what we are teaching, the substance of it. Having parts to teach makes us feel safe because, quite simply, it makes us feel like we have *something* to teach. But if teaching begins with the wholeness of vision, the parts won't go away. Think about the charts Emily and Lisa and their students generated from their studies. They are full of parts, parts that mean so much more to the students because they know where they came from, they know what they are parts *of*. Writers write well because they have clear vision of the writing they are trying to do, not because they've been careful—in an operational sense at least—to piece together all the parts they've been taught to include that make writing good.

What About Teacher Modeling?

The importance of students seeing their teachers as writers and of teacher modeling is well documented in the professional literature about the teaching of writing (Atwell 1998; Graves 1989; Ray 2002; Routman 2005). The modeling a teacher does, however, looks different depending on which teaching stance is taken. Sometimes when teachers write they are trying to create a *model* more in the noun sense of the word than in the verb sense. They want their writing to serve as a model for what the students will write. But when teachers work from an inquiry stance, they have decided that the *model* for the writing will come from the stack of gathered texts. And of course it's not just one model—there's a stack of texts there—which is why the word *vision* is probably a better word for what they want their students to have.

When quality texts anchor the teaching, students don't need their teachers to create a model of what the writing should look like, but this doesn't mean that modeling isn't important. As the inquiry progressed, Emily showed her students how to take what they were learning and turn it into possibilities for their own writing. She let them inside her head as she made decisions while creating her own piece of commentary. What Emily modeled was the *process* she wanted her students to go through rather than the product she wanted them to produce. Similarly, Lisa was careful always to nudge her students to think about how they might use what they were learning about punctuation in their own writing.

By modeling the process of moving from the study of texts to their own writing, Emily and Lisa showed their students the "value of the discipline required to learn a discipline" (Wiggins and McTighe 2001, 55). And in a very real way, what these two teachers were really teaching their students was how to carry on with their learning without needing a teacher. Because their teachers modeled "off" whatever the students discovered in their inquiry and not from their own predetermined qualities of good writing, the students could see how it is that writers learn to write from *reading* rather than from *teaching*.

Related to this, teachers who consistently model the process of writing develop empathy for the work of a writer, and I don't think the value of this should be underestimated. Teachers who have empathy for the work of a writer are able to teach more than just process; they can help students understand what it's like to be a writer engaged in the process, and that's so different. For example, it's one thing to know, in an intellectual sort of way, that people who write often have to rewrite and rework a draft over and over to get it right. It's quite another thing to understand, in an emotional sort of way, how hard it is to actually do that. When what you know about "people who write" becomes what you know "as a person who writes," what you know *changes*.

Closing Thoughts

I've come to the end of the line of thinking that grounds the work you'll read about in *Study Driven*, so first let me summarize the main ideas I've written about in this chapter. As you read forward in the book, my hope is that you'll return to these main ideas often and find them helpful reminders as you ground your own thinking.

Teaching from an inquiry stance:

• asks students to read like writers, developing a habit of mind that will potentially teach them how to write well throughout their lives;

• ensures that the content for writing is grounded in the realities of both product and process;

• expands the teacher's knowledge base as she learns alongside students;

• helps students develop vision for writing before they're asked to engage in *re*vision;

• asks the teacher to model the process of writing, rather than create a model for what the writing should look like when it's finished.

And finally, a closing thought. "Let's just talk. What are you thinking about an ellipsis?"

Imagine what it would be like to go to school every day as a six-year-old or a sixteen-year-old, and to know how important your thinking is to what will happen in the classroom that day. To know that your teacher is waiting there for you and your classmates, and that her lesson "plans" for the day have huge spaces in them that she's waiting for you to fill with your thinking.

I didn't go to school this way when I was six or sixteen, so I can only imagine it, but when I do, I realize how much this is not just about the teaching of writing. It's about the teaching of *being*. At its very core, teaching from an inquiry stance is an ongoing, loaded invitation to construct a particular identity. And I realize that the invitation is not just extended to students, either. Inquiry is an invitation for teachers to construct different identities, too. Perhaps that's why thinking about working in this way with students causes an emotional stir in so many of us as teachers—a stir that can go either way depending on how we see ourselves in our classrooms.

I end this chapter with this thought to remind myself of the implications of what I'm writing about, and to write my way forward into the next chapters with respect for these implications.

Craft Pause

This is a short excerpt from Carolyn Coman's (2000, 117–18) young adult novel *Many Stones*. A father and his teenage daughter are traveling in Africa, and this is a scene where they're arriving at a bed and breakfast.

> We sail through the stone pillars that mark the driveway of Rocky End Bed and Breakfast. A group of black men, workers, are gathered near one of the pillars. We kick up driveway dust in our rented car, and I feel embarrassed and white and rich.
>
> As soon as we step out of the car and into the hot afternoon, a very blond, very tan woman dressed in tight white cotton pants and a shirt tied in a knot above her bellybutton comes out the door to greet us. I turn to Dad, and catch him pulling in his gut, straightening to his full height.
>
> Blondie leads us into the main house and shows us around and gets us settled. It's like we've landed in some place out of a magazine, a million miles away from any place called Africa, all these chunky pine tables and cabinets and baskets and checkered napkins and pottery with tiny Dutch people in clogs painted all over them. It's Martha Stewart does Africa, only our Martha is named Suzanne and has a clipped little accent.

INSIGHTS ABOUT CRAFT

I highlighted this excerpt the very first time I read *Many Stones* because I felt these three little paragraphs were just brilliant, well-crafted fiction. We learn so much about these three characters in this little space of text, and very little of it (she's blonde and tan) is in a direct way. First, that dad, pulling in his gut and straightening up at the sight of a beautiful woman. Actions *do* speak louder than words, and this is perhaps one of the greatest lessons for fiction writers to remember. We learn so much about the father from that single, tiny action. It's "show, don't tell" in its highest form. We also learn a whole lot about the woman who's come out to greet them from the simple details of what she's wearing and from the peek inside her house. Showing what surrounds a character can help the reader understand a lot about the character.

And finally, the narrator, the teenage daughter. Even if you've never read *Many Stones*, this small excerpt probably gives you a pretty good sense of her character. I believe, particularly, the reference to "Blondie" for the woman she's just met tells us worlds about her. Writers of fiction can reveal so many facets of the character of the narrator by letting the "inside voice" of this character—with all its biases and particular ways of seeing the world—narrate what's happening. The choice to have a first-person narrator affords the writer this nonobjective luxury of insight about the character.

Before *Revision*, Vision

What Have You Read That Is Like What You're Trying to Write?

Awhile back, Ralph Fletcher and I were both teaching at a summer institute in Idaho. When I learned that he had a new book coming out and that it was a memoir, I was excited. I couldn't wait to see what he would do with this wonderful genre I've grown to love so much. "So Ralph," I asked, "What's it like? Your memoir?"

He thought for just a moment, and then he said, "It's sort of like *House on Mango Street*, but without the craft."

We had a good laugh at this. I knew that Ralph couldn't write a memoir "without the craft" if he tried. His memoir would be carefully and delightfully crafted as all his writing is. But because I know *House on Mango Street* (Cisneros 1989), I knew a lot more than this too. I had a clear picture of how Ralph's memoir would "read." I knew that it would most likely be written as a series of vignettes, and that these vignettes would be in the form of prose, but with many of the lyrical qualities of poetry. I knew that I would be able to read the vignettes as satisfying, stand-alone pieces, but that when I read across the whole of them, people, places, and ideas would reappear in different ones. Read together, the vignettes would work to form the "bigger picture" of the memoir. And I knew, perhaps most importantly, that I couldn't wait for Ralph's memoir, *Marshfield Dreams* (2005).

This was a tiny little interaction between Ralph and me, a single question and a single answer, but the lessons about writing I find in this interaction are significant. First of all, consider the significance of the question itself: *So Ralph, what's it like? Your memoir?* I suppose some people might think that question a little rude, my presuming that Ralph Fletcher would be writing a memoir that is *like* something else. Some people might think I was insulting the integrity of Ralph's personal writing style with my question. But I didn't think it was rude at all, and I knew Ralph would be able to answer it and that he wouldn't be offended by it. People who write well know how their writing fits into the world of written texts. Even when they are trying to be experimental and do something *different* with writing, they have to know what it is different *from* in the world of written texts.

Second, consider the significance of the answer Ralph gave. He was unapologetically clear and specific in his answer, naming an actual text he thought I would know to help me understand what his writing was like. And think about the significance of my response to his answer. Because of his answer, I couldn't wait to get my hands on Ralph's new book. Because of his answer, I could envision a memoir that I would just love to read. And more importantly, what I would like to suggest here, is that because of his answer, because of his *vision* for the writing he did, Ralph Fletcher was able to write a memoir that lots of people will just love to read.

Reading and Its Connection to Vision

In the last chapter I explained all the reasons I believe an inquiry stance is important in the teaching of writing. One of those lines of reasoning was that the deep reading students do during the immersion phase of inquiry helps them to develop a vision for the writing they are going to do, the kind of vision Ralph Fletcher has when he writes. The purpose of this chapter is to crack open the idea of vision even more.

If a person ever hopes to write well, there may be no more important question for him or her to answer than this: *What have you read that is like what you are trying to write?* For the recursive processes of drafting and *revision* to lead to good writing, writers have to have a clear vision of the good writing they want to do. Now, writers may have this clear vision from the outset, prewriting with it in mind, or the vision may gain clarity during the process of drafting, but either way, at some point, writers have to have a vision of the kind of writing "thing" they are making as they compose text. And as I said in the last chapter, I'm not sure we have done a very good job, historically, of helping our students know how to answer that question about the writing we've wanted them to do. I'm not sure we've understood how to help them answer that question in fairly specific ways with responses like these:

- This is a review of a new Outkast CD like you would read in *Entertainment Weekly*.

- This is a sports feature piece like Rick Reilly writes in the back of *Sports Illustrated* or like they have in the Sunday sports section of the paper.

- This is a short story like you'd find in a collection of short stories like Angela Johnson and Gary Soto write.

- This is an interview like they sometimes have in *People* magazine as a feature piece on a famous person. But it's about my grandfather.

- This is a how-to piece about making dolls like you'd read in *Southern Living* or *Good Housekeeping*.

- This is a memoir that would probably work well as a picture book, something along the lines of *Saturdays and Teacakes* (Laminack), *Grandma's Records* (Velasquez), or *The Range Eternal* (Erdrich).

- "This is a memoir—sort of like *House on Mango Street*, but without the craft."

Notice how contextualized these answers are, each one set somewhere in the actual world of writing. The content that writers choose to pursue, the "what" of what the writing is about, is certainly individual, but the vision for how that content will be developed into a finished piece of writing is borrowed from the larger world of writing. Plain and simple, visions of good writing that help people write well come from reading.

Reading, and the clear vision that writers have because they read, is so critical to good writing because there can be no *revision* without vision. Perhaps this is why so many of us learned so little about revision in our school experiences with writing. When we were in school we did endless *papers*. What was a *paper* exactly? For me it was a bunch of paragraphs about some topic I'd chosen or been assigned. It wasn't anything, really. The word *paper*, and my thinking about what I was making with the writing, wasn't linked to anything I'd read.

As a starting point, teachers of writing need to force the issue of connecting students' reading to their writing. When students are just writing on their own in writing workshops, they must learn to answer this essential question, *What have you read that is like what you are trying to write?* Their answers, of course, will be limited to their experiences as readers. This is why we teach our youngest writers in kindergarten and first grade to answer this question very simply as "I'm making a book." A book is something they know, so we staple a few pages together so it looks like a book and ask them to make books like the picture books we are reading to them (Ray 2004). As students move along in the grades and begin to read more different kinds of texts, however, they'll be able to answer this vision question in more specific ways, like the examples I gave earlier. When a rich variety of writing is available for students to look at during writing workshop it helps them have a breadth of vision for the writing they might do.

In a classwide study of a particular kind of writing, the stack of texts essentially answers—in a general way—the question, *what have you read that is like what you are trying to write?* Students are asked to write something *like* what's been gathered for the study. But students still must develop a specific vision for the actual writing they will produce, and this is what will come out of the close study of the texts we gather.

To understand this, think about the two focal points of Ralph Fletcher's vision for his book *Marshfield Dreams*. On one level he was writing memoir. If he were a student in a writing workshop, that's the kind of vision he would get from a classwide study of memoir. His teacher would have gathered a variety of memoirs for everyone to read and study, perhaps asking the students to help with this gathering, and then she would have required each of them to write something that would fit (as memoir) in the stack. But the more specific vision of wanting it to read "sort of like *House on Mango Street*" came from a decision Ralph had to make on his own.

Students Writing with Clear Vision

To understand the impact of vision on the writing that students do, let's look at a few examples of what it looks like when children know exactly the kind of thing they are "making" with their writing. We'll start in kindergarten because vision is just as important for beginning writers as it is for experienced writers. (See Figure 3.1.)

"A very good number book for you to see" is a counting book and this beginning writer shows us she knows a lot about how counting books are written. Her book fits with other books like this as Samantha uses many of the techniques she's seen in this kind of writing:

- Counting books generally ask readers to participate in the counting.
- Counting books often use repetitive sentence patterns as they move through a series of numbers.
- A break in the pattern of sentences is a crafting move that makes the counting book more interesting to read (I see six sticks. Then it starts to rain).
- Counting books "picture" the number in the illustrations.

Samantha also makes some decisions in writing this book that are more general crafting decisions and not as specific to the genre: putting a related picture on

FIGURE 3.1 *Samantha's Counting Book "A very good number book for you to see."*

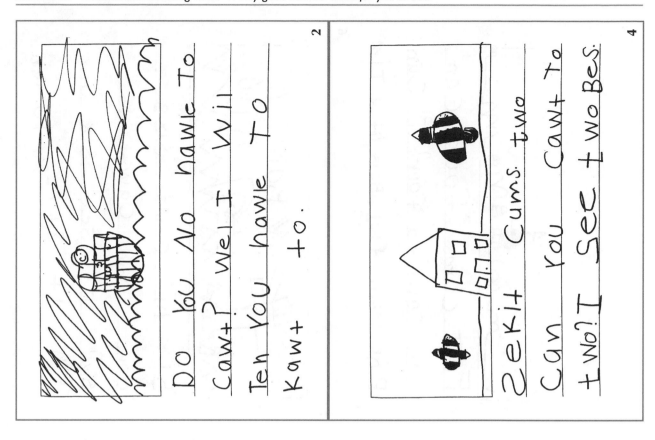

Page 1 (right panel):

3' 1 2 3 4 5 6 1 8 9 10 11 12 13
a 9 Vare God hob r 14
2g book for You Tə 17
21 2 ee 22 21 20 19 18
2ə 22 24 23

BY Sqmar+na
Ilysradd BY Sqmqntha

Page 2 (left panel):

Do You No hawie To
Cawt? Well I Will
Ten You hawie To
Kawt to.

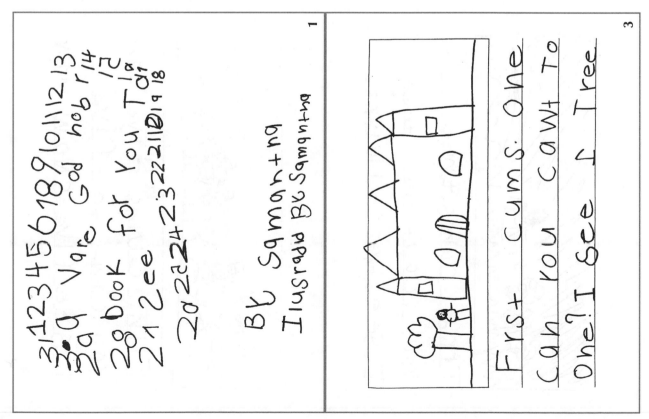

Page 3 (right panel):

Frst Cums One
Can You Cawt To
One? I See 1 Tree

Page 4 (left panel):

2ekit Cums two
Can You Cawt To
two? I See twoBes.

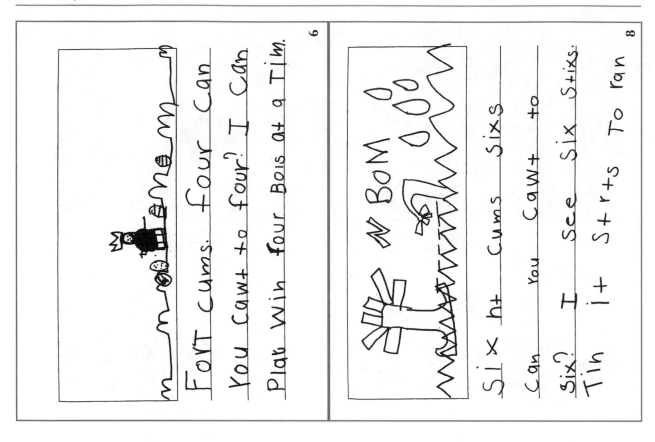

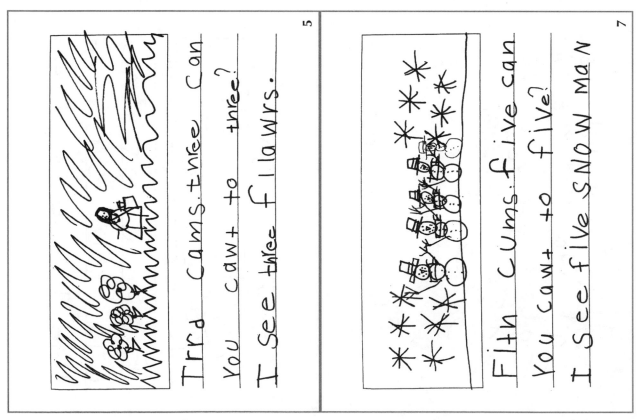

5

Irrd cams.tnee Can

You cawt to three?

I See tnee filawrs.

6

Fort cums. four Can

You Cawt to four? I Can

Plat Win four Bois at q Tim.

7

Filtn Cums.five can

You cawt to five?

I See five SNOW MAN

8

Six ht Cums Sixs

Can You Cawt to

Six? I See Six Stixs.

Tin it Strts To ran

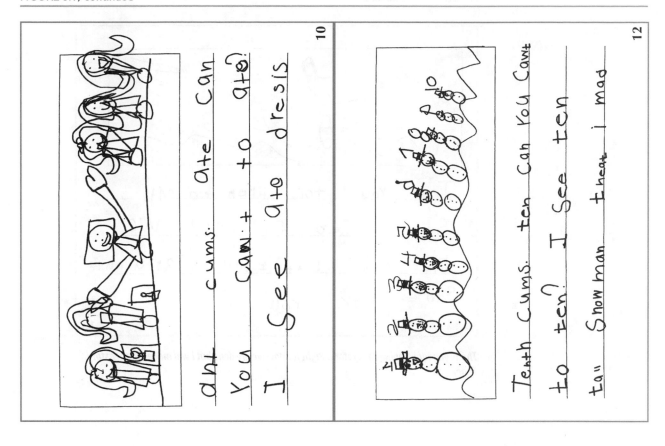

10

Ant cums. Ate Can
You Can·t to ate?
I See ate dresis

9

Zevint cums. sevih.
Can You cant to Sevih.
I See sevin Appous.

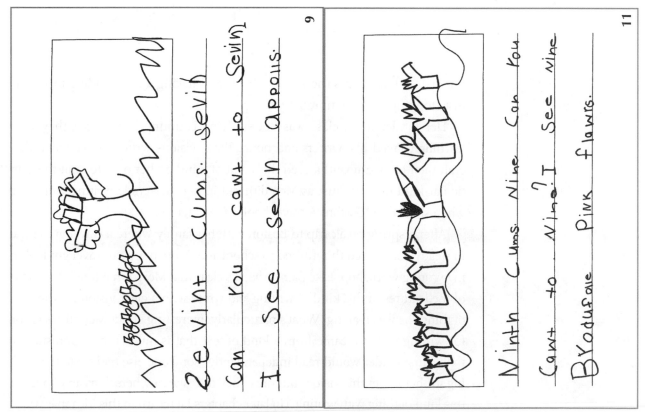

12

Tenth Cums. ten Can You Cant
to ten? I See ten
tou Snow man thear i mad

11

Ninth Cums. Nine Can You
Cant to Nine? I See nine
Broduroue Pink flawrs.

Tan you for linen to My Stor Rev for naW We rae dun but I wil MaKa nutr Store ToK You

13

Thank you for listening to my story. Right for now we are done but I will make another story. Thank you.

the first and last pages (herself in a boat) and having a clear ending instead of just stopping with the number ten.

Her kindergarten class was not studying counting books, but they were learning to read like writers and notice the decisions writers make when they craft their texts. Samantha used this habit of mind on her own to craft this particular kind of book, just as Meredith did in her first-grade writing workshop when she wrote "Boston: A travel book." (See Figure 3.2.)

After a spring break trip to Boston with her family where a travel guide was in steady use, Meredith returned to school and wrote her own travel guide during writing workshop. Like Samantha, it's clear that Meredith attended to many of the features of this kind of writing and wrote with a clear vision for the kind of thing she was making. What's particularly interesting about Meredith's vision for writing is that it came from a kind of text that is much more sophisticated than a first grader would read independently. Someone else had to do the reading for her to get this vision, but once they did, she saw herself as able to make this kind of thing with writing. (In later chapters I'll return to this idea that young

FIGURE 3.2 *Meredith's Travel Guidebook to Boston*

Bston
a chruvl
book

By Meredith

1

Boston—A Travel Book

Name Holtels   Date

Radusin

The Radusin holtel is very - VERY gob. The pool gave it morru pons because it was rely wome. 7/7 pons

2

Hotels—The Radisson hotel is very, very good. The pool gave it more points because it was really warm. 7/7 points.

Name Restrons   Date

Sea food

The restront I went to once was not as god as the Rodsin. I didint like it. I think it is cold Seafood. 4/7

3

Restaurants—The restaurant I went to once was not as good as the Radisson. I didn't like it. I think it is cold seafood. 4/7.

Name The parcks   Date

I thot that the porcks war fun just to wak thruw. Thdy war not like play porcks thay war thruw. Porcks you wak thruw. 7/7

4

The Parks—I thought that the parks were fun just to walk through. They were not play parks. They were parks you walk through. 7/7.

Museums—I thought that all of the museums were perfect. The science museum, the art museum, and the children's museum. Points 7/7.

The Pilgrims—I thought that the people were funny and just great. Fantastic job pilgrims! Points 7/7.

I love all the things—I love Boston.

children need access to more sophisticated texts than they can read on their own to support their development as writers.)

Jessica wrote "The Garden State: The Best Places to Go in New Jersey" during a study of feature articles in her fourth-grade class. (See Figure 3.3.)

Jenifer Smith, Jessica's teacher, had her students look at a range of kinds of "work" feature articles could do and then decide which kind of article they wanted to write. Some of them wrote articles that gave advice, others were informative, and still others were how-to pieces that walked the reader through the steps of something. Jessica chose to write a travel article that serves as a guide, and it reads a lot like the travel articles I find each month in the magazines I buy. She focuses on the two main things that interest travelers: food and fun.

FIGURE 3.3 *Jessica's Travel Feature Article*

The Garden State
The best places to go in
New Jersey By Jessica

In New Jersey there are a lot of things to go do and see, just like any other place. The places in this article are some of my favorite places in New Jersey.

DENVILLE DAIRY

Denville dairy is a great place to go. It is an ice cream store downtown.

The ice cream is absolutely delicious! There is chocolate, vanilla, strawberry, mint chocolate chip, cookie doe, rocky road, and anything else that you can imagine! They even have ice cream cakes!

Now you might not believe this if you live in Missouri, but EVERY time you go, you have to take a ticket in order to get your ice cream! There is AT LEAST 45 people there every time! You can imagine how busy that can get. The wait is usually at least up to 1 hour.

But if you are in Denville, New Jersey, you HAVE to go to Denville Dairy.

TRAVELER'S DINER

At Traveler's diner you can grab a cup of coffee, or you can sit down and enjoy a nice breakfast or lunch. For breakfast some things they have are: waffles, pancakes, sausage, a cup of coffee, juice or milk.

For lunch, some things they have are: sandwiches, salads, soups, and more. When you're done eating, and go up to he counter to pay, you can get a lollypop. It's a great place to eat!

It is located in Dover on Route 46, and is only a few minutes away from Denville. Enjoy!

SATURN PLAYGROUND

If you want to go spend the day at the playground, then you should go to Saturn playground.

It has very nice equipment, and even a field so that you can play soccer, base ball, or fly a kite...

Some of the equipment is: swings, monkey bars, tunnels, slides, and also some kinds of equipment that you may have never seen before!

It is a good size playground. Not too big [so that you don't lose anybody], and not too small [so that no one gets squished]. This playground is good for kids of all ages. [there's also bathroom's in case you got to go] And water fountains also!

This place is located in Denville. So get out and play!

ROCKAWAY MALL

Rockaway mall is another great place to visit in New Jersey. It's big, cool, and exciting!

One of the of the great stores there that you could go to is "Build A Bear Workshop." It's a cool store to visit because you get to actually make your own stuffed animal! The cool thing is that you get to pick out whatever kind of stuffed animal that they have. [you even get to stuff it yourself, and then you put a little soft heart in it.]

Next is the fountain. The fountain is cool. If you want to you can throw a coin in the fountain and make a wish. It's a lot of fun!

and last but not least, IT IS HUGE! There are 2 floors, elevators, escalators, and stairs.

so come and visit!

INDIAN LAKE

At Indian Lake, it is a whole bunch of fun! Here are some things that you can do there: Swimming. You can go swimming for as long as you want! It is very fun to ride on a boogie board or kick board against the waves.

#2. The snack bar

The snack bar is good! Some of the things they have are: ice cream, hot dogs, nacho's...[etc]

So you have to come and eat!

#3. Fire works on 4th of July

On the Fourth of July you can go down to Indian Lake and watch the fire works. They are SO pretty. They are very big and bright. You have to see how beautiful they really are yourself!

Come and visit Indian lake so you can see for yourself how beautiful it is!

Now do you want to go to New Jersey?

She gives helpful advice, a range of optional activities, and even a little bit of location information—"located in Dover on Route 46." I love her use of parenthetical asides to her reader, and her enthusiasm for New Jersey is contagious (and this from a writer in Missouri!).

What all these writers have in common is *vision*. Each of them knows the answer, just as Ralph Fletcher knew the answer, to the one very important question that writers must be able to answer: *What have you read that is like what you're trying to write?*

Before Vision, Intention

While it may seem odd that I am placing this at the end of this chapter, I wanted to make the idea of vision as clear as possible before I explained that I don't believe good writing starts with vision. I believe good writing starts with the passion of purpose, with some good reason a writer has found to want to write or to *need* to write. In his chapter titled, "The Tyranny of the Final Product," William Zinsser (2001) explains that too many people who want to be writers begin with visions of the final product before they have clarity of purpose. He advises, "If your values are sound, your writing will be sound. It all begins with intention. Figure out what you want to do and how you want to do it, and work your way with humanity and integrity to the completed article" (264).

I believe that long before Ralph Fletcher developed the clear vision for the kind of writing he would do in *Marshfield Dreams*, he was first drawn to his memories of that place and time in his life and the impact they have on who he is today. He was drawn to the idea first, and then, purposefully, to a kind of writing he knew that would serve his writing intentions: memoir.

One of the key responsibilities teachers of writing have is helping students develop intentions as writers. So much of the talking work and the writer's notebook work (Buckner 2005; Calkins 1990; Fletcher 1996a) with students is done in the service of helping them develop intentions and reasons to want to write things. But once students have these, then the teacher's job is to help them develop vision for a kind of writing that might serve those intentions. It's the kind of help I was able to give nine-year-old Harrison when he wrote *War Poems for Doctor Green*.

Harrison had interviewed Dr. Green as part of an assignment related to Veteran's Day, and what he'd learned in the interview about this surgeon's time in Kosovo was compelling to him. He was looking for ideas for how he might write about it in an interesting way. There were several kinds of writing I could have suggested, but I knew he was interested in poetry and had been reading a lot of it around this time, so I suggested he look at poets who use the form to write about people in short, almost biographical sketchlike pieces: Tony Medina in *Love to Langston*, Marilyn Nelson in *Carver: A Life in Poems*, Charles R. Smith, Jr. in *Hoop Queens* and *Hoop Kings*, and any others he might find. *Love to Langston* was particularly influential in helping Harrison have vision for crafting his material into literature, and the result of that vision was *War Poems for Dr. Green*. (See Figure 3.4.)

I'd like to suggest that as a teacher of writing, the short stack of texts I recommended to this individual writer is every bit as important, and probably even more, than any stack of texts I might gather for a classwide genre study. I was helping Harrison do what Zinsser says he (and many, many others) did in learning how to write, "I learned by reading the men and women who were doing the kind of writing *I* wanted to do and trying to figure out how they did it" (2001, 35). If you know *Love to Langston*, you can see that Harrison learned many things from Tony Medina. He figured out "how she did it" and used that to help him write this starkly beautiful collection of poems about a time of war.

I've seen lots of students who grab hold of a topic that interests them and their interest is so clear. You can see it in their eyes and hear it in their voices when they talk about it. But when they try and write about it, fully intending to make the writing match the interest, the intention falls short. Intention without vision leads them nowhere. They still love the topic, but they don't love the writing.

In the resource chapters at the end of this book, you will see that I use a writer's intentions as my defining language for different kinds of writing in the world. I do this because I believe so strongly in the idea that writing starts with intention and moves toward vision. If one of the ways teachers understand different kinds of writing is connected to *why* people choose particular genres, then they can do a better job of helping children find genres to match their intentions.

The Tension in Intention

Having said all this about intention, I must be honest when I say there is tension for me in the idea of whole-class genre study because it forces the intention to come from the vision of a kind of writing, and not the other way around. It's a tension I accept, however, for two reasons.

First, the tension is grounded in the reality of at least some writers' real-world work. Leonard Pitts, for example, is a syndicated columnist and must write three columns a week for *The Miami Herald*. He has learned to live in the world like a person who must write three columns a week and has developed strategies for finding ideas that compel him and give him intention for this kind of writing he's expected to do. He told me once when I asked him how he gets ideas

FIGURE 3.4 *Harrison's War Poems*

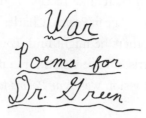

Missing My Family

One day the phone rang,
I answered it with out thinking a thing.
But when I heard those dreadful words,
I wasn't lying in my bed.

I was surprised,
and so was my family.
I said good-bye,
for I had to go to war,

I missed my family,
especially when they called,
I got letters, e-mails, and phone calls,
from my family, and they were at home

Friends

I made a lot of friends at war,
we liked the same thing.
But when we had a patient,
we weren't laughing at jokes, or playing around.

My friends and I,
saved many lives.
We were called,
and didn't waste time to go and get to work.

My friends and I,
had some spare time.
We went to a place,
with pool and ping pong.
But I mostly read books,
in the library there.

Lives

I saved a lot of lives at war.
The main thing was that bomb,
that dreadful bomb,
and on that day, was when it
   happened.
The day, that I saved some lives.
I was focused,
and didn't think about anything,
but the operation.
It was hard,
but I was I confident,
and we did it.
Me and my friends,
had found the strength,
to save a lot of lives,
to hand their soul back to ordinary,
and perfectly innocent people.
It felt good,
to know,
that I saved some lives.

Food at War

Foods at war were like space food.
In the bag was food called MRE,
quick and ready to be eaten.

It would say, "Hot Dog"...
looked like sausage.
The taste was the same.
I didn't mind,
just to know that was helping my
country was enough.

Some people didn't like
some of the food.
I didn't like some either.
But none of us cared.

Danger

I wasn't scared.
I was protected
with a bulletproof vest
and a gun.
I was safe.

I had to always be prepared,
on guard.
The conditions were different
than a hospital in your home town.

I was safe,
but something could always happen.
I saved many lives
so they wanted me to be protected.

Danger in Kosovo,
and the people were treated poorly.
Many people died.
Thank goodness I wasn't one of them.

Dangerous things around every corner,
bombs
guns
and terrorist attacks.
I didn't like to see people die just because of where they
lived.
It was very dangerous in the war.

Notes About the Poems

Missing My Family

At war Bart Green missed his family very much. He had to talk to them on the phone for a short amount of time or email his family. He also got letters from home that made him miss his family even more. But he fought through it all and saved people's lives from being a great doctor and very brave.

Friends

Dr. Green made many friends at war. He made friends with doctors and nurses. They were important and I think it helped him during hard times.

Lives

Once Dr. Green and other nurses and doctors got called and got rushed to the terrorist attack. A bomb had gone off on a bus and Dr. Green saved many people's lives. They were perfectly normal people.

Food at War

Food at war was eaten from a bag called MRE. They were not very good but the cafeteria food was really good.

Danger

When Dr. Green was at war he was not in any great danger but he had to wear a bulletproof vest and a gun. Something could always happen. So there was always a slight chance of getting injured.

that he makes sure he's at the water fountain when everyone else is taking a break, he's a voracious news reader, and he drops into Internet chat rooms to see what people are talking about. He lives in a way that leads him to intentions. So teaching students to find intentions to match a kind of writing in the world is teaching them to do what at least some writers have to do.

Second, I believe that one of the purposes of genre study is to expose students to a range of writing that people use to serve different human intentions. If a person doesn't even know a particular kind of writing exists, or more commonly, knows it exists but has never looked at it with an eye toward writing it, he may not even realize he's got intentions that could be served by writing that kind of thing. Most of the students in Emily Steffans' fifth-grade class knew very little about commentary and the work it does in the world, so they couldn't really understand the function of this kind of writing until they were exposed to it as readers.

When I think about finding intentions to match a kind of writing, I can't help but think about one of the newest genres I know, the *blog*. Think about the way so many, in such a short span of time, have embraced this kind of self-published writing and used it in such intentional ways. And less than a decade ago, the genre didn't even exist.

Genre study can help students imagine fulfilling intentions with writing that they might not have realized were possible. And as students return to studies of certain kinds of writing over time and deepen their understandings, their abilities to wield power with particular kinds of writing deepen as well. The key, I think, is a healthy balance of time. In a year of writing, students need time to follow their own intentions with writing and time for deep study into the promise and possibility of different kinds of writing through genre study. Units of study other than genre (like the one Lisa Cleaveland planned around punctuation) are important studies both for the curriculum they offer and because they give students an opportunity to choose both topics and genres. In a yearlong framework then, genre study certainly needs to be balanced with units of study other than genre for this reason.

Craft Pause

NOTICE

The lead to Veronica Chamber's *Celia Cruz, Queen of Salsa* (2005):

> In the fabled land of Havana, where rhythm grows, sweet and juicy, like oranges in Florida, there lived a girl. She looked like a girl and talked like a girl, but everyone who ever met her agreed, she sang like a bird.
>
> When Celia Cruz was a girl growing up in Cuba, she could never hear the magic others claimed was in her voice. When she opened her mouth to sing, she heard a girl like any other. But when she sang . . .
>
> Her father heard thunder.
> Her cousins heard the call of the sea.
> Her neighbors heard a hummingbird.

The lead to Amy Ehrlich's *Rachel: The Story of Rachel Carson* (2003):

> Rachel's house was far from the ocean, hundreds of miles inland at a bend on the Allegheny River in Pennsylvania. There were no seagulls there, no sharks or whales. But one day she found a fossil, a single dark spiral lodged in a rock at her feet. She brought it to show her mother, and they looked it up in a book. The fossil was a sea creature, her mother said. Millions of years ago the ocean had covered their land and left it behind.
>
> Imagine! Beyond the fields and orchards, beyond the woods where she played with her dogs, beyond the Allegheny and the town of Springdale and the city of Pittsburgh, there was a vast ocean even now. At night Rachel lay in bed, her thoughts turning like waves.

The lead from M.T. Anderson's *Handel Who Knew What He Liked* (2001)*:

> This is George Frideric Handel. He looks very satisfied with things. He's smiling a little, as if he's very sure of himself. You'd have to be sure of yourself to wear a wig that gigantic.
>
> Right from an early age, Handel knew just what he liked. He wanted to study music. His father said he couldn't. His father said nobody ever made any money as a musician. He told the boy to study something that would make him money.
>
> Handel's father was a doctor.
>
> But little Handel knew what he liked. What he liked was music.

INSIGHTS ABOUT CRAFT

Picture book biographies, by design, need to be quite focused. One way to focus these books is to establish a theme right from the start, and then choose anecdotes and information to illustrate that theme across the person's life. (You can see the follow-through of the themes established in these leads if you look at the texts in their entirety.)

*A special thanks to M.T. Anderson and the session on picture book biography at the 2005 NCTE national conference in Pittsburgh. He taught me to notice this organizational structure (by theme) that is common in so many picture book biographies.

Understanding the Difference
Between Mode and Genre

I don't think Gary Paulsen, beginning a new novel, thinks to himself, "Okay, let me get started on some *narrative* writing today."

I don't think Leonard Pitts sits down to do a little *persuasive* writing three times a week when he writes his syndicated column for *The Miami Herald*.

And I'm sure as I'm working on an article for *Language Arts* or a chapter for a book, I don't think of what I'm writing as *expository* writing. I think of them as an article for *Language Arts* or a chapter for the book I'm writing.

Playful semantics? Perhaps. But I believe the point I am making has significant instructional implications. As I explained in Chapter 3, good writers know what kind of thing they are making with writing. They can answer the question, should someone ask, "What have I read in the world that is like what you are trying to write?" No one I know would answer that question with words like *narrative* or *persuasive* or *expository*. These words simply aren't operational for people who write. They aren't the terms writers use to talk about or think about the writing they are producing. And as my friend Isoke Nia says, you don't go into a bookstore and ask the clerk if he can help you find some expository writing.

And yet, in the world of writing in schools, these words *rule*. Both curriculum documents and large-scale writing assessments use these words to name what writers should be able to produce, and as a result, these words are commonly used to frame instruction in writing. Children are asked to produce descriptive writing and persuasive writing and expository writing, and the words used for these tasks are rarely questioned. I believe, however, that in the service of offering students better writing instruction, they're worth questioning. I don't think we need new words. I simply think we need more clarity and understanding about the words we are using.

Understanding Mode and Genre

First let's consider the difference between *mode* and *genre*. The words most often used in school to describe different kinds of writing are names for different *modes* of writing. They describe the meaning "work" that a writer is doing in a text, and they come from the historical influence of traditional studies in rhetoric (Gere, Christenbury, and Sassi 2005, 62–63). The four traditional modes and the meaning work they do are:

Mode	The Writing Work This of Mode
Narration	tells a story
Exposition	explains an idea; conveys information
Description	creates an impression of something (sight, sound, feel, taste, smell)
Argumentation	makes a case for the validity of an idea or opinion

Because these terms also imply text structures that are inherent in the different modes, they are often used interchangeably to talk about the structure of a text.

Curriculum documents, writing tests, and materials made for schools use other mode words as well, words like *procedure, definition, summary, persuasion, clarification.* Citing the work of James Briton, Dorn and Soffos (2001) say they emphasize three modes of writing in teaching young children: *expressive, transactional,* and *poetic* (26). And there are others. Basically, any words that name the meaning work a writer is doing in a text are describing the *mode* of the writing.

As I pointed out earlier, mode words don't actually name the kinds of things people *make* with writing, so by themselves they don't give anyone vision for writing. Genre words do that work much better. The word *genre* means, simply, "kind, sort." It's what we say when someone asks, "What kind of writing is it?" It's what we ask for in the bookstore or the library when we want help finding something. In an email I got from my friend Amy Ludwig-Vanderwater recently, she updated me on her writing life. She wrote, "I am going to read another essay at our local NPR affiliate on Friday, and have written another. These are fun shortish memoiry things, and I like having them to hold onto as well." *Fun shortish memoiry things.* That's genre-talk. Perhaps not the high literary sort, but the real way people who write talk about what they're writing.

Gary Paulsen writes novels or, more specifically, adolescent fiction, mostly realistic. Leonard Pitts writes a syndicated column of mostly social commentary for *The Miami Herald*, but he is also the author of a wonderful chapter-book–length memoir, *Becoming Dad* (1999). And I write, well . . . what would you call what

I write exactly? I've always struggled with this. When laypeople find out I am a writer and ask what kind of writing I do, I always have trouble answering. I usually say, "I write professional books for teachers," but the response I often get is, "Oh, you write *text*books." And then I have to try and explain how they are not *text*books. But what are they, exactly?

The thing is, genre words have limitations, too. First of all, there aren't enough of them to name, in a one-word-label sort of way, every kind of writing we know in the world. For example, what do you call those articles in magazines and newspapers with titles like "Eight Reasons to Go Camping in Yellowstone" and "Five Books You Don't Want to Miss If You're a Romantic" and "Ten Hot Night Spots for Summer Fun"? Certainly in the broadest sense they are feature articles, but they are a particular kind of feature article. Anyone who reads magazines knows exactly the kind of article I'm talking about, and yet I'm not sure exactly what to call them.

My bookshelves are full of picture books that I'm not quite sure how to label. What should I call *In November* (2000), for example, by Cynthia Rylant? The text is certainly not a short story; the primary mode at work in the book is description—seven small "pictures" made of words describing life in the month of November. There really isn't any factual content, and the Library of Congress distinction is of no help at all (as is so often the case), labeling the book simply "fiction." I can't just call it a picture book because that simply tells me the kind of container it's in, not the kind of writing it is.

I'm not sure what I should call this kind of writing or what I would ask for if I wanted to find more of it at the bookstore, but here is something I can do. I can make a stack of other books that are like this one, other books where authors must have had similar intentions as Rylant had when she crafted the text for *In November*. Here are a few books that would be in my stack:

Mud (1996) by Mary Lyn Ray, illustrated by Lauren Stringer
Scarecrow (1998) by Cynthia Rylant, illustrated by Lauren Stringer
The Barn Owls (2000) by Tony Johnston, illustrated by Deborah Koogan Ray
Uptown (2000) by Brian Collier
Water (1995) by Frank Asch

Not knowing what to call the kind of writing I find in this stack doesn't stop me from believing in the existence of this kind of writing. In other words, I don't have to have a one-word-label for it as long as I can describe it well enough and show someone examples of the kind of writing I am talking about. This is where my problem explaining my writing to laypeople gets difficult; I can't really name other books and say, "You know, it's like the stuff Janet Angelillo writes or Carl Anderson writes." People who aren't teachers haven't read their books either.

Vision = Lots of Words to Name the Genre

The difficulties I've encountered searching for just the right genre word for every sort of writing I know, including the kind I do myself, have been the catalyst for coming to believe so strongly in the importance of the question I discussed in the last chapter: *What have you read that is like what you're trying to write?* Or as a teacher of writing: *What have I read that is like what I want my students to write?* In other words, forget what it's called; just tell me where I might have read something like it. Describe it to me. Show me some examples of it. Use lots and lots of words to tell me what it is, if you need them.

In Lisa Cleaveland's first-grade writing workshop, she uses two separate stacks of picture books to help her students understand the difference between what they call "regular nonfiction" and "literary nonfiction." The first stack has books with straight, factual information in them. They are books readers seek out because they want to learn more about specific topics. They're reference books, in a way. The second stack, the *literary* nonfiction books, also have factual information in them, but the facts are embedded in texts where writers seem to work hard to engage readers and make them think, "Wow, this is a very interesting topic." In these books the writers convey a certain sense of awe and wonder for the topics they are addressing. They are what Lee Gutkind (1997) would call "creative nonfiction," though she has used this term more in a journalistic sense rather than applying it to the world of picture books.

Now, I doubt Lisa could go into the picture book section at her local bookstore armed with nothing but the labels "regular nonfiction" and "literary nonfiction" and get much assistance. She would probably have to describe the kinds of books she's looking for, maybe something like, "I want some books with just facts in them, no commentary or flowery stories, just facts." And if she brought a few along with her that were like the kind she wanted, she could get help even more easily. The point is, she might need a lot of words, rather than a label, to find what she wanted.

If there are clearly defined and widely accepted labels for the kinds of writing she wants to show her students, Lisa uses them. But often there aren't, as was certainly the case with the nuanced distinction between different kinds of nonfiction. Teachers need not shy away from certain kinds of writing because they don't know what to call them. If you can make a stack of texts where writers seem to be fulfilling like intentions, let the definition come from the characteristics those texts share. The "name" of what you're studying will take up a lot more room on your curriculum calendar because you'll need more words to say it, but that's okay. Use all the words you need.

In addition to helping writers get past the label problem, answering the question, "What have you read that is like what you're trying to write?" forces the issue of more specific vision inside a genre. It leads to answers like this: "I'm writing a feature article about a young woman in my hometown who survived cancer, sort of like what you read in *Redbook* or *Ladies' Home Journal*. It's her story, mostly, but around her story I'm going to include some of the factual information I've been gathering about cancer prevention. I'm hoping her story will inspire people to take action and get early screening." Look at all those words to say what it is. All in all, we can start with the genre words we have, but I think it helps to use more words rather than fewer words when we set out to name a particular kind of writing in the world. The clarity of vision comes when writers say as much as they can to describe the kind of writing they have in mind.

Different Modes at Work

Now I need to go back to the idea of mode. You may remember that I said modes describe the meaning work that a piece of writing is doing at any given place in the text. The thing is, in a single text, writers usually move among different modes in order to accomplish their purposes, to help them *make* whatever it is they are making with the writing.

Take, for example, my book *What You Know by Heart: How to Develop Curriculum for Your Writing Workshop* (2002). It's a professional book for teachers (not a textbook). The main mode I employ in the book is certainly the expository mode. I explain a lot of ideas. But the first page of the first chapter of the book is actually written in the narrative mode, present tense, as if it's happening as you read it:

> I am sitting in the airport in Charlotte, North Carolina, and I notice a man sitting near me. He is so like most of the other men I see in airports—briefcase, loosened tie, cell phone. He's obviously on his way to or from a business meeting, like hundreds of others in the airport this night. He is so like the men I am used to seeing, except for one thing: he is hunched over a colorful piece of material and his hands are carefully cross-stitching.
>
> *Cross-stitching.* I stare for a while. He doesn't notice me; he's intent on his work. I pull out my notebook and I write an entry. (1)

And it goes on. I use this little story from my life to make a point, and I actually do this all the time when I'm writing. Telling a story is one of the main ways I explain an idea. So while *What You Know by Heart* is clearly not a storybook, it has lots of stories in it that do other work. And lots of other writers who aren't writing stories—writers of feature articles and essays and commentaries—use the narrative mode as well. In a single professional book or article for teachers, in addition to telling stories, I might also need to do the work of descriptive or procedural or persuasive writing to help me achieve my bigger purpose of explaining my ideas.

To think of it another way, a novel is clearly, at its core, narrative driven in terms of mode. It must tell a story, but in doing so, the writer of a novel might also need to describe or explain or walk the reader through a procedure for some reason. Novelists will employ these different modes of writing in the midst of a narrative, suspending the story's movement through time while other work gets done. The following are two examples from a recent novel I read, Meg Rosoff's *How I Live Now* (2004), winner of the American Library Association's Michael Printz Award for Excellence in Young Adult Literature.

By page six of the novel we learn that our narrator, Daisy, has arrived in England (from New York) where she will stay for the summer with her aunt and four cousins whom she's never met. When Daisy arrives at her cousins' house, they all come out to greet her, and then the text reads like this:

> Before I tell you what happened then, I have to tell you about the house, which is practically indescribable if the only sort of houses you've lived in before are apartments in New York City. (6)

Through the voice of the narrator, the writer has let us know that she is suspending the story for a moment—"Before I tell you what happened then. . . . " She's told us she is switching modes. What follows, then, are six paragraphs of richly descriptive writing. Here's an excerpt of one of them:

> First, let's get it clear that the house is practically falling down, but for some reason that doesn't make any difference to how beautiful it is. It's made out of big chunks of yellowish stone, and has a steep roof, and is shaped like an *L* around a big courtyard with fat pebbles set in the ground. The short part of the *L* has a wide arched doorway and it used to be the stable, but now it's the kitchen and it's huge, with zigzag brick floors and big windows all across the front. . . . (6–7)

It's a beautiful passage of description that makes a very clear picture of the house and surrounding gardens in my mind's eye. The descriptive mode of writing does lots of useful work for the writer of fiction.

Here's another example. Later in the novel as Daisy and her cousin Piper are making their way home, trying to go undetected in a time of war, Daisy (the narrator) says:

> I was starting to think if we didn't have something different to eat we might die of despair even before we died of hunger so we decided to cook our first meal of mushrooms and salami and here's how we did it.

First we set up our so-called tent and waited until sundown so no one would see the smoke, then we collected some dried dead weeds and made a pile of them and next to it a pile of twigs and little bits of branches that were completely dead and dry, then we got some stones from the riverbank and made a circle and saved a few stones that we could balance our little metal bowl on, then we lit the dry weeds with one of our matches and waited till they caught and then added twigs slowly, and although it took two tries and four matches and the twigs weren't as dry as they should have been, we had a pretty nice fire going after about twenty minutes. (133)

In the midst of the narrative, the mode is clearly procedural here, moving through the steps of a process so the reader is informed about how something was accomplished. The writer's decision to punctuate it as a single sentence matches the desperate, things-running-out-of-control mood of the story at this particular juncture.

The point I'm making, that writers employ different modes of writing in a single text, is not some groundbreaking discovery I've made. Anyone who reads must be thinking, "Well, of course that's true." I'm simply pointing something out that has always been true of writing. But the issue is, too often in schools, the concept of mode is grossly oversimplified. When students are taught to think about writing in terms of mode rather than genre, this teaching belies the complexity of how different modes of writing are used to compose a short story or feature article or personal essay (see Figure 4.1). I believe, in fact, that the oversimplification of the concept of mode actually results in flawed curriculum. The content is off in a close-but-not-quite-right sort of way.

The resolution to this is simple. If the point of departure in teaching is genre rather than mode, if the move toward a draft begins with an answer to the question, "What have you read that is like what you're trying to write?" the complexity of mode will be intact. It can't *not* be intact because this is how things get written in the world outside school. It's as simple as shifting from teaching students to do persuasive writing and descriptive writing and expository writing, to teaching them to write short stories and book reviews and commentary and "those feature articles that walk you through a list of something—eight great books for summer or ten cities that are great for pets—you know those kinds of articles. I'm not sure what they're called, but. . . . " It's as simple as knowing exactly the kind of thing you'd like your students to write, and showing it to them.

Now I need to be very clear here. Because of the importance of vision, I believe that genre (and all the words we need to name it) rather than mode needs to be the point of departure in the teaching of writing, but understandings about the various modes of writing aren't irrelevant. As students and teachers study good examples of the kinds of writing they want to do, one important line of

"Real Trees: Where They Come From. And Where They Came From"
Timothy Harper

Delta's *Sky* magazine, December 2004, 108–9

It was a couple of days before the Christmas when I was 4 or 5 years old. My folks wanted to drive across town to see Aunt Carrie's "real" Christmas tree. I couldn't understand the big deal. We had a Christmas tree at home, and it seemed pretty real.

When we walked from Aunt Carrie's kitchen into her tiny living room, already dusky in the late afternoon, her tree literally took my breath away. It was a normal tree for back then—kind of scrawny compared with today's big bushy evergreens—but it glittered with dozens of tiny candles: real candles, each carefully nested on a thin branch, each with a tiny flame that flickered and danced. I stood fixated, staring at the tree, then shuffled back and forth to see it from different angles, until the grownups put out the candles. They did this by licking their fingers and lightly pinching each tiny flame into a hiss of smoke. It was magic, every bit of it.

Aunt Carrie is long gone, and I'll probably never walk into another private home and see a Christmas tree decorated with real candles. Who would be crazy enough nowadays to build a perfect firetrap in the family room? But Aunt Carrie's tree will always be a part of Christmas for me.

Recently, my wife, Nancy, and I took a Sunday drive out into the New Jersey countryside, near the land where a farmer started the cut-your-own tradition a century ago. That farmer planted row upon row of Norway spruce seedlings and then, six years later, let people come in and chop down their trees for a dollar apiece.

Nancy and I arrive at Yuletide Christmas Tree Farm on Evergreen Road just outside the hamlet of New Egypt. John Perry, who has been raising and selling Christmas trees with his brother Alan for 35 years, is happy to show us around. The 20-acre "cut'n'choose" farm sells about 1,000 to 1,200 trees annually—a tiny fraction of the 25 million "real" Christmas trees Americans buy each year. (The number is going down as the population ages and more people—about 29 percent in 2003—buy artificial trees. Fake trees can cost over $1,000 these days, and the best ones come with imperfections, and even extra needles to scatter on the floor, to make them look more real.)

John Perry shows us his 20,000 trees: blue spruce, white pine, Norway spruce, Douglas fir, white fir and others. He seems to like them all equally, but notes that blue spruce have a nice color, a pleasant aroma and full shape, and are sturdy enough to support heavy ornaments. And their prickly needles discourage curious pets.

We stroll into Perry's fragrant private forest, and he points out trees that are 20 years old but are still only 2 feet tall, and trees that are only 10 years old that are 12 feet tall. Both the trees that are too small and those that are too large will be cut down and put into the chipper for mulch—though more of the larger trees are being sold

these days for new family rooms with cathedral ceilings. Perry seems to look almost fondly at some of the more misshapen trees, and says he'll give them another year or two. "Some people come in and ask for 'Charlie Brown' trees," he says, referring to the small, lopsided tree from the beloved holiday TV special "A Charlie Brown Christmas." "Some want a tree they can put against a wall or in a corner. There's a tree for everybody."

Perry tells Nancy and me about the rhythm of a Christmas tree farm. Not much happens in January and February. March is devoted to treating plants to ward off disease and insects. Seedlings are planted in April to fill in the spots where trees have been cut down. The summer is to focus on weed control and shearing the trees. It's that shaping—"Each tree gets a haircut every year," Perry says—rather than fertilizers or biogenetics that gives today's Christmas trees their full, conical shape. More seedlings, 2,500 in all each year, are planted in October. In November Perry finishes his Christmas shopping and fills in groundhog holes so that nobody trips or falls.

The weekend after Thanksgiving, the farm opens for business. Orange cones are set out to show where to park cars. A 38-foot inflatable snowman is raised—both to draw in crowds from the highway and as a landmark to help city slickers find their way back to their cars—a mere 200 yards from the trees. Customers are given a sharp bow saw and one of the farm's 21 narrow, trough-shaped, 5-foot-long wagons to pull up and down the rows. The littlest child in the family usually jumps right in the wagon, and the family tromps off into the trees.

Perry's description reminds me of the first time Nancy and I went to a farm and cut down a tree 10 years ago. Our son Jonny was about the same age I was when I saw Aunt Carrie's tree. It was a bitterly cold day, and at one point he burst into tears and wailed, "My face hurts." We tried to get him to stop, but his tears froze and he was miserable till we got him some hot chocolate next to a potbellied stove.

That tree was one of the tallest and fullest we ever had. Back home, I had to hack off several inches, using extremely un-Christmassy language at times, to get it into the stand. I finally wrestled it into the house with barely enough room on top for the exquisite angel, with her velvet dress, flowing blond hair and hand-painted wax face. Nancy's relatives in Germany, where the tradition of handmade ornaments started, gave us that angel.

I ask Jonny, now 15, what he remembers of past Christmas trees. He immediately mentions that first time we went to cut down a tree ourselves. But he doesn't say anything about crying because it was so cold. "That," he says, "was a great tree."

In recent years, we tell Perry, we have been partial to the Fraser fir, a premium tree known for keeping its color and needles and for being able to hold the many ornaments we pile on. Ornaments from when Nancy was a child. Ornaments from trips we've taken to Europe, and even from the Middle East and China. Antique glass ornaments from garage sales. The wooden Santa who's an inch tall but has a foot-long hat. The banana moon. The furry little reindeer. The brassy musical instruments. Best of all, ornaments from our friends and ornaments our children made.

We like to bring the tree into the house and let it spread for a few days before we decorate. The decorating often takes hours, with breaks to eat and drink. Friends and relatives frequently come over for this ritual. When a Jewish neighbor told us, "You know, I always wished I could have a Christmas tree," we invited her over to help decorate, and she and her husband now come every year.

Back on the farm, Perry loves the way families show up together on weekends—he can tell when the big football game is over on Sunday because the cars start pouring in—and how parents and children are always excited and happy. He tries to close at 4 o'clock, but is often helping tie trees to cars after dark. Perry closes the lot for good on December 23 and takes Christmas Eve off. He gets his own tree the second or third week of December, and it takes him "about five minutes" to find the one he likes.

"Most people take an hour or so; some take three or four hours," Perry says. "They head way off toward the back of the farm, where the big trees are." People keep looking, he says, because the perfect tree might be just a little farther on, in the next row.

"The perfect tree is elusive," he says, laughing.

No, it's not, I thought.

All I have to do is close my eyes and think back to the perfect tree we had in our living room last year. And the year before. And all those other perfect trees, back to Aunt Carrie's. Sometimes I can even smell those trees of Christmas past.

This year's tree is going to be the best ever.

---

thinking should be "What kind of meaning work is the writer doing here?" and the language of mode is very much a part of that discussion. Remember the origins of these words. As Gere, Christenbury, and Sassi (2005) point out, "When Aristotle wrote his *Rhetoric* in 350 B.C.E., the Greeks had been using rhetorical processes for some time. Aristotle simply developed a way to describe what speakers of his age were *already* doing" (62, emphasis mine). The thing to remember is: mode is a descriptive device, not a prescriptive one.

In later chapters I'll return to the idea of mode and genre as it relates to deciding which kinds of writing to study with students.

Closing Thoughts

Iris is the daughter of our friends from Florida who come up to the mountains of North Carolina a couple of times each year. This past summer when I saw her, Iris had just finished fourth grade. She knows I like to know all about her reading and writing lives, so she gave me a report. She started with reading and told me how she had read so many books this past year that she'd gotten a top award for reading. We talked about some of the titles she liked best, and luckily I knew a fair number of them so I could carry my side of the conversation. "And writing," I asked, "How did it go with writing this year?"

"It was okay, I guess," she said. "I passed the writing test." She paused long enough for me to nod my approval. And then she added, "But I just don't like expository writing."

My heart sank. I wanted to turn back the clock for Iris and show her the wonderful promise of the work this mode of writing can do in the world. I wanted to thumb through magazines like *Ranger Rick* and *Time for Kids* with her. I wanted to read aloud to her from Cynthia Rylant's *Appalachia* (1991), and show her my collection of beautiful "literary nonfiction" picture books that almost always end with interesting, well-written notes on the subject of the book. I wanted to show her the article I'd recently printed off the MSN website explaining what to do if you're attacked by a shark. In the world outside school, writers employ the expository mode to delight and entertain readers in myriad interesting ways, but Iris hadn't learned that.

I wanted to confer with Iris and help her see how her life was rich and full of possibilities for this kind of writing. Iris is actually a child who loves to be outside exploring, roaming through woods and wading in creeks and digging in sand, seeing what she can find. Iris knows lots about animals and soccer and the aerodynamics of red wagons on the sides of mountains. Iris knows how to drive a boat, for heaven's sake. How could she leave school thinking she doesn't like writing about all these interesting topics she knows so much about?

The word *expository*, the idea of the word and the sense of what she should be doing to serve the word, left Iris with no vision for her writing. And since vision is what gives writers energy, it should be no surprise, I suppose, that Iris didn't like expository writing. She's an energetic kind of girl.

Interestingly enough, I told my husband, voracious reader of newspapers and magazines, about my conversation with Iris and that she said she didn't like expository writing. He asked, "What kind of writing is that?"

My point, exactly.

Craft Pause

NOTICE

This is an excerpt from Cynthia Rylant's vignette "On Beginning School" in the collection of memoir by various authors, *The Milestones Project*, edited by Richard Steckel and Michele Steckel (2004, 43). The vignette is about how her grandfather used to watch her as she walked off in the dark mornings to catch the school bus.

> He waited until he saw my small figure walking up the other side of the hill. He waited until he saw the lights of the school bus. He waited until I was safely on.

This is an excerpt from a Leonard Pitts commentary posted on April 29, 2005, in *The Miami Herald*. He's writing about the kindergartener caught on tape having a tantrum in Florida classroom who was later led away in handcuffs by the police.

> This wasn't stomping and shouting and throwing a fit. This was walking over to a shelf and sweeping items off it. Walking to a wall and snatching photos down. Walking across the room to pick things up and break them. Walking back and forth, in no apparent hurry, methodically wrecking the room with the calm deliberateness of someone who knows you can't do anything to stop her.

INSIGHTS ABOUT CRAFT

Repetition, in some form or fashion, is very common in well-crafted writing. In these two examples, both Rylant and Pitts chose to repeat the same verb in a series of sentences, and because they are action verbs, the repetition is even more significant. You get the sense of the action repeating itself in almost methodical ways because the verb used to capture it is repeated. Both writers could have combined these sentences to cut down on or eliminate the repetition all together, but both chose not to do this, making it clear they wanted the actions to stand out through repetition.

Pitts made another interesting crafting decision to let his sentences share the subject and verb from the first sentence in the series, "[This was] Walking. . . . "

5

The World Is Full of Writing

Finding Texts for Teaching

As I was reading the *Asheville Citizen-Times* I had to get up from my breakfast and go get the scissors. On the front of Section D—the "Fitness" section on Tuesdays—the layout of a feature article caught my eye. The title of the article was "Prepare to Bare" and there was a photo of a yellow bikini top and bottom framing the article in between. The margins of the text itself had been manipulated to look like a well-shaped body with a slim waistline inside the bikini. "Cool," I thought, but before I made the decision to go and get the scissors I had to read a little bit first. The writing was good, too, the author taking an obviously active stance to crafting the short piece about "fitballs" in an interesting way. I clipped it and tried to figure out a way to copy it so it would fit in my big blue three-ring binder of writing I collect for teaching.

I read like a teacher of writing (Ray 2002) even when I'm reading the morning paper, and I see rich text possibilities all around me. Because I believe so strongly in the need to show students examples of all kinds of texts, I'm always on the lookout for interesting writing. Sometimes my gathering is quite purposeful, as it was back before Christmas last year when I was scheduled to work three days with students and teachers in a school in Connecticut. I learned that one of the classes I would be teaching for the three days would be at the beginning of a study of how to write catalogue copy. I had never studied this particular kind of writing before, so I set out to gather as much of it as I could. Luckily it was the month before Christmas and I was getting two or three catalogues a day in the mail. It was very interesting for me to look at the catalogues with my writer's eyes instead of my shopper's eyes. I saw all kinds of things I'd never noticed before. I searched purposefully for good catalogue copy because I needed it for this teaching. At other times though, I simply carry on in my reading life just as I would if I weren't a teacher of writing, but I'm always on the lookout for things I might use in teaching.

Gathering a stack of texts that represents the kind of writing students will do is the first move a teacher makes when planning a study. The teacher gathers the texts knowing that whatever ends up in the stack will form the vision toward which students will draft, and that the stack will help students know where their writing "fits" in the larger world of writing. The word *world* is important in gathering. If you have a kind of writing in mind that you want your students to do and you can't find any examples of it in the world of writing outside school, then you probably need to rethink whether this kind of writing is worth doing.

In this chapter I'd like to consider six very common kinds of publications where I find a rich variety of short texts that I gather for teaching writing: newspapers, magazines, picture books, collections, excerpts, and Internet sites. But first, a note on why I look for *short* texts.

The Issue of Length

How long does it have to be? This is a question most of us remember asking as students ourselves, and inevitably we've been asked this question by our own students. The thing is, though, this isn't a question a teacher needs to answer when she's teaching from an inquiry stance. Length is part of the inquiry. Once you've gathered a stack of texts representing a certain kind of writing, one of the questions you'll ask is "How long are these texts?" The answer to "how long does it have to be?" depends on what kind of writing it is and how long it typically is in its published form.

Length guidelines are very much a part of the world of writing outside school. Depending on where the writing will be published, writers must work within specified guidelines. A feature article about hurricanes will be much shorter in *Time for Kids* than it will be in *National Geographic*. A memoir that will be published as a picture book will probably be much shorter than a memoir that will be published in a chapter book collection of memoirs. An essay published on the back page of *Newsweek* will be much shorter than an essay published over a series of pages in *The New Yorker*. And lots of composition-type writing that isn't published in this more traditional sense must be kept within word limits, too. The demands of my husband's business writing—letters, product reports, proposals, and so on—almost always require him to attend to length guidelines.

Recently I've written three articles for professional journals with three different word limits: 6500 (*Language Arts*), 3500 (*Educational Leadership*) and 1500 (*School Talk*). The different numbers of words present quite different writing challenges, and the bottom line is, I have to control the whole of the text—beginning, middle, and end (for lack of better words)—in the space I'm given.

As a teacher of writing, you'll want to think about length when you're gathering texts. You need examples that are about the length you actually expect students to write, sometimes a little longer than that (especially for the youngest writers), but not much. The selection and organization of ideas and their relationship to length is part of the vision students will get from immersing themselves in reading the texts. So even though second graders and eighth graders might both be studying feature articles, second graders will need shorter, more focused examples of this kind of writing for their study.

Length is a particular challenge when we want students to write in a genre they know well as readers, but they know it mostly in longer texts. Take fiction, for example. By the middle elementary years, most readers have moved into chapter books of fiction, but in a classwide study of fiction, you wouldn't want students to write chapter books. The scope of that writing would be too big in terms of volume and time for you to address as a class. For a fiction study you'd need to gather short stories because even though the students may know a lot about fiction from their reading of chapter books, they would need to see how writers control a whole story in a much more compressed format.

Now I'll walk through the places I go to find a variety of short, rich texts for teaching. As you read about these places, you might be slightly *under*whelmed by my ideas, and actually I hope that's the case! So much of what you need to teach students how to write well is right at your fingertips—and lots of it is free. If you just carry on with your everyday reading life you can fill notebooks with wonderful writing examples, and then with a little specialized searching every now and then, you can find everything you'll ever need.

Newspapers

I love *USA Today*. Because I travel a lot, I frequently get this paper delivered right outside my hotel room door and it is always a treat. I know it's not the most literary or erudite newspaper in the country, but I love it and perhaps more than any other reason, I love it because I am a teacher of writing. The writing I find there is accessible, often well crafted and it covers a wide range of interests. *USA Today* and any other newspaper are publishing containers just filled with all kinds of writing. I like that word *container* because "newspaper writing" is not a kind of writing in and of itself; a newspaper is simply a format where all kinds of writing are laid out in particular, familiar ways.

Inside *USA Today*, I find straight, who-what-when-where news stories of varying lengths. I find all kinds of feature articles, investigative reports, personal essays, travel articles, and op-ed pieces. There are book, movie, theatre, dance, and music reviews, and I love the two editorials that take opposite sides on current issues, "Our View" and "Opposing View." There is almost always fabulous sports reporting, especially during college basketball season when my interest in this kind of writing is at its peak, and I love all the different layout features that embed charts and timelines and maps as reference tools for the various articles. I just love *USA Today*.

As a teacher of writing, I am always on the lookout for short, interesting texts when I read *any* newspaper. And of course in today's world, most major newspapers are archived on their websites so I can keep tabs on my favorite columnists who write their delightfully short, 500- to 800-word columns a couple of times each week. If I want to see what Mitch Albom has written lately, I simply go to the *Detroit Free Press* site (*www.freep.com*) and find out. When I'm not traveling, I check in on Craig Wilson, the wonderful "slice of life" columnist for *USA Today*, at *www.usatoday.com*. And if I'm longing for a little something New York, I find William Safire at *www.nytimes.com* or if I want a good laugh I look up Dave Barry at *The Miami Herald* site (*www.miamiherald.com*). It's so *easy* to access so much wonderful writing from newspapers around the country, and an easy-to-print format is usually just a single click away.

At certain times I find specialized kinds of writing in the newspaper that aren't a part of the regular paper—the end of the year photo essays for example (or end of a football season, end of a century, end of a former president's life, end of the Olympics, etc.), or the pieces of short memoir published around the December holidays. While not usually a regular feature, sometimes papers will publish extensive interviews with people: political candidates, local people who've made it big, returning soldiers, and so on. I keep an eye out for these and other surprises I might find on a more infrequent basis in the daily paper.

While national newspapers have great writing in them, I keep a check on local papers as well, simply because some of the kinds of writing I'm interested in are specific to the locale in which I live and work. Reviews of local restaurants and area theatre, for example, and feature articles on people, places, and things of local interest. Our local paper, the *Asheville Citizen-Times*, has a regular weekly feature on some aspect of area history, so I often cut these out to go in a stack of historical essays or feature articles about history.

Many papers across the country have special sections (often published once or twice a week) devoted to young readers with a variety of kinds of writing in them. A recent edition of the two-page "Kidsday" section in New York's *Newsday* featured two interviews, an article on a school program about peace, a product review of something called the DreamPearls Keepsake Package, two recipes, and a column covering a variety of kids' opinions on the value of TV commercials. Children's sections like this can be great places to gather shorter texts for our youngest writers, and many of them have feature pieces that are actually written by children. The quality of these varies a good bit, but I'm always on the lookout for good writing in the children's sections.

Magazines

Because it holds many of the same kinds of writing (feature articles, reviews, essays, etc.) a magazine is a very similar container to a newspaper, only glossier. As a teacher of writing, I'm happy that our national attention span seems to have shortened and that magazines have lots and lots of one-page texts in them these days. Because of their compressed length, these are great texts to gather for teaching.

Most magazines have regular columnists we can follow, just like newspapers. I love Gary Smith and Rick Reilly of *Sports Illustrated*, Anna Quindlen at *Newsweek*, and Roger Rosenblatt who often writes for *Time*. There are also regular features we can return to again and again in magazines. The back pages of *Time* and *Newsweek*, for example, almost always have essays on them. The back page of my *Southern Living* is often a piece of memoir or sometimes a slice-of-life personal essay. I love the "My Turn" column in *Newsweek* where readers can have a go at publishing an essay. The *New York Times Magazine* has regular columns on language, food, style, ethics, and my favorite, "lives," which often has a one-page piece of memoir on it. Some magazines regularly publish works of short fiction.

Just like newspapers, most magazines now have websites and archives of articles. Some of them have free, unlimited access, and some of them require you to be a subscriber. Often, however, you simply need to enter an address of someone who subscribes, so if your school subscribes, you can use that address to get into the archives.

One of my favorite things about magazines is the number of specialty ones that exist. Basically, if there is even a small group of people in this country who are passionate about something, then there is probably a magazine devoted to their passion. I love craft magazines like *Beadwork* and *Pottery Making Illustrated* because they are full of articles that teach readers how to make things and do things. I sometimes buy *Backpacker* because I love its articles that are written as lists—"11 New Routes in the Rockies" and "20 Quick Family Getaways." I'll pick up *Biography* magazine from time to time because it has so many articles written as biographical sketches and interviews. Barnes & Noble publishes *Book* magazine and it's full of reviews and literary essays. If I taught high school, I'd have to subscribe to *Rolling Stone* because, well, it's just so cool.

An interesting line of thinking in the magazine world is to follow a topic across a number of different magazines and see how it is handled. Specialty magazines have much more select audiences than those with more general readerships. Because of its audience, *Backpacker* magazine would have a different take on "20 Quick Family Getaways" than say, *Travel and Leisure* would have, and their take would be different than what you would find in a summer issue of *Ladies Home Journal* on great family getaways. Randy Bomer (1995) defines a feature article as "something written to inform readers that they never realized a topic could be so complex and interesting" (175). Readers of specialty magazines already find the topics in them to be complex and interesting, that's why they buy the magazines in the first place, so writers of the texts in these containers have a little different work to do than in a general read kind of magazine.

And of course, one of the huge things magazines offer us as teachers of writing is the wide variety of them that are devoted to children. The articles in children's magazines are generally of high interest, they're often very well written, and many, many of them are also delightfully *short*. The very first stacks of feature articles that you'll use to give second and third graders their first visions for this kind of writing will likely be the three- or four-paragraph articles found in *Ranger Rick*, *National Geographic World*, and *Time for Kids*. Magazines like *Spider*, *Stone Soup*, and *Cricket* publish a variety of short fiction, and there are also children's magazines devoted to special interests such as *Dig*, which is all about archaeology, and *Young Rider*, which is devoted to horseback riding.

A few other magazines for children filled with great writing:

American Girl	*Family Fun*
Ask: Art and Sciences for Kids	*Highlights for Children*
Boy's Life	*Jack & Jill*
Calliope	*Muse*
Click: Opening Windows for Young Minds	*Odyssey: Adventures in Science*
Cobblestone	*U.S. Kids*
Faces: People, Places, Culture	*Your Big Backyard*

Picture Books

As a teacher of writing, I love picture books, of course, probably even more than I love *USA Today*. I love them at any grade level at which I work, but especially in teaching the very youngest writers because picture books open up worlds of possibilities for introducing them to all sorts of interesting writing. A picture book is a format in which words and illustrations (of some kind) work together to convey meaning. I have a collection of hundreds of these books, and inside many of them are complex, interesting texts that are fine, fine accomplishments in writing well. And, most wonderfully, they contain relatively *short* texts. In this beautiful container known as the picture book we find all kinds of fiction (realistic, fantasy, historical, etc.), memoir, poetry, slice-of-life writing, biographical sketches, and other kinds of writing that take lots of words to name.

In picture books I also find writing that is a lot like writing in other containers. This is especially true when I stack texts by what it seems the writer is trying *to do* with the writing. This is an idea I'll come back to again later in this book, but for now let's just think about it in a small way. In his book *Time for Meaning* (1995), I like that Randy Bomer defines different types of nonfiction by different intentions a writer might have. This helps me so much in my thinking as a teacher of writing. Take the feature article definition that I mentioned earlier, for example. Again, Bomer defines a feature article as something written to inform readers about a topic they never realized could be so complex and interesting. This seems to be what many writers of pictures books are intending to do. James Prosek's *A Good Day's Fishing* (2004), for example, takes the reader on a lively tour through a tackle box and then provides a rich glossary of information about the items in the box at the end. It's a very interesting book to read, it is very informative, and it seems to be driven by the same writerly intentions as the feature article.

Bomer defines an essay as something written to take readers on a journey of thought as the writer tries out an idea. Sometimes writers of picture books seem to have this kind of writing as their goal. For example, I think Geraldine Mc-Caughrean's book *My Grandmother's Clock* (2002) is a book like this. While the journey of thought happens in the frame of a conversation between a child and a grandmother, McCaughrean certainly seems to be "trying out an idea," the idea that time can be measured in ways that don't have anything to do with clocks or other traditional measures of time. And an editorial or argument, which Bomer defines as something written to persuade readers to believe as the writer believes, certainly seems to be a big part of David J. Smith's intention in the book *If the World Were a Village* (2002). His text and the notes at the end seem designed to nudge readers to believe in a particular worldview. He says, "This book is about 'world-mindedness,' which is an attitude, an approach to life. It is the sense that our planet is actually a village . . . Knowing who our neighbors are, where they live and how they live, will help us live in peace" (30).

My point is, picture books are not just story books, a serious overgeneralization that doesn't help us as teachers of writing at all. Writers of picture book texts realize all sorts of intentions in this format. Thinking about them in this way—as an act of intention on the part of a writer—helps us in two main ways that I can see. First, when we share stacks of these texts with our youngest writers in kindergarten and first grade, we realize we are laying important groundwork for them to understand a variety of sophisticated writing intentions that will grow with them as they grow, both as people and as people who write. If a kindergartner learns, for example, that one kind of writing people do in the world is a kind where a reader is entertained in some way but also learns important information about a topic, this is a precursor to so much of the writing he'll be asked to do later in school and in life.

The second way looking at writers' intentions behind texts helps us is that we can gather a stack of texts that might include picture books alongside writing we've found in other containers like newspapers and magazines. This is especially powerful in the upper elementary grades and beyond as it really helps students come to understand how the different containers in which writing can be published simply offer different ways to have the same intentions realized (in terms of visual images, design features, length of text, audience, etc.).

Collections

Collections are another container for shorter texts of various kinds of writing. Short stories are probably the most familiar kind of collection and of course they are essential to studies of fiction because of the length issue. I find that it is actually fairly challenging to find collections of short stories that are truly *short*. Many of them are technically short stories, certainly much shorter than novels, but still a good bit longer than what I would actually expect upper elementary students to write. I think so much like a teacher of writing that when I pick up a new short story collection I first look at the page numbers in the table of contents just to see how long the stories are! A classic collection I know many teachers have used is Cynthia Rylant's *Every Living Thing* (1985), but I also like Angela Johnson's *Gone from Home: Short Takes* (1998), and *Tripping over the Lunch Lady and Other School Stories* (2004) edited by Nancy Mercado.

There are wonderful collections of memoir like the two edited by Amy Ehrlich, *When I Was Your Age: Original Stories About Growing Up,* Volumes 1 (1996) and 2 (1999), written by different authors of popular children's fiction. *Grand Fathers* (1999) and *Grand Mothers: Poems, Reminiscences and Short Stories About the Keepers of Our Traditions* (1994), both edited by Nikki Giovanni, are collections of different kinds of writing but all coming from writers digging into their memories. *Linda Brown, You Are Not Alone* (Thomas 2003) is a collection of memoir by different authors and all focused on a particular historical event, the *Brown vs. the Board of Education* decision and the impact it had on public schools.

Don Wulffson's *Toys! Amazing Stories Behind Some Great Inventions* (2000) and *The Kid Who Invented the Trampoline: More Surprising Stories About Inventions* (2001) are collections of short informational pieces (most like feature articles) about the origins of various inventions. I have collections of essays like Barbara Kingsolver's *Small Wonder* (2002) and Naomi Shihab Nye's *Never in a Hurry: Essays on People and Places* (1996), and collections of columns written by some of my favorite columnists like *The Life of Reilly* (2000) by Rick Reilly, *Paradise Screwed* (2001) by Carl Hiaasen, and *Thinking Out Loud* (1993) by Anna Quindlen. I have a wonderful collection of sports writing by Gary Smith, *Beyond the Game* (2000), a collection of famous speeches, *In Our Own Words* (Torricelli

1999), and I even have a collection of "rants" by Dennis Miller, *I Rant, Therefore I Am* (2000).

Excerpts

Excerpts from longer texts sometimes make great additions to a stack I'm gathering for teaching. In genre studies I'm usually looking for what I would call the "stand alone" excerpt, meaning one that feels complete without relying on the rest of the text. Take memoir, for example. Tomie dePaola's memoir *26 Fairmont Avenue* (1999) is chapter book in length, not a long chapter book, but still longer than what I would expect students to actually write. Chapter Three, though, about a trip to see *Snow White and the Seven Dwarfs* at the movies, stands alone nicely as a memoir example. Chapter book memoirs often have a lot of excerpts that work well by themselves because they are actually made up of many smaller stories tied together in the longer structure of chapter divisions.

Nonfiction chapter books also often have excerpts that stand alone well, usually because they address and cover all the writer will say about some aspect of a larger topic. The chapters in Karen Magnuson Beil's *Fire in their Eyes: Wildfires and the People Who Fight Them* (1999) stand nicely on their own, as do the chapters in Stephen R. Swinburne's *Coyote: North America's Dog* (1999).

I find it to be much more of a challenge to pull a stand alone excerpt from fiction that can serve as an example of *fiction*, simply because it's the nature of the genre for the bits and pieces of a story to rely on one another for their wholeness. What I often collect in excerpt form from fiction, however, are sections of text where a writer is attending to some particular aspect of craft I might want to study with students. Some of these will be fairly specific to the genre of fiction, things like shifting the pace of movement through time or developing subtle nuances of character. I love the first chapter of Jerry Spinelli's *Stargirl* (2000) for both these aspects of fiction. But many of the excerpts I collect from fiction are more general examples of crafting that aren't specific to this genre: interesting punctuation moves (anything Gary Paulsen writes) and purposeful, compelling descriptions (the beginning of chapter three in *Charlotte's Web*), for instance. These kinds of excerpts can be pulled from all kinds of writing, actually, not just fiction.

The Internet

Access to the World Wide Web has changed my life in so many ways, and this is certainly true for me as a teacher of writing. I think my three favorite words in the English language are *printer friendly format!* First, there is the easy access to the archives of so many magazines and newspapers I've already mentioned. But in addition to this, I can go to sites like *www.rottentomatoes.com* and get immediate links to movie reviews in newspapers and magazines from all over the country. I can Google something like "children's short stories" and find a site like *www.eastoftheweb.com* where a variety of short stories of varying lengths appear in their entirety on the site.

My Internet browser was preset to go to MSN each time I log on, and I've never changed it because as a teacher of writing I love this site (almost as much as I love *USA Today* and picture books). If I spend just a few minutes pointing and clicking around the site, I can find all sorts of short, interesting articles on a wide variety of topics and links to even more. For example, *Slate*, an online magazine connected to MSN's site, has wonderful articles in it. On the particular day that I am writing this I take a time-out and go on and find, among other things, a feature article about guinea pigs being raised as a food product in Peru and an essay about how horrible ponchos are as a fashion fad. Both of them are well written and certainly high interest, so I print them off and add them to my notebook.

In addition to being an invaluable resource to find writing that has been published in more traditional formats, there is also the *website* itself as a relatively new form of publication in the world. I haven't done any work with students around writing to be published on a website, but I know others have and have found it to be very interesting, heady writing work for students. When you think of writing (as we have been thinking of it) as beginning with some intentions a writer has, then a website is just another option with different kinds of potential for how that writing might be presented in the world to fulfill those intentions. I certainly imagine that within the span of many of our teaching careers, the potential for publishing writing on the World Wide Web will continue to expand and as teachers of writing, we'll have to stay abreast of the implications this has for understanding writing in the world outside school.

It's a World of Layout

Six different containers for all kinds of writing: newspapers, magazines, picture books, collections, excerpts, and the Internet. What these different containers offer writers, more than anything else, are different potentials and possibilities for layout and presentation. The children we teach will grow to be experienced writers in a world dominated by layout and the potential of graphics to enhance the meanings of written texts. Our students will be called on to fashion texts in a world of seemingly endless font possibilities, boxes, icons, graphs, charts, insets, motion, sound, color. . . . Vision for writing is not just vision for how the words can go anymore; it's a presentation vision too, and I believe students are underserved by writing instruction that doesn't ask them to think about layout when crafting their texts. The "what have you read that is like what you are trying to write?" question is as much one of layout and presentation as it is of genre and form.

Imagine, for example, that I wanted to write a memoir about the old railroad bell that sat on our back porch and that my mother used to ring to call us in from play each day. My vision for this memoir changes when I think of it as a picture book, then as the back page of *Southern Living*, then in a collection of short memoirs by women who grew up in the South, then as a feature in our local paper known as "Our Stories." The topic doesn't change and the genre doesn't change, but the vision of the finished writing shifts some. Some of the shifting vision has to do with the text itself, especially when I think about the different kinds of people who read those different texts. Certainly my vision for length shifts some for each container, but a lot of the shifting vision has to do with the layout possibilities for my memoir that are possible in those different containers. And even if I decided I didn't want to send the memoir out into the world, I just wanted to send it to my mom, I'd be thinking about how I might present it to her. Perhaps as a voice-over for a DVD compilation of pictures of my siblings and I playing as children . . . now there's a good idea!

Related to this, one question I'm often asked about children's writing in the primary grades has to do with the amount of time and attention young children spend thinking about their illustrations versus their written texts. In response I usually ask about how much composition intention children are bringing to the illustrations. Are they using the illustrations to make meanings that aren't in the words? If the answer is yes, I tend not to be quite as concerned, perhaps, as some might be that more meaning isn't carried with the words. Again, the definition of composition that these children need to understand is much broader than the one I knew at their age, and I'm comfortable with them exploring the edges of that definition with graphics other than words.

Starting a Collection of Writing for Teaching

One of my most prized possessions in this world, one of the first things I'd grab in case of a fire, is my big, blue, ever-expanding notebook of things I cut from newspapers and magazines and things I've printed off the Internet. The notebook is divided into sections. Some of my favorite newspaper and magazine writers have their own personal sections of the notebook—Craig, Leonard, Rick, Anna— and everything else is divided into sections with labels such as interviews, travel articles, movie reviews, essays, articles that are lists of things, and so on. These labels sometimes change as I develop new nuances of understanding about different kinds of writing.

For example, I once had only one section for articles that explain how to do something. Then I engaged in a study of this kind of writing and realized there needed to be two sections for this kind of writing. One is a section for articles written with the expectation that the reader should actually be able to do what's being explained after reading the piece—make a mirror with mosaic tiles or start a compost pile in the backyard. The other section contains articles that explain exactly how something is done, but there is clearly no expectation that the reader will be able to do it—how cloning is done, for example, or how maple syrup is harvested. The purpose of these articles is to *inform* readers about how something is done, not teach them how to do it. Two kinds of how-to articles, both very driven by the procedural mode, but written with clearly different intentions.

My blue notebook contains, for the most part, the things I clip from my adult reading life that I want for any teaching I might do with children in the upper elementary grades and beyond. I would encourage all teachers of writers in the upper elementary, middle, and high school grades to begin their own collections of writing that will give students vision. Teachers can collaborate on these collections and they'll grow faster than anyone might imagine. And of course, don't forget to invite your students to help you find good examples of writing you might add to your collection. Students can be a wonderful resource for gathering texts because they often know about magazines and websites that we've never heard about.

You may be wondering why I don't just publish my collection of writing for others to use when it would save busy teachers so much time and energy. Well, there are three main reasons why I don't do that. First, it would be very, very expensive. Permissions to reprint writing in another publication cost money. Quite simply, I can't afford to publish my notebook full of writing. Second, though I know it takes time and energy to collect examples, you will be a different teacher of writing after going through the process of collecting. You'll understand things about writing that you didn't understand before you started trying to find real-world texts to support your teaching. And third, the topics of many pieces become dated very quickly, particularly things like reviews and commentary because they are written in direct response to what's happening in the world at a given time. Examples of these kinds of writing have to be continually updated if we want them to remain high interest for students.

In addition to all the things I cut and place in my notebook, because I'm not housed in a school I also subscribe on my own to a variety of children's magazines. I keep these magazines in their entirety (as opposed to cutting out just the articles I want for my notebook) because they are simply treasure troves of good examples of writing. A single issue of *Ranger Rick*, for example, usually has seven or eight different feature articles and often each one shows a different interesting approach to this kind of writing. A class could do a whole study of this kind of writing (informative but also engaging) from a single issue. I would encourage you to spend a little time looking through the magazines in your school library as a teacher of writing would look at them. What kinds of writing do you find there? Consider asking the media specialist to order even more as you explain why you'd like to use them for the teaching of writing.

If you can use money to buy some subscriptions you can keep in your class, all the better. Ask your students to donate to the class any children's magazines they might have from home and are finished reading. For magazines you do have in your classroom, consider having students go through them and label the different kinds of writing they find there—using words that will give other writers vision, of course.

I would love to tell everyone to start an extensive collection of picture books to support the teaching of writing, but of course, picture books are expensive. Instead, consider talking with your media specialists about stacking texts. Explain how you want to be able to show students multiple examples of specific kinds of writing. Explain how you may need lots of words to say exactly the kind of writing you are looking for, but if you can say all those words, can she or he please help you find that kind of writing. Enlist this person in helping you stack texts by the kind of writing represented in those texts.

One of my greatest pleasures in life is being able to share my own picture books in this way with my teaching friends. Several times each year I load up a couple of bags of books and head out to Jonathan Valley Elementary where my friend Lisa Cleaveland teaches first grade. I love that moment when I walk through the door with the books and the children spot me all loaded down. Because Lisa's teaching has become so familiar to them, because they recognize the rhythms of this teaching over time, they know exactly why Ms. Katie has come bearing books. The looks on their faces at that moment are simply priceless to me.

Craft Pause

This excerpt of commentary from a Leonard Pitts column in *The Miami Herald*, posted on August 2, 2004, reflecting on his trip to Seirra Leon and Niger in West Africa.

Around us, Kroo Bay goes about its business. A mangy dog with open sores sleeps on a sidewalk. Gray water trickles in a stream filled with garbage. The air is pungent with the smoke from cook fires. An old man sits in front of his home smoking his pipe. He lives in a shanty with a roof made from corrugated metal. There are rocks on it to keep it from blowing away in a high wind.

This excerpt from Cynthia Rylant's picture book memoir *Christmas in the Country* (2002).

Winter in the country is so quiet. The snow slows everything down. Birds are silent and serious. Dogs stay in their warm houses. Children want cocoa and blankets. Everyone is ready for something really special. Everyone is ready for Christmas.

In each of these excerpts, the first sentence makes a sort of general, descriptive statement, and then the short sentences that follow it bring the idea to life. To put it another way, the first sentence tells, and the short sentences that follow it *show*.

In many ways, I also believe the way sentences like these work together creates a sense of voice in texts. We often do this when we're telling someone about something. We'll make a sort of general claim about something ("You would not believe how crowded the mall was on Saturday"), and then, realizing the need to make ourselves believable in this claim, we'll supply specific details of information to back us up—often whole, quick lists of them just as you see in these crafting examples ("We circled the parking lot for at least half an hour before we found a spot. People were six deep waiting to check out in Dillards. We couldn't even walk side by side there were so many people."). Listen carefully, and I'm sure you can hear yourself or someone you know using language in just this way.

Deciding What to Study from a World of Possibilities

When I sit in front of my bookshelf, I can't help it, I dream of studies.

In a perfect teaching world, I'd plan an author study of Marilyn Nelson and how she uses poetry as a way to explore history in books like *A Wreath for Emmett Till* (2005), *Fortune's Bones: The Manumission Requiem* (2004), and *Carver: A Life in Poems* (2001).

I'd plan a study of how writers combine words with responses to photographs to create all sorts of interesting texts: Toni Morrison in *Remember: The Journey to School Integration* (2004), Carole Boston Weatherford in *Remember the Bridge* (2002), Cynthia Rylant in *Something Permanent* (1994), and Walter Dean Myers in *Here in Harlem* (2004).

I'd plan of study of all the different ways writers can achieve the work of an essay and take readers on a journey of thought: Julius Lester in *Let's Talk About Race* (2005), Mem Fox in *Whoever You Are* (1997) and Cynthia Rylant in the poetry collection *God Went to Beauty School* (2003).

I'd plan a study of rich language use and anchor it in nothing but excerpts from Gary Paulsen's *Clabbered Dirt, Sweet Grass* (1992). I think I could study that book for a whole school year and never tire of it.

I'd plan a study of memoir written as a collection of short vignettes: Kathi Appelt in *My Father's Summers—A Daughter's Memoir* (2004), Ralph Fletcher in *Marshfield Dreams* (2005), and Eric Carle in *Flora and Tiger: 19 Very Short Stories from My Life* (1997).

I'd set students loose in the library for a few days and have them search for kinds of writing or things about writing they'd like to study. Then I'd plan a whole range of options for study based on their findings and let them each choose the study they wanted.

I have no trouble making plans for inquiry in a perfect teaching world. But in the somewhat less than perfect world where teaching really happens, how do teachers decide what makes sense to study in a writing workshop across a school year? How do they put together a year of study like the one you see on the curriculum calendar in Figure 6.1?

In addressing this question, I'll assume the inquiry happens in a writing workshop that includes time most every day for three things (and yes, I do believe these are essential—even in the less than perfect world where teaching really happens):

- a whole-class gathering for teacher-led conversation, demonstration, or inquiry
- independent writing and writing-related work (teacher conferencing)
- talking and sharing about the process of writing

Planning from a Larger Sense of Purpose

First and foremost, in making decisions about what to study, I think it is important for teachers of writing to know what their goals are for the teaching they'll be doing over time in a workshop setting. Quality, day-to-day work with young writers begins with a much larger sense of purpose. Interestingly enough, I have basically the same goals, the same larger sense of purpose, whether I'm

FIGURE 6.1 *Sample Year of Study in an Upper-Grades Writing Workshop*

Unit One	Making Plans for Writing Across the Year
Unit Two	Genre Study: Feature Articles with Strong Narrative Qualities
Unit Three	Making Our Notebooks Better Toolboxes for Writing
Unit Four	Genre Study: Slice-of-Life Stories from Our Lives
Unit Five	Punctuation as a Tool to Craft Our Writing
Unit Six	Genre Study: Short Stories (realistic fiction)
Unit Seven	Revision Strategies
Unit Eight	Genre Study: How-to Feature Articles
Unit Nine	Revision as Recasting (writing an old piece in a new genre)
Unit Ten	Looking Back, Looking Forward (assessing the year of writing)

teaching a group of writers in kindergarten or in college. Over time in any writing workshop, my goals are to see students developing:

A. a sense of self as writers, as well as personal writing processes that work for them;
B. ways of reading the world like writers, collecting ideas with variety, volume, and thoughtfulness;
C. a sense of thoughtful, deliberate purpose about their work as writers and a willingness to linger with those purposes;
D. their membership in a responsive, literate community;
E. ways of reading texts like writers, developing a sense of craft, genre, and form in writing; and
F. a sense of audience and an understanding of how to prepare conventional writing to go into the world (Ray 1999; Ray 2001; Ray 2004).

When teachers are clear about their larger sense of purpose, then it's not a stretch to see how almost any study in writing can help them work toward these kinds of goals. This is true, of course, because the inquiry happens in the writing workshop and the workshop itself, by design, supports children growing in all these ways. A whole-class study is simply an overlay to the day-to-day writing work that supports children's growth as writers.

To understand this, I sometimes ask teachers to think about a writing workshop as a time each day when there is no explicit teaching at all, only management of student work. And let me be clear, this is only an *intellectual exercise*; I'm not suggesting that a writing workshop with no explicit teaching is a good idea. That being said, imagine a workshop with just these essentials:

Time	A regularly scheduled, healthy chunk of time when students work on pieces of writing and develop stamina for the process.
Talk	A predictable time and space where students talk with others about their writing.
Expectation	An expectation that students will regularly finish pieces of writing, filling a portfolio by year's end.
Vision	An expectation that students will write with vision and that for their finished pieces of writing they can answer the question, "What have I read that is like what you're trying to write?"

The writing students would produce with these essentials in place might or might not be any good, but they could certainly do the writing work. The interesting thing is, if a teacher simply managed this writing every day then students would be working toward all the goals I outlined earlier. And if that teacher ritualized what it means to be finished so that students had to account for their process each time, then the workshop format would do even more teaching without explicit teaching. That ritual might look something like the form you see in Figure 6.2, and I've noted the teaching goals that are particularly supported by asking students these questions.

Because writing is something people do, it's impossible to ask students to write and not also be asking them to *learn how to write* at the same time. As a matter of fact, students probably learn more from the experience of writing a lot over time than from anything else. The lines between curriculum and instruction are all but indistinguishable when you think about it this way.

When teachers recognize that it is the *work* of the *work*shop that does the most important teaching across the year, deciding what to study as a whole class becomes a different sort of decision than is typically made when planning for other content areas. Teachers of writing aren't relying on units of study to "cover" everything students need to know about writing. As long as the inquiry happens in a writing workshop context, almost any study can raise the level of work students are doing and still help everyone grow in all the "big picture" ways they need to be growing. And of course, units of study don't do all the teaching either. In daily writing conferences, teachers offer a wealth of essential writing curriculum that is specific and differentiated for individual student needs.

In many ways, then, dreams of studies don't have to be just dreams. Teachers of writing can gather texts and plan some studies during the year to follow their particular interests and the needs and interests of their students. Let's think now about the different kinds of study you'll want to support in your writing workshop.

Plan for Independent Writers First

First, to support as many different independent intentions as you can imagine in a class filled with different children, you'll need a rich variety of different kinds of writing available. You may remember back to Chapter 3 when I showed writing that came not from whole-class studies but from the individual intentions of three different students: Samantha's counting book, Meredith's travel guide, and Harrison's collection of poems. These young writers had to have access to these kinds of texts before they could write them. So if you expect students to answer thoughtfully when you ask, "What have you read that is like what

FIGURE 6.2 *Student Questionnaire*

Your Name _____ **Date** _____

Title of Your Piece _____

Kind of Writing _____

_____

1. How did the idea for this piece start? (Goals B and C)

2. What kinds of things did you do to develop this idea before you began drafting it? Any nonwriting work like research, gathering, etc.? What notebook entries did you do to support this draft? (Goals B and C)

3. What have you read that is like what you are trying to write? What kind of person reads the kind of thing you've written (audience)? (Goals E and F)

4. Describe your process for drafting and revision. Explain some actual decisions you made while drafting and revising this piece. Include details about any specific crafting decisions you made. (Goals A, C, and E)

5. Describe your process for proofreading. Can you honestly say you've copyedited as well as you possibly can? (Goal F)

6. How did you decide on the format for publishing the piece? (Goal F)

7. How does this piece fit into the journey of your writing life? What did you learn from writing it? (Goal A)

Be sure to show all artifacts from the process you describe.

you're trying to write?" they'll need some writing around to give them the vision with which to answer.

I will sometimes add a piece of writing to my collection for just this reason—so I have it on hand if an individual writer needs to see it—not because I expect to study that type of writing with a whole class of students. Consider paying attention, for example, to things like notes that come with new music CDs. You may encounter students who are very into music and when you do, it's good to have some of this kind of writing about music on hand. You might buy neat cookbooks, collections of plays, or magazines devoted to video games for the same reason, just to have them around as possibilities. Individual students or small groups of students can pursue their own studies of different kinds of writing when a variety of writing is available, and you'll find many opportunities in writing conferences to suggest students look at particular texts to help them get vision for their writing.

Decisions About Whole-Class Studies

Basically there are two main kinds of studies that make sense for a writing workshop: studies that have something to do with the *process* of writing (and what it means to be a writer living through the process) or studies that have something to do with the *products* of writing. In the year of studies you saw in Figure 6.1, there is a healthy balance between these two kinds of studies. Genre study is really a marriage of the two because you study both the process of writing in the genre (and yes, the process is slightly different for different genres) and you study examples of the genre (the product) closely, too. Some product studies zoom in and look at a particular aspect of crafting texts such as punctuating in interesting ways or using a strong text structure to organize. Chapter 12 will give you other ideas for process studies, and then the entire collection of resource sections will give you ideas for product studies in both genre and craft. How will you decide?

Studies That Come from Students' Needs and Interests

Some of what you decide to study during the year may come from what you learn interests your students as writers. Believe it or not, many students are interested in issues that could lead to units of study in writing. We just need to listen to them with our ears open for possibilities.

For example, my niece who's in middle school and I had an interesting conversation about how books get turned into movies. It seems she had been discussing this at school, particularly as it relates to the newest Harry Potter movie and *Chronicles of Narnia*. If this conversation had happened amongst the students in my writing workshop, seeing their interest, I might ask if they'd be up for studying how books are turned into screen plays. I'd have some work to do to get access to screen plays that had first been books, but if the interest was there, I'm sure my students could help me figure out how to get them and off we'd go. This would be a very big study, one where I'd have to learn along with the students, so we'd want to be sure it was something we wanted to tackle as a whole class.

As we assess our students and their work as writers, we'll also realize that certain studies make sense because students need them. They might need to be introduced to an important idea about writing such as how to read like a writer or how to keep a writer's notebook, or they might need to deepen their understandings in these areas so they can do more sophisticated writing work with them. Interestingly enough, what you see students need as writers will have a lot to do with your own knowledge base about the curriculum of writing. In my first years as a teacher of writing, it would never have occurred to me that students might need to learn how to read like writers or use a writer's notebook because I didn't know anything about either one of these. As your knowledge base grows about writing, you'll see more and more possibilities for studies that might deepen the work your students are doing.

Studies Based on Curriculum Guidelines and Mandated Assessments

Beyond understanding that whole-class studies in writing workshop can be planned to support students' needs and interests, teachers of writing also need to be very familiar with their state and local curriculum guidelines (not the ones tied to language arts textbooks) and with the kinds of writing students are going to be expected to produce on mandated assessments of writing. When I study these guidelines for my particular locale in North Carolina, I find that many of them are quite similar to my personal goals for teaching and are similarly supported by the day-to-day work of the writing workshop. For example, consider the language of general guidelines such as:

The learner will:

- Explore a wide range of texts and their distinguishing features.
- Write for a variety of purposes and audiences and use writing as a tool for learning.
- Use increasingly sophisticated knowledge of grammar and language conventions in oral and written products and presentations.

> (North Carolina Standard Course of Study, Fourth Grade English Language Arts Objectives, revised 2004)

All the studies I can imagine—as long as they are tied to immersion and the study of well-written texts—would support students in fulfilling these objectives in the context of a writing workshop.

I generally find a range of specificity in curriculum guidelines, with a general trend that they become more specific, particularly with respect to genre, as students move into higher grades. For example, in North Carolina's standard course of study for first grade, there are only two goals connected to genre. One (4.6) says, "The learner will compose a variety of products using a writing process," which leaves lots of room for teacher decision making about the kinds of writing to study. The other (4.2) seems to indicate that writing in the narrative mode needs to be included as it says, "The learner will use words that describe, name characters and settings, and tell action and events in simple texts." The most obvious study to support this goal would be a study of writing slice-of-life stories, but savvy teachers will realize they might also support this goal in a study of literary nonfiction by choosing books or feature articles that engage readers in a story but also provide factual information, books like Jonathan London's *Panther: Shadow of the Swamp* (2000) and *Baby Whale's Journey* (1999). In Figure 6.3 you see a piece of literary nonfiction from *Click* magazine that has a strong narrative quality in the writing.

As students move up in the grades, the kinds of writing they should be studying, particularly for mandated assessments, get more specific. The problem is, curriculum documents are not often written in ways that make it easy to know what kind of writing to ask for when you go into the library or bookstore to find it. As I mentioned in Chapter 4, both curriculum documents and large-scale writing assessments tend to use the language of mode to name what it is students should be doing with writing. Figuring out what to gather to support children in learning about these different kinds of writing involves an act of *curriculum translation* on the part of teachers of writing.

CURRICULUM TRANSLATION

As an example, let's look at one of the writing performance descriptions found in the New Standards' guide entitled *Performance Standards*, a document published by a group of educators representing the National Center on Education and the Economy and the University of Pittsburgh's Learning Research and Development Center (1997). The *Performance Standards* were developed from the national content standards of the leading professional organizations in various fields of study: for language arts, the National Council of Teachers of English and the International Reading Association. As a demonstration, let me walk you through my thinking as a teacher of writing when I look at this sort of document. My hope is that seeing *how* I think about this will help you as you study the curriculum guidelines specific to your teaching situation.

"Cheetah Chase"
Susan Yoder Ackerman

Click, July/August 2005

Heat rises off the African grassland. Duma and her cubs sprawl under a thorn tree. They are well hidden as they sleep. Their yellow-gray fur, covered with dark round spots, blends into the shadows and dry grass.

The sun is lower now. Duma opens her eyes and stretches, purring and chirping to her cubs. Late afternoon is hunting time for cheetahs.

Duma sharpens her claws at the base of the thorn tree. Other cats can tuck their claws into their paw pads when they're not hunting, but a cheetah's claws are out all the time. Duma's long, strong claws will help keep her feet from slipping as she races after her prey.

Duma starts down into the valley. The cubs dash ahead. Duma keeps an eye on her cubs. On the last hunt, they chased a hippopotamus by mistake, an animal much too big for a cheetah to capture. But they're learning.

Duma's sharp eyes spot gazelles grazing in the distance. A gazelle is Duma's favorite meal. Gazelles can run faster than anything—except a cheetah.

Everything about a cheetah makes it fast. Cheetahs are long, light, and muscular. They have small heads and narrow shoulders and hips. Their joints are loose and their spines flexible so they can stretch out to take giant strides. Cheetahs have almost no fat on their bodies. Being so lean saves weight, but unlike big lions and tigers, cheetahs must eat every two or three days or they will starve.

A cheetah can take off in an instant. In three seconds, Duma has passed her cubs, traveling at a speed of more than 45 miles per hour. Duma runs so fast that only one foot touches the earth at a time. Every second she takes three big strides, each one longer than a car.

The gazelles scatter in all directions when they see the cheetah. Duma follows the nearest one. The cheetah is full of energy for the chase. The bulge in Duma's skull between her eyes provides an extrawide passage for sucking in air as she runs. Her big, bushy tail helps Duma keep her balance when the gazelle turns sharply, trying to escape.

The gazelle is fast, but Duma stays right behind. Duma has saved just enough energy for the final sprint. With a burst of speed, she flies across the ground at 70 miles an hour, faster than a car on the highway. Again and again, her spine bends and stretches out like a spring, pushing her forward and making her long legs reach even farther with every bound.

Duma strikes with her paw and misses. The gazelle disappears into a stand of trees. The hunt is over. The cubs catch up with their mother, disappointed.

Tomorrow the cheetahs will run again. But for now, hot and exhausted, Duma must rest all through the African night.

One of the four writing performance descriptions for fourth graders reads like this:

The student produces a narrative procedure that:

• engages the reader by establishing a context, creating a persona, and otherwise developing reader interest;

• provides a guide to action that anticipates a reader's needs; creates expectations through predictable structures, e.g., headings; and provides transitions between steps;

• makes use of appropriate writing strategies such as creating a visual hierarchy and using white space and graphics as appropriate;

• includes relevant information;

• excludes extraneous information;

- anticipates problems, mistakes, and misunderstandings that might arise for the reader;
- provides a sense of closure to the writing.

When I looked at this the first time my response was, "Oh, my . . . what is this exactly?" The label "narrative procedure" was not familiar. I mean, I knew both those words, but I didn't really know them together. As I looked at the descriptors under the label, I couldn't figure out why the word *narrative* had been used because I didn't see anything that really supported the idea that there had to be narrative work in the writing—only that the procedure be interesting to read. Perhaps the word *narrative* was being used in the sense of narrating the steps of the procedure. One thing I knew for sure, *narrative procedure* was not something I could go into a bookstore or library and ask to be shown. I would need more words, and so I focused on the descriptors themselves. Reading down the list, I tried to imagine, "What have I read that is like this?"

Next, I looked at the list of examples provided in the document underneath the descriptors. The list gives examples of what students might do to demonstrate achievement in writing a narrative procedure, but even these didn't help me decide right away what kind of writing I needed. The examples are really more topic-embedded assignments for writing rather than a category of writing from the world I might study with students. Here's the list of the suggestions given in the *New Standards* with my thoughts as a teacher of writing in italics after each one.

Examples of narrative procedures include:

- A set of rules for organizing a class meeting. (*This might make sense as a shared writing engagement for the class. But I can't imagine having a whole class study of written rules or protocols for meetings. That's a too-specific kind of writing.*)

- A chapter book developed around procedures, for example, how to have a safe vacation, with chapters on safe swimming, safe games, and other issues of safety. (*Chapter books are too long. I'd rather have a shorter kind of text we could study so students could write their own entire text rather than just a chapter of a collaborative chapter book.*)

- A how-to report to accompany a board game. (*I've never seen this kind of writing before. Maybe they mean something like what you find in those magazines about video games? "How to get to level nine in Zelda's Quest" or something like that. Is report the right word for this?*)

- A set of procedures for accessing information in the library. (*Could we write procedures, guides really, for topics of our own choosing rather than this one? Where could I get good guides as examples?*)

• A rewrite of video game instructions for a younger reader. (*Where could I get examples of very simple video guides? Does such a thing exist? Might we use simple how-to picture books that aren't about video games to get vision for this? Then we could broaden the instructions into all kinds of topics.*)

As I thought about these examples, I realized I needed to do the work of untying these suggestions from the topic ideas embedded in each one. When I did this, I was left with a set of rules, a chapter book–length guide book about how to do something, a how-to report, a set of procedures, and instructions. This helped me get closer, though I still hadn't put my finger on exactly what I needed yet.

The idea of studying written instructions and directions for things seemed right at first glance, but when I really thought about what the descriptors said, there were just lots of things that didn't fit. Most sets of instructions or directions that come with things don't do any work at all to engage a reader's interest. Most people who have gotten to the point of opening them up and reading them have interest already built in—they want to get this thing put together or up and running! Most of them don't provide any sense of closure either, and the ones I use never seem to anticipate *my* needs. Instructions and directions, as I know them in the world, have some of the features of this kind of writing, but not enough that I would want to devote a whole study to them in the writing workshop. Perhaps students could do this purely instructional kind of writing in another content area?

What really helped me was actually the suggestion of a how-to report to accompany a board game. Now, I don't really think of these as reports and I don't think I've ever actually seen one about a board game, but certainly I know that my *Southern Living* magazine is filled each month with highly engaging, one-page articles that walk me through how to do something or make something. *Ranger Rick*, the kids' magazine I love so much, has some kind of how-to article like this in it each month. Even our local paper has articles in its "Living" section that are about how to do things. Take a look at the piece from *Ranger Rick* in Figure 6.4. I believe it has all the qualities of writing outlined in the descriptors for *narrative procedure*.

Once I realized that articles like "Backyard Campout" truly fit the descriptors for this kind of writing, I was on my way. I knew where I could find lots of examples of this kind of writing that students might study to support this goal.

Curriculum translation, then, is the process of studying a curriculum document or a set of standards and figuring out what kinds of writing to gather from the world to support studies that will help your students meet the objectives set out for them. And this translation doesn't have to lead you to just one kind of writing. Understanding the distinction between mode and genre should help you see that a variety of kinds of writing can serve different purposes.

"Backyard Campout"
Gerry Bishop

Ranger Rick, September 2004, 18–19

Summer's fading fast, and soon school will rule. So why not make the most of summer's end and go camping in your own backyard? It's really easy—and it could be something you'll never forget. (We mean that in a *good* way.)

GET THE GEAR

You'll need very little stuff for a whole lot of fun. Here's a checklist for keeping dry and warm:

- ❏ tent (or a blanket, tarp, or big sheet of plastic draped over a clothesline, with corners held down with rocks)
- ❏ sleeping bag (or a sheet and blankets)
- ❏ sleeping pad or air mattress (or just a plastic sheet over old newspapers to keep out the chill)
- ❏ warm clothes

Other stuff you'll need:

- ❏ flashlight and extra batteries, red plastic (optional)
- ❏ bug juice (insect repellent)
- ❏ bottle of water
- ❏ camera with a flash

GRAB THE GRUB

If you have an adult to help, you can make dinner outside. Barbecue, anyone? But it may be easier to eat inside, and *then* go out to camp. Making a backyard campfire is a job for a grown-up. And a good place to make one is in a portable charcoal grill. Or build a campfire in a metal trashcan, a large metal bucket, or even a metal wheelbarrow.

Tip: Make sure your town or city allows open fires. And don't have a fire if there's a drought in your area.

FUN IN THE DARK

If you're a scout or you go to summer camp, you probably know lots of fun things to do around a campfire—things such as singing songs and playing games and telling stories. But here are some ideas for having a truly "wild" camping experience:

✳ **Red Lights at Night.** You can go "red-lighting" for big earthworms called night crawlers. Cover the end of your flashlight with a piece of red plastic. This makes the light invisible to the worms and lots of other night creatures too. Then search the ground in front of you while you walk as softly as you can.

If you see a night crawler, stop and crouch down to watch it. What is it doing? Eating? Mating? Now stamp your foot on the ground nearby. See how quickly the worm can pull itself back into its burrow?

Tip: Keep an eye out for other night creatures, such as crickets and beetles, that appear in your red beam of light.

✳ **Go on a Sounds-and-Smells Scavenger Hunt.** Nighttime is a great time for discovering new sounds and smells. Lie quietly for five or ten minutes and list all the sounds you can hear. (Cup your hands behind your ears to hear better.) Do you know what's making each sound? If not, write down what you *think* it sounds like. Do the same thing for smells. Then compare notes with your camping friends. Did you hear and smell things that other's didn't?

✳ **Play Night Survivor!** If you like TV survivor shows, make up your own. Make up challenges that test your "survival" skills, and then see who can meet them.

Example: See who can be first to find a night crawler with a flashlight, catch it, and bring it back to camp. (No, you don't have to eat it—unless you want to!)

✳ **Bring on the Bugs.** Hang a white sheet under a porch light (white light, not yellow). Or hang it over a clothesline or between two trees and set up a bright light to shine on it. Moths, beetles, and other cool insects will gather on the sheet in no time.

Tip: A "blacklight" works even better to attract insects.

MORE TIPS, MORE FUN

Go to *nwf.org/gowild* for more "wild" things to do while backyard camping. And check this website for a great book called *Night Science for Kids*, by Terry Krautwurst. You also may be able to find it at a library.

In North Carolina, for example, the state assessment of writing in fourth grade continues to ask students to write in the narrative mode (remember earlier I showed that this was true in first grade as well). While certainly studies of short fiction, memoir, and slice-of-life stories make sense to prepare students for this assessment, students might also study feature articles that contain strong narrative work as a way of engaging the reader. Consider the following lead, for example, in a *Time for Kids* October 29, 1999 article about the growing grizzly population in Yellowstone National Park.

> On a crisp morning last May, Jennifer Bales, 14, got up at 6:00 A.M. to feed her lambs. The sky was brightening in her home in a valley near Cody, Wyoming. In the past, other lambs that Jennifer had raised had won ribbons at the county fair. She had high hopes for her four new lambs.
>
> She filled a bucket with water and walked across her yard toward the lamb pen. An eerie silence warned her something was wrong.

A study of feature articles that all use narrative writing in some part as a way to engage the reader would make perfect sense for a group of students expected to show proficiency in writing in this mode. Students would then be expected to write feature articles and explain how and where in their articles they used narrative writing to engage the reader.

In my big blue notebook I have all kinds of examples of writers using the narrative mode in essays, reviews, commentary, how-to articles. I have a "narrative radar" that goes off when I'm reading because of my home state's expectation that students show proficiency in this mode of writing. You'll want to develop your own radar that goes off when you're reading and helps you find the kinds of writing work you need to show your students.

Studies That Bring Rigor and Challenge to the Writing Workshop

Finally, I believe it is important to decide on some studies simply because they will bring rigor and challenge to the writing workshop. I wonder how many of you thought while reading about Emily Steffans' study of commentary in her fifth-grade class in Chapter 1, "My students are just not ready for a study like that. I'll need something simpler." If you had that thought, I'd like to ask you to reconsider. Here's my line of reasoning.

In kindergarten and first-grade writing workshops, teachers have a solid understanding of the role approximation must play in children's learning, and not just in conventions like spelling and handwriting. They understand approximation in genre and crafting, too. For teachers to plan a study of say, literary nonfiction, and then anchor that study in books by Nicola Davies and Jonathan

London, books most of the children in the room aren't even able to read independently yet, they must know right from the start that what the children will do out of this study will be an approximation of what most people consider to be literary nonfiction in the world.

These teachers know that their students will have to write literary nonfiction like six-year-olds, but that's perfectly okay. That's all they're asking them to do. Most every study in kindergarten and first grade asks teachers to accept lots of approximations in children's work because it is just such a rich, heady learning time in children's lives. And because their teachers accept their approximations, these very young children really believe themselves to be the kinds of people who write literary nonfiction, memoir, poetry, and all the other rich kinds of writing they study during the year.

Somewhere along the way, though, often around third grade, many teachers seem to lose their understanding of the value of approximation in learning, and I think with it comes the loss of "rich heady learning" for older writers. Teachers don't need to shy away from challenging work because they fear students won't be able to do it. They just need to accept that students will do the work as well as they can. Approximations are an indication that learning is happening, not that the teaching wasn't effective. If a teacher stays within the safe confines of curriculum she thinks students can easily handle, there can't possibly be as much learning taking place as if she asks them to work in an area where she knows full well she'll have to value their approximations.

Perhaps most importantly, we need to value approximation in the upper grades so that students can believe more in themselves as writers. I was so impressed with the students I conferred with during the study of commentary in Emily Steffans' writing workshop. Her fifth graders had that same swagger of confidence I see in so many first graders when they describe to me the very big work they are doing in writing—authoring plays and chapter books and series. By bringing in the very best in the world to mentor them, Emily had helped these ten-year-olds believe they could write something like a Pulitzer prize winner, and her belief in them set their learning in motion. They were willing to try something really challenging because they knew that was what Emily was asking them to do and their trying would be valued.

The question then, as you consider whether a unit of study makes sense for your students, is not "Can they do it?" but "What would it look like if they tried it?" "Can they do it?" is not even a legitimate question because you're not talking about something that can be determined to be *done*. The word doesn't even fit the conversation. What you are asking students to do is to try and write something *like* what you've been studying and every one of them can do that. *Being like* something has so many different manifestations that every student can achieve some quality of like-ness in his or her writing. When you look at it this way, worlds of possibilities simply open up for what you might take on as study in the writing workshop.

Deciding What to Teach: Pulling It All Together

To summarize, when the attention of the whole class is pulled together around some big topic of interest to people who write, that topic should come from one or more of these lines of decision making:

- the interests of writers in the workshop
- the needs of writers in the workshop
- state or local curriculum objectives or mandated assessments
- a desire to bring rigor and challenge to the writing workshop

There is no magical right answer to what students should be studying at different grade levels at different times of the year. The design of the writing workshop itself, a place where students work over time to complete personally meaningful writing projects, gives rise to the most important curriculum as students develop the understandings and strategies of writers at work.

My best advice would be to make sure every year, at least once, you plan a study of something that simply fascinates you as a teacher of writing. What an amazing thing for students to see their teacher as a person who is fascinated by something. And what energy you'll find in being that kind of person in front of them.

Craft Pause

NOTICE

The following excerpt is from the Pulitzer prize–winning novel *Middlesex*. Author Jeffrey Eugenides (2002, 95–96) describes Lefty Stephanides' job at a Detroit auto assembly factory.

> Every fourteen seconds Wierzbicki reams a bearing and Stephanides grinds a bearing and O'Malley attaches a bearing to a camshaft. This camshaft travels away on a conveyor, curling around the factory, through its clouds of metal dust, its acid fogs, until another worker fifty yards on reaches up and removes the camshaft, fitting it onto the engine block (twenty seconds). Simultaneously, other men are unhooking parts from adjacent conveyors—the carburetor, the distributor, the intake manifold—and connecting them to the engine block. Above their bent heads, huge spindles pound steam-powered fists. No one says a word. Wierzbicki reams a bearing and Stephanides grinds a bearing and O'Malley attaches a bearing to a camshaft. The camshaft circles around the main floor until a hand reaches up to take it down and attach it to the engine block, growing increasingly eccentric now with swooshes of pipe and the plumage of fan blades. Wierzbicki reams a bearing and Stephanides grinds a bearing and O'Malley attaches a bearing to a camshaft.

The following excerpt is from Jack Gantos' *Joey Pigza Swallowed the Key* (1998, 5–6; a National Book Award finalist) where Joey has been sent out into the hall at school because he's out of control.

"You glue your feet to the floor for five whole minutes or you can just spin yourself down to the principal's office," she said. "Now, what is your choice going to be?"

"Can I get back to you on that?" I asked.

Her face turned all red. "Five minutes," she said. "Settle down for five, and you can rejoin the class."

I nodded, and when she was gone I wrapped the belt and laces around my middle and gave it a good tug and began to spin and spin and slam into the lockers and I got going so good the gum I had under my tongue flew out and my Superball slipped out of my hand and went bouncing down the hall and I kept going and going like when you roll down a steep hill and before long I was bumping on the glass walls around the principal's office like a dizzy fish in a tank. Then the principal came out and pinned me against the wall and we had a little talk about my behavior goals and I spent the rest of the day on her office floor sorting out all the used crayons that the kindergartners kept in big plastic tubs until I had separate piles of blue and green and red and yellow and you know the rest.

And, one from Eloise Greenfield and Lessie Jones Little's memoir *Childtimes* (1979, 174–75).

Family. All this running through my mind. . . .

Saturday Sunday mornings Daddy making pancakes big as the plate Daddy Making fat hamburgers leftover stuffed with rice green peas enough for everybody. Hot nights leave our hot one room sleep till midnight pillows blankets grass bed beside the river.

Lincoln Park evenings Mama other mothers bench-talk children playing.

Give Mama her lesson take my piano lesson teach Mama. Downtown Wilbur Gerald Eloise wait in the car have fun get mad have fun get mad. Go for a ride park car New York Avenue hill dark watch trains wave passengers sitting in lighted window squares sliding by. Gerald tell us the movie tell us show us be the gangster be the good guy be the funny guy tell us show us. Look out the window wait wait snow stopping Daddy going to make snow ice cream ready to eat without freezing.

INSIGHTS ABOUT CRAFT

In all three passages, the way the sentences are crafted actually match the meanings they convey: the dull, repetitive feel of assembly-line work in a factory, a little boy who's out of control, and a memoirist with thoughts *running* through her mind. Writers can employ a variety of crafting techniques—sentence structure, punctuation, repetition—in order to make the way sentences are written match the meanings in the text.

Selecting Texts to Anchor Close Study

I don't know about you, but when I go into a children's bookstore, selection is a real problem for me. Of course, now that I think about it, I have the same problem in a shoe store. I want to buy them all, or at least I want to buy way more than I can afford to buy. I usually make a big stack while I'm browsing and then as checkout time looms closer, I begin to put things back, making decisions about what I absolutely must have. Sometimes I wait until I'm actually checking out and I make decisions based on the total that is ringing up in front of me. I wish I could buy everything, or cut and save everything in my blue notebook, but I can't of course, so selecting texts for teaching is something I'm often thinking about.

In this chapter that's what I'd like to consider: text selection for the teaching of writing. Once you've decided what you'd like to study, text selection to support the study is the next important consideration. What makes a text a good text to anchor a study? How do you select good examples from so many possibilities? Other than them being short (as explained in Chapter 5), what are you looking for in a text?

Some Criteria for Selecting Texts

Before I walk you through my thinking about these questions, let me first say that in any study you want to aim for both breadth and depth. You'll need enough examples so students can see a good range representing a particular kind of writing in the world. This range will give the study breadth, and you don't need to be quite as particular about the selection of texts that serve this purpose. But the texts you'll ask students to study closely need to be selected with more care, and you'll only need a few of them. These texts will anchor the study and it's important they show students the best the world has to offer (that you can realistically gather) for a particular kind of writing.

To help me explain text selection, I'll return to Emily Steffans' study of commentary described in Chapter 1 and one of the texts she selected to anchor her students' close study. Before we even look at the text itself, I should note once again that Emily chose a Pulitzer prize winner and a ten time national sports writer of the year as mentors for her students—the best the world has to offer. The piece you see in Figure 7.1 was written by Leonard Pitts of *The Miami Herald* and posted on November 17, 2003. It was in the packet Emily's fifth graders received. Take a few moments to read "Ready-Made Sandwich Just Too Convenient."

While I didn't select this text for teaching, Emily did, it has all the qualities of text I look for when I am the one in charge of selection. Before I walk you through these qualities, let me suggest you do something. Take a few moments, reread the piece, and make a list of all the qualities of the writing that strike you as interesting. Why do you think Emily and I would choose this particular column as an anchor text for a study of commentary?

Text Reality

The first quality I look for is the easiest to explain. I call it the "real text" quality. Emily found "Ready-Made Sandwich" in *The Miami Herald* columnists' archives. She left behind commercial textbooks and other materials made to be used in schools and went into the world outside school to gather texts. In many ways, this represents the ultimate "preparing students for the real world" stance. As I've explained in earlier chapters, selecting texts from outside school ensures that the teaching will be grounded, and it is critical for this reason.

High Interest

I always try to find examples of writing that address topics I think students will find interesting. Whether it's a great collection of poems about origami like Kristine O'Connell George's *Fold Me a Poem* (2005) that I want to show kindergartners, a collection of rock star sketches to use in a study with middle school students like *The Book of Rock Stars: 24 Musical Icons That Shine Through History* (Krull 2003), a personal essay from *Time* about a young black man making peace with his love of "white music" like "Black Guy, White Music" by Ta-Nehisi Paul Coates, August 22, 2005, or a bawdy collection of memoir that boys might find appealing like *Guys Write for Guys Read* (Scieszka 2005), I try to find topics that I think will engage students first as readers. This involves some speculation on my part, and certainly sometimes I miss the mark and select things that just fall flat, but I try. If students can't connect at all as readers with the topics, it is difficult for them to imagine fulfilling similar intentions for themselves as writers.

"Ready-Made Sandwich Just Too Convenient"
Leonard Pitts

The Miami Herald, posted on November 17, 2003, *www.miamiherald.com*

How long do you figure it would take you to make a peanut butter and jelly sandwich?

Not trying to set a land speed record, mind you. Just working at a normal pace, slapping jelly on one slice of bread, peanut butter on the other. How long do you figure it would take, start to finish? Thirty seconds? Forty-five?

Do you really have that kind of time to waste?

PJ Squares is betting that you don't. So the company, born—it swears!—in Sandwich, Ill., is offering a solution for time-pressed Americans. A PJ Square, you see, is a two-sided slice of "peanut butter flavor layer" and a second, jelly-like layer made of fruit juice. It comes individually packaged like that shiny fake orange cheese in the dairy case. You slap one down between bread or crackers and presto! Not a PB&J, but an incredible simulation.

PJ Squares are said to be available in "select" supermarkets and Target stores nationwide, but I didn't have to go that far to find one. A co-worker—let's call him "Bob," since that's his name—brought some in the other day, whereupon some of us spent a few minutes not putting out the newspaper. Instead, we had an impromptu taste test.

The consensus? They are not disgusting. If you were trapped on a desert island and had to choose between one of these or shoe leather, you would pick the Square in a heartbeat. And yet by their very existence, PJ Squares raise a question of pressing concern:

How lazy do you have to be to need a shortcut to a peanut butter and jelly sandwich?!

I'm sorry. Did I say lazy? I meant, "time-pressed." Granted, some of us are too effort-challenged to fan away the flies, and I'm sure PJ Squares will find a nice market among those folks, assuming they can make it to the store. But for most of us, the issue is simply time and the lack thereof. We stagger through sleep-deprived days trying to figure out how to do the same things in fewer minutes.

As the PJ Squares website puts it, "[I]f you only have a few minutes to give the kids a snack, find the missing soccer shorts and get to a game, you can grab a box of PJ Squares and get on the road." In other words, they're convenient.

Heaven help us.

I mean, when "convenience" became a Madison Avenue mantra 50 years ago, the idea was that it would give us more leisure time. Instant coffee, instant oatmeal, hands-free mops and wrinkle-free slacks, self-propelled lawn mowers, frozen foods and microwave ovens . . . the promise, sometimes implicit, sometimes stated, was that they would make life's mundane chores a breeze, that they would free us to read and chat, to paint or play the piano or just pause and sniff those darned roses. Life would be better.

So here we are, a half century later. What are you doing with all your extra time?

Yeah, that's a good one, isn't it? We get the same 24 hours previous generations did and yet ours seem to have been short-changed. You want to demand a recount. While their days seemed merely busy, ours feel . . . *crammed*. Stuffed to the breaking point with deadlines, demands, presentations, Net surfing, business trips, soccer practices, things that all have to be done right now.

And there is never enough "now" to go around.

I blame convenience. Because with more time has come an implicit expectation of more accomplishment. What excuse is there for lingering over the morning meal when breakfast is a bar you can munch in the car? How can you justify relaxing with a book in the airport lounge when the big report can be downloaded to your PDA?

Woe unto the unstructured moment, the moment not spent planning, racing, rushing, doing. The moment you spend just being.

The paradoxical thing is, we had more of them when life was less convenient.

Yeah, maybe I exaggerate, but this much I know: If you're too busy to make a peanut butter and jelly sandwich, you're too busy.

"Ready-Made Sandwich" and the other pieces of commentary Emily gathered were selected with this criteria in mind, and I remember thinking when I first saw what she had in the packet how interesting they were as a collection. She knew her students and their interests, knew their history of conversations across the year, knew what they had studied in other content areas, and she used all this knowledge to make selections she thought would interest them. One of the Rick Reilly columns in the packet, for example, addressed childhood obesity. Emily and her students had just finished an interesting study of nutrition in science and health, and so she knew this column would resonate for her students because of that. Making topic connections to other content areas is a good idea when it's possible, even though the study will be about how the texts are written rather than what they are about.

One of the best ways to gather high-interest texts is to invite students to help you find them. Whatever the genre—book or movie reviews, poetry, feature articles, short stories, memoir, and so on—students know better than anyone else what interests them and other people like them.

Readability

It may surprise you that one thing I don't worry much about is whether students can read the gathered texts independently. This is particularly true for the youngest writers in grades K and 1. These students need a much richer diet of texts to give them vision as writers than they can yet tackle as readers, so teachers have to do the reading for them in writing workshop. The youngest writers can actually out-write themselves as readers for quite some time because they know so many words orally that they don't yet recognize in print. By approximating the spellings for these words, they can write much richer texts than they would be able to read independently. And of course, the richness of new vocabulary in well-written texts is so critical to all facets of language development that it's just essential young writers be exposed to literature they cannot yet read for themselves.

Certainly as students become more independent readers, they can and should carry more of the weight for reading texts on their own in inquiry. Having said this, however, in any classroom there will likely be some students who need more support with reading than others, and you'll want to plan ways to lend them this support so they have access to the same texts everyone else has. In other words, to support their growth in writing, don't give these students less well-written texts simply because they're easier for them to read independently. Exposure to rich, well-written texts is as critical to their writing development as texts they can read independently are to their reading development.

Related to this issue, sometimes the genre you'd like to study is not a kind of writing students have read independently even if they are able, so they will need some support in understanding the genre and the work it does in the world of written texts. This was certainly true for most of Emily's fifth graders who were encountering commentary for the first time as readers. Many of the students could read most of the words in the commentary they were studying, but of course reading is about more than just knowing the words. They needed help understanding why people write and read commentary. The reading immersion phase of the study had to have more whole-class support than it would if the type of writing had been more familiar to the students.

Representative of the Genre

I actually wouldn't place one of my favorite Leonard Pitts columns in a stack of commentary meant to introduce students to this genre. It's a piece he wrote after winning the Pulitzer prize in 2004 and it's titled, "My First Reader." It's a tribute to his mother, and it's written with such eloquence that it brings tears to my eyes every time I read it. It would tuck nicely into a stack of writing in varied genres meant to show close attention to crafting, but in a genre study of commentary it would be a little problematic.

Here's my reasoning. One of the purposes of genre study is to help students understand how different kinds of writing in the world help people fulfill different sorts of intentions. For this reason, particularly in studies that *introduce* students to a genre, I would look for examples that are representative of the typical intentions served by the kind of writing under study. "My First Reader," though incredibly well written, is not a typical example of the work commentary does in the world. While certainly there is commentary in the piece, particularly about the strength of women through hardship, the question of why the writer decided to pursue this topic—because he won the Pulitzer prize and wanted to thank his mother—is too exceptional. I've got far too many other good examples of commentary from Pitts and other writers that would better help students understand the more typical work of this kind of writing in the world.

Related to this, when I think about examples being representative of a genre, I am also thinking about form. When introducing students to a genre, I want the texts we study closely to be representative of the form the writing generally takes. So while I would certainly include some of Rick Reilly's sports commentary in our stack just as Emily did, there are a few of his pieces in my collection I'd leave out of the introductory study. For example, Reilly's "In Order of Importance," December 3, 2001, is written entirely as a series of lists of things like "Best actual rodeo names" and "Sentences that have never been uttered." The last list in the piece, "Lamest column ideas," has only one item on it: *lists*. I'd also leave out his May 27, 2002 column—which I love—titled "Never Again." It was published to look like an angry Detroit Red Wings fan had handwritten derogatory comments all over it. They're fun pieces, and largely they're fun because of the form in which they're written, but neither piece is representative of typical commentary form.

As I consider choosing examples that are representative of the genre, I must admit there is some tension in my thinking. I can't help but ask myself, "To be grounded, shouldn't the understandings about what is typical come from the inquiry?" I know that teachers of writing can only make this judgment and use it as a guideline for gathering texts if they have read widely in the genre themselves. I believe students would probably own the understandings about what's representative more if teachers let them figure it out the same way they had, through extensive reading. But that reading takes time and decisions have to be made about where to spend the time and energy in any study. I've come to believe teachers get more than they give up when they go ahead and do some of this culling work in the gathering of texts. Students still have to figure out what the texts have in common and how they are both similar and different from other kinds of writing in the world. And when students do encounter an atypical example of the genre, they'll recognize it precisely because they've seen lots of representative examples.

Of course, if the genre is new to the teacher as well as the students, then there will be no choice but to work together, through inquiry, to determine what is representative writing in the genre. Together there will have to be a lot of "best guess gathering" (Nia 1999) and sorting through examples to figure out what is representative of the genre. That's not a bad thing, it just means a chunk of the time and energy of the study will be spent figuring this out, leaving less time for other lines of inquiry that might be interesting to follow. If this is the case, the study can be revisited later in the year because there is still so much untapped potential for learning around it.

Now, having said all this about examples being representative of the genre, it is also true that for students who know a lot about a particular kind of writing and have experience both reading and writing it, studying examples that *are not* as representative is a good way to stretch students' understandings of the potential of the genre. For example, fifth graders who've been through more than one genre study of memoir and poetry in earlier grades might grow their understandings of both these kinds of writing by looking at writers who've combined the potentials of the two. Angela Johnson's *The Other Side: Shorter Poems* (1998) and Cynthia Rylant's *Waiting to Waltz: A Childhood* (1984) would fit easily into a stack of texts they might study for this reason.

An Obvious, Active Stance to Crafting the Writing

Texts that anchor an inquiry and will be studied closely need to show writers taking an obvious, active stance to crafting the writing. Look for texts that are striking as much for how they're written as for what they are about. Look for writers who are what Mem Fox calls, "Powerful communicators . . . [who] understand intimately that the choosing of words and the placement of words has an *affective* impact on meaning—that response to meaning comes not only from minds but from hearts as well" (1993, 105).

As you think about this quality of the writing, remember that the craft of writing, what writers know how to do with words and sentences and the organization of ideas, is something that *crosses* genres. The writer of a memoir published in a picture book intended for children might "choose and place words" in exactly the same way a writer crafting an essay for the back page of *Time* magazine chooses and places words. For example, look at the following excerpt from one of Anne Lamott's personal essays in her wonderful collection of essays written for adults, *Traveling Mercies*. The chapter about her struggle with an eating disorder opens like this:

> This is the story of how, at the age of thirty-three, I learned to feed myself.
> To begin with, here's what I did until then: I ate, starved, binged, purged, grew fat, grew thin, grew fat, grew thin, binged, purged, dieted, was good, was bad, grew fat, grew thin, grew thinner.
> I had been a lean and energetic girl, always hungry, always eating, always thin. But I weighed 100 pounds at thirteen, 130 at fourteen. For the next ten years, I dieted. It is a long, dull story. (1999, 190)

Lamott shows such a comfortable, easy knowledge of the work of the verb. The verb is it, the verb is where the action is and it can do so much work, all by itself. It can cover seasons and seasons of time if it needs to, as it does in this single sentence capturing the first thirty-three years of Lamott's life.

Jerry Spinelli is doing the same kind of crafting in his children's novel *Loser* (2002, 162–63) in this passage where the main character, Donald Zinkoff, is trying to get through the summer so he can start middle school.

> They go away for summer vacation: three days at the beach. They stroll the boardwalk. He shakes hands with Mr. Peanut and eats an ice cream and waffle sandwich and a chocolate-covered frozen banana. While Polly digs holes in the sand, he hunkers in the surf and dares the ocean waves to knock him over.
> Back home, he pesters his parents to join the swim club, but they say it's too expensive. So he does what a kid has to do: He smells the cedar chest in his parents' bedroom, he decapitates dandelions, seesaws at the park, licks the mixing bowl, rides his bike, counts railroad cars, holds his breath, clucks his tongue, tastes tofu, touches moss, daydreams, looks back, looks ahead, wishes, wonders . . . and before he knows it, miraculously, the summer is over.

The ellipses is actually in the text; Spinelli uses it to show that the list sort of fades away into time. His crafting here pulls from the same knowledge about how language works as Lamott, and Cynthia Rylant pulls from the same knowledge in this beautiful sentence where seasons of time pass in her beautiful picture book text, *Scarecrow* (1998):

> The earth has rained and snowed and blossomed and wilted and yellowed and greened and vined itself all around him. (n.p.)

Because craft crosses genre, finding texts rich with craft-teaching potential is critical because the teaching has no boundaries. In other words, what students learn about writing well in one genre can help them write well in many other genres. "Ready-Made Sandwich" is clearly rich with craft-teaching potential. When I look at it as a teacher of writing, I get excited about the possibility of studying it with a group of students. I find myself noticing all kinds of interesting things I'd like to talk about if I studied this text closely with other writers. Have a look back at "Ready-Made Sandwich" (p. 97) as you read this list of things that interest me as a teacher of writing:

• All the different ways Pitts uses questioning to engage me as a reader off and on throughout the text. There is rich variety in the work he's doing with questions.

• All the interesting punctuation work, particularly the way it helps me "hear" the piece as if Pitts is talking to me. The piece could anchor a study of how writers use punctuation in interesting ways to craft their texts just as well as it anchors the study of commentary. Not only does he use lots of different marks doing different kinds of meaning work in the piece, he also uses some marks in interesting, unexpected ways.

• The creative phrase choices like *incredible simulation*, *impromptu taste test*, and *individually packaged*, and how with these phrases he cleverly manages to mock the advertising industry by using their language as his language.

• His formatting decisions like paragraph breaks and font are significant. Paragraph breaks are always more numerous in texts published in newspapers because the columns are narrow and things get long fast. However, in "Ready-Made Sandwich" there are a few short sentences punctuated as single paragraphs that clearly represent a writer's decision making.

• Humor—the piece is clearly funny in places and I'd love to study it. But "it's funny" is my response to it as a reader and I'm not sure "funny" can be understood as writing craft. A sense of humor has to do with how a person sees the world. In other words, if a person is funny, he's funny whether he's writing or not. I do believe, however, that how to put funny down on paper involves craft, and that's what I'd like to study.

• The "presence" of the writer in the piece, for lack of a better way of saying it. Conversational comments like "I'm sorry. Did I say lazy?" and "Yeah, that's a good one isn't it?" and "Heaven help us."

- Some very interesting sentence work catches my attention. There are a few series of sentences that could be studies in and of themselves, so rich are they in language work. I particularly like the paragraph about the Madison Avenue mantra: the wonderful list, the rhythm of the list, the move from single phrases to paired ones, the repetition of words, the reliance on understood connections to make the listing sentence grammatically complete, the surprise of such a short sentence after such a long one, and of course the punctuation here is so artful too. I also love the sentence work in the "unstructured moment" paragraph for some of the same reasons.

- The interesting positioning of the "main idea" at the end of the piece and how Pitts takes us on a journey of thought (Bomer 1995) leading to this main idea.

Without a doubt, it looks like Leonard Pitts crafted "Ready-Made Sandwich" with great intention and it would make an excellent text to anchor a study of commentary. You may be wondering why I say "it looks like" he crafted it with great intention. I say this because I actually know that much of what goes down on paper when writers draft is not a conscious act of crafting. Much of the knowledge writers have about the craft of writing becomes operationally implicit over time, meaning they don't even think about it when they're writing. They may think more explicitly about crafting during revision, but sometimes even then changes are made to drafts, making them more artful, and the writers haven't thought in an explicit way about *why* they're making them.

So why do we talk about writer's craft as if it were an act of decision making? Because it still is. A writer must always decide when to say, "I'm finished. I've done all I can do to make this as good as I can make it." And whatever is left in the text is there because the writer decided to leave it there. Craft study—in an explicit way—helps students write with an ever-growing sense of what's possible to leave in a text (or add to, change, rearrange) and make it good. But over time, you should expect that more and more crafting decisions will become operationally implicit for students just as they are for experienced writers.

While you might think that texts showing an obvious, active crafting stance to the writing would be less important for beginning writers, I would caution you not to underestimate them as learners. Many very young children who are exposed to talk around richly crafted writing will begin to craft in ways that are operationally implicit rather than explicit. The lead in six-year-old Anna Serenius' memoir, "Disney World," about the moment she and her mom first saw the Disney characters is a good example (Figure 7.2).

Anna has internalized the sound of language working in this way, ". . . my mom was almost in tears. Happy tears." And she also has developed vision for

FIGURE 7.2 *The first page of Anna's memoir about Disney World.*

how language like this can go down on paper. Her punctuation is right-on for a sentence construction like this.

What to Look for in Texts: A Summary List

To pull this line of thinking together, then, I've explained five things to think about when gathering texts for an inquiry:

1. Text reality—it should come from the world outside school.
2. High interest—the topic is appealing.
3. Readability—it's okay for the text to be challenging for students as readers.
4. Representative—a consideration for genre study only.
5. Obvious, active crafting stance—the text has lots of potential for learning about the craft of writing.

The good news is, the world is full of fabulous writing that is easily accessible to us as teachers of writing. The bad news is, the more you know about fabulous writing the harder it becomes to decide which texts are the right texts for your teaching. But, alas, more good news: there are no right texts. Some are better than others, for sure. Just look for ones that are better than others.

Craft Pause

This passage of description is from the Newbery award–winning novel *Missing May* (1992, 7–8) by Cynthia Rylant.

> . . . May turned me to the kitchen, where she pulled open all the cabinet doors, plus the refrigerator, and she said, "Summer, whatever you like you can have and whatever you like that isn't here Uncle Ob will go down to Ellet's Grocery and get you. We want you to eat honey. . . .
>
> My eyes went over May's wildly colorful cabinets, and I was free again. I saw Oreos and Ruffles and big bags of Snickers. Those little cardboard boxes of juice that I had always, just once, wanted to try. I saw fat bags of marshmallows and cans of SpaghettiOs and a little plastic bear full of honey. There were real glass bottles of Coke looking cold as ice in the refrigerator and a great big half of a watermelon taking up space. And, best of all, a carton of real chocolate milk that said Hershey's.
>
> Whirligigs of Fire and Dreams, glistening Coke bottles and chocolate milk cartons to greet me. I was six years old and I had come home.

INSIGHTS ABOUT CRAFT

Over time in my teaching, I have probably read *Missing May* aloud to students more than thirty times. This passage, early in the book, teaches me so much about the crafting of description. First, it has the listing, "look around the scene" quality so common in passages of description. But in so many ways what makes this list so vivid is Rylant's use of proper nouns. Try reading it and replacing each of the proper nouns with a common noun. The description is not nearly as vivid that way; there's a big difference between *cookies* and Oreos and *candy* and Snickers. Proper nouns, particularly when they name familiar items, are much more descriptive.

The other significant aspect of crafting description I learn from this passage is how the writer helps us see the scene through the character's eyes. Good description is not about including every possible detail; it's about selecting details that help the reader take in the scene with the same feelings the character is experiencing. Just before this scene when the little girl (and narrator), Summer, walked into May and Ob's trailer for the first time, she said she felt "like Alice who had fallen into Wonderland." What we see in the kitchen helps us capture this feeling. Surely there was salt and pepper out somewhere, a tub of Crisco shortening, perhaps a big jar of Tums on the counter, but these aren't included. Only the things a six-year-old—who felt like Alice in Wonderland—would see are included.

section
TWO

Informed
Practice

Setting the Stage

8

On a Monday morning in March in Lisa Cleaveland's first-grade writing workshop, the children are gathered in the meeting area. Lisa has a plastic tub next to her filled with brightly colored picture books, all of them poetry anthologies by poets who've chosen single topics and written collections of poems on those topics. Lisa tries to pull each book out slowly, but little hands keep reaching around her trying to get at other books in the tub. As I videotape what's happening, I notice that Lisa responds to the children with understanding. She's not unhappy with them, she knows they're just excited and her attempt to slowly reveal the contents of the tub just isn't going to work.

This Monday in March is the first day of new study in writing workshop in this first-grade class, and what strikes me as especially significant on this morning is that the children know what today means to the tomorrows of this classroom. They understand the journey they are getting ready to take as writers. They *recognize* the teaching because they have been down this road before with other studies. It is March, after all, and all year long they've been going about their studies in basically the same way each time. As I think about what the children understand is happening, I realize there are several layers of understandings in place. The children understand that:

- What's in that plastic tub is likely to be good stuff. Lisa chooses books to anchor her studies with intention: she wants them to be high-quality books that she knows the students will enjoy reading.

- They will be studying those books over the next few weeks. Lisa will read them aloud, and they will also get their hands on them and be allowed to look at them closely.

- They will be expected to help their teacher notice as many things as they can about how these books are written. They know they will carry a lot of the weight of this work, and that what they notice will go on the now-blank chart that says only "Poetry" at the top.

- They are expected to begin writing something that is like what they're studying. They understand that they will all eventually write at least one book that could fit with the others in the plastic tub.

- They see themselves as being *like* Kristine O'Connell George, Charles R. Smith, Jr., Jane Yolen, Nikki Grimes, and the other poets who have collections in the tub.

What a powerful image, those first graders' hands reaching for those books, knowing they hold such promise for them as writers. Think about the significance of children recognizing teaching as it is happening. The teaching—and of course the learning that comes from it—is not something the teacher alone holds in her hands. The children aren't sitting passively waiting to see what new lesson their teacher has for them today. Instead, they see the "lesson" as the time each day when they work with her to fill their charts with interesting things they're learning about whatever the subject of study happens to be.

At this point in March, though Lisa is beginning a new study with her first graders, there's nothing really new at all about what they're doing. They are very much in the *middle* of an ongoing conversation that started the first day of writing workshop. The conversation is about how people write well and it continues and builds day after day. This is simply a new direction that it will take for a while: how people write *poetry* well.

Inquiry as Predictable Teaching

The purpose of this and the next few chapters is to suggest predictable ways of working that help generate important writing curriculum and create vision for the work students do out of a study. The important word here is *predictable*. When teaching has a predictable rhythm to it, students recognize what's happening and can engage with the whole process of teaching and learning much more intentionally because it is so familiar. Now, the fact that it is predictable doesn't mean in any way that it is redundant or boring. The way you go about a study is predictable, but the content that comes from the study is anything but predictable. The teaching is "structured for surprise" (Graves 2001, 51) and it's the promise of what you might discover together that gives both students and teachers energy for the study.

You may remember this overview chart from Chapter 1. It's a generalized representation of the work Lisa Cleaveland was embarking on that morning in March with her first graders.

Gathering Texts	The teacher, sometimes along with students, gathers examples of the kind of writing students will do.
Setting the Stage	As the study gets underway, the teacher makes sure students know they will be required to finish a piece of writing that shows the influence of the study. All reading is done with an eye toward, "We're going to write something like this. . . ."
Immersion	The teacher and students spend time reading and getting to know the texts they'll study. They make notes of things they notice about how the texts are written.
Close Study	The class revisits some of these texts and frames their talk with the question, "What do we notice about how these texts are written?" Teacher and students work together to use specific language to say what they now know about writing from this close study. They record it somehow and, most importantly, they envision using what they have learned in their own writing. The teacher, through modeling, takes a strong lead in helping students envision possibilities.
Writing Under the Influence	Students (and often the teacher, too) finish a piece of writing that shows the influence of the study in writing. Students are expected to show very specific ways in which the study influenced their writing.

These predictable ways of working are at the heart of the instructional expertise I discussed in Chapter 2, and they are not particular to any grade or experience level of students. With just a few variations in teaching support, kindergarteners and college students alike can use this same framework for study in the writing workshop. As a matter of fact, I love to imagine how incredibly savvy high school students might be if they had experienced the study of writing the same way since they were in kindergarten. Imagine how solidly they'd understand how to learn to write from their reading. Imagine how deeply they'd get the idea that teachers don't hold the answers to what makes good writing *good*, texts do. One of my hopes for this book, actually, is that it will make it more likely that these high school students of my imagination will exist someday.

Another important point is that while this instructional framework clearly makes sense for genre study, any issue related to how texts are written can be studied in this same way. In Lisa Cleaveland's first-grade workshop, for example, they use this same predictable way of working to study things like how writers use punctuation in interesting ways to craft their texts, how illustrations and layout add to the meaning of texts, and how writers structure texts in interesting ways. Students across grade levels might use the framework to study issues such as how writers make paragraphing decisions, how language can be used in surprising ways, how time moves when writing in the narrative mode—anything, really, that is text based. These are all studies that are not specific to any one genre of writing. Each study simply starts with a short stack of texts or text excerpts that show writers doing whatever it is you'd like to study.

Set down as it is in the previous chart, this instructional framework for study appears to be a linear process, and certainly there are some aspects of it that are linear in nature. For example, students need to know right from the start that they'll be doing the kind of writing you're studying, and it's important to save the actual writing of a finished piece until later because the immersion and close study are what give students a vision toward which they can draft. But in between these beginning and ending points for the study, the process of inquiry is usually much more recursive than it is linear as the class moves in and out around reading, noticing, talking, charting insights, and planning drafts.

Figuring out how to write about this process as it plays out in actual classrooms and do it in a way that keeps it true to the essence of genuine study has been a real challenge. I can't just write a day-by-day guide for it; the very nature of the teaching—that it is inquiry based—belies this. What I can do is share with you a menu of possibilities for kinds of things you might do with students in each phase of the study to help you generate important content together. I think of what I offer here and in the next few chapters as a menu because I imagine it being used in this way. As you plan and engage in an inquiry with your students, you'll want to select ways of working that make sense in your teaching context and that fit with what unfolds as the study moves through time. The energy of one day should feed into the next. I also expect you'll imagine other ways of working (that I haven't yet imagined) that will serve the same goal of helping students develop vision for the writing they will do.

I also think of what I offer here as a menu because it sort of reads like a menu. I've made no attempt to connect the "items" on the menu in the same way that paragraphs generally connect in texts. Each possibility simply represents another way of getting the same work of the study accomplished. The possibilities, you'll notice, are generic and don't apply to any one kind of writing or writing issue specifically. My hope is that you can use this chapter alongside the resource section that suggests specific studies (at the end of the book) and begin to make plans for the day-to-day work in an unit of study.

As I write about different ways of working through the different phases of study, each new possibility I suggest is likely to leave you with some questions about how everything works together or what would make the most sense in your particular teaching context. While I'll try to anticipate some of your questions along the way, please know that I also trust you as an instructional decision maker. I trust that by this point in *Study Driven*, the "big picture" of this work makes sense to you (or else it doesn't, which means you've probably already abandoned reading), and that you're ready to think in specific ways about how unit of study might look in your classroom. I trust that I can write about possibilities in each "phase" of study and you can figure them out in ways that make sense for you and your students.

Context for Inquiry Work

Before I begin, I should point out once again that the inquiry I'm writing about happens in the context of a writing workshop as it's somewhat universally described in the professional literature on the teaching of writing (see Appendix A). Writing workshops exist in *time*, and to do the kind of teaching you are reading about in this book, there must be time for students to engage deeply with both the study of writing and with writing itself. Teachers doing this work have decided the investment of time makes sense and invest anywhere from 45 minutes to an hour or more in the teaching of writing on a regular basis.

During the time allotted for writing workshop, students should be accustomed to working in a number of different configurations. First, they should know how to work independently in a variety of ways that support their writing: researching, developing ideas in writers' notebooks, drafting and finishing writing projects, working in collaborative ways with other students (pairs or small groups), and reading to support the writing they will do. During this independent writing time, students should be accustomed to being interrupted for writing conferences with their teacher on a regular basis.

In the context of the writing workshop, students should also be used to a variety of things they do while gathered as a whole class: engaging in discussions related to inquiry, listening to a teacher-directed lesson or read-aloud, and listening and responding as other students share their thinking about their work. These whole-class gatherings generally open and close the workshop time. As I present this menu of possibilities, I'll ask you to imagine this work happening in all these different configurations.

Gathering Texts

All the chapters up to this point have been about possibilities for gathering texts, so I won't offer any new ones here. A decision must be made about what will be studied, and then examples of that kind of writing or examples showing that quality of writing must be gathered. Once the texts have been gathered, the biggest teaching decision you must make revolves around how students will gain access to the texts you've gathered. Here are some possibilities to consider for helping children gain access to the gathered texts.

POSSIBILITY

You can have single copies of different texts gathered in baskets or some kind of holders and have them out in the room. Single copies mean, of course, that only one or two students can be reading the same text at any given time during their independent work. In this case, you'll need to make sure individuals or pairs of students also get access to different texts as the study moves along.

POSSIBILITY

Multiple copies of texts are easy to come by. You can type out the written texts of picture books to go with the single copies of the books you have, and of course, things from newspapers, magazines, collections, and excerpts are easy to photocopy for classroom use, especially those pulled from Internet archives that have the printer friendly versions. If you use multiple copies of texts, you'll have to decide whether you want all your students to have their own copies of the main texts you'll be studying, or whether you just want multiple sets of them available for classroom use at tables or in small groups. Personally, I'm partial to students having their own copies of each of the main texts anchoring the study because I like them to make notes on them of things they notice. But they can make notes in their notebooks or on sticky notes, however, so they don't have to have their own copies.

POSSIBILITY

If you teach beginning readers, you'll almost certainly be using texts that most of the students cannot yet read independently, so there is really no need for them to have their own copies. In this case you can simply keep the gathered texts in a basket or tub at the meeting area and give students access to them during writing workshop and at other times of the day.

Setting the Stage

Once the texts have been gathered and readied, you'll need to set the stage for the study that will follow. Setting the stage isn't really a phase of the study, it's simply a launching time when the study gets underway, you turn your students' thinking in a particular direction, and you let them know what they will be expected to produce out of the study. Remember that over time as students come to recognize the predictable rhythm of your teaching, you won't have to do much to set the stage other than get them looking at the texts. They will understand where they are headed in a study because they've been there before. Here are some possibilities for kinds of things you might do to turn students' attention toward the study and to make requirements and expectations clear.

Turning Students' Attention Toward the Study

POSSIBILITY

You can give students a beginning, working definition of what you have gathered for the study and the kind of writing or writing issue it represents in the world. This definition will be a work in progress because over the course of the study you and your students will continue to flesh out your understandings about it.

POSSIBILITY

As you talk about what you'll be studying, you can show your students the texts you've gathered and talk a little about each one in a "preview" sort of way. Call the authors of the texts by name as you talk about them, and don't be afraid to show your enthusiasm for the collection and the promise it holds for the good work you can do together around it.

POSSIBILITY

If you have them available, you can show students examples of writing other students have done in a similar study. These would be in addition to the examples you've gathered from professional writers, not in place of those. If you don't have any student samples because it's your first time studying with students in this way, be sure to save some for this purpose for future years.

POSSIBILITY

Reading aloud from at least one knock-your-socks-off text in your stack is a great way to set the stage for a study, even those we typically don't think of as texts to be read aloud, commentary, for instance, or movie reviews, essays, and feature articles. As you read to your students, think about the fact that you have begun—in collaboration with the author of the text—to teach your students how to write. Attend to the rhythms of the text created by punctuation, sentence structure, and word choice. Through your reading, you'll be helping students know what good writing of this kind *sounds* like, and tuning their ears to hear this will be one of the best tools they'll have to help them draft and revise well.

POSSIBILITY

You can talk with your students (as a whole class or in small groups) about their histories as readers and writers with the kind of writing or writing issue you'll be studying. Find out what they already know about it, and what (if any) hopes they might have for growing their understandings.

POSSIBILITY

You can invite students to add texts to those you've gathered if they think they know other good examples. Isoke Nia calls this gathering that students help you do "best guess gathering" (1999). This expression hints at the fact that some texts students add to the stack will represent a "best guess," but they may not be the kind of thing you decide you want to write. Often, the discussions around students' missed guesses help everyone deepen their understandings about the kind of writing you are studying. The other benefit of students adding texts to the study is their additions help broaden everyone's vision of what's possible.

POSSIBILITY

To give students a sense of the kinds of things they'll be learning about, you might look at charts other classes have made in similar studies and discuss them before you start your own. Doing this actually sends two important messages about the nature of writing curriculum and inquiry itself. First, it shows that you don't think of the content as something that is set or frozen in any way. "This is what they discovered. Let's go see what we can learn about this." And second, all good research begins with a "review of the literature" to see what others have found when they studied the same topic the researcher is setting out to study. In many ways, this matches that move that researchers make.

POSSIBILITY

You can let students get their hands on the texts you've gathered and just look them over as a way of setting the stage for the study. This is especially useful when the texts are in containers where there are lots of graphics to go along with the written words—picture books and magazines, for instance. "Getting their hands on the texts" is useful even for students who aren't able to read all the words independently as it helps them envision what the finished writing they're about to study looks like in the world of texts. If you send students out to look at texts, be sure to bring them back and ask them about their first impressions.

POSSIBILITY

You might want to announce to other people in your school that you are launching a new study and invite them to share resources and experiences with you if they have them from their own writing study.

POSSIBILITY

If you send out any sort of parent notifications, like newsletters, you can announce the study as well. This kind of communication is very useful in terms of helping parents understand the work you're doing in writing workshop.

Requirements and Expectations

POSSIBILITY

For more experienced writers, you might consider making a handout with formal requirements and due dates for work in the study. Figures 8.1 and 8.2 show a sample set of quite formal guidelines for a feature article study and a punctuation study.

These are samples of what's possible and are meant, more than anything else, to give you some vision for how you might outline the requirements of a study. You might ask fewer, more, or different kinds of questions depending on the emphasis of your teaching. You might use different language for your questions. You might spread the questions out in intermediate handouts along the way to help students pace their work, especially students who would be overwhelmed by so much detail in a single handout.

POSSIBILITY

You can develop charts and forms to help students report on their work during the study. Figure 8.3 shows an example of one sort of form like this. It's for students to show their work developing an idea in a writer's notebook. With anything you design, you'll likely need verbal reminders along with the handouts to help students remember what they are to be doing in the course of they study.

POSSIBILITY

With very young writers, it's probably best to have expectations rather than formal requirements. You might simply say, "Over the next few weeks as we study these different kinds of ABC books, each of you can create ABC books about topics you love, just as these writers have." This invitation, coupled with the continued reading and talking and studying, is usually enough to get most young writers up and trying the kind of writing you're studying. A few of them may need a little help from a supportive adult to get started and try the work of the study, but they will show you they need this if you don't see them trying it on their own.

Thinking Point: Setting the Stage

One question I'm sometimes asked is if it dampens the spirits of students to announce the requirements for writing so early in the study. "Shouldn't they just

FIGURE 8.1 *Sample Requirements and Expectations: Feature Article Study*

Feature Article Genre Study

Overview

Our study in writing workshop for the month of February will be *how to write a feature article.* Using good examples of feature articles from magazines and newspapers to guide us, we'll focus our study around these guiding questions:

✦ What kinds of topics are appropriate for feature articles?

✦ What kinds of prewriting work do writers of feature articles do?

✦ How are feature articles *crafted* in ways that make them compelling for readers?

Expectations

By the end of the study, each student will be expected to publish one feature article on a topic of his/her choosing. In addition, each of you will be expected to participate in the inquiry part of the study during writing workshop, and to turn in all the reflective writing about process and evidence of work along the way (outlined below). During writing conferences, please remember that I will ask to see evidence that you are trying the work of the minilessons on a regular basis.

As in every classwide unit of study, you may choose to work on "back-up" work during writing workshop after the work of the study has been completed.

Monday, February 9

1. Describe the topic you have chosen for your feature article. Explain in as much detail as you can how and why you have chosen this topic for this feature article project.

2. Tell me about what material you already have in your writer's notebook related to your topic. Then, write about the plans you have for the notebook work you want to do in the coming days to support you in writing your feature article.

Monday, February 16

1. Show evidence of all the notebook work you have done with your seed idea up until this point. Tell a little about how each separate entry of this work came to be. You may use the big sticky notes to do this if you'd like. You may photocopy your entries or turn in your notebook to me. If you turn your notebook in, I'll be sure you have it to work with during writing workshop.

2. Provide a copy of the feature article you are using as a touchstone text for your writing. Explain why you admire the writing and selected it as a touchstone text, and detail three specific things you have learned about crafting a feature article from the writer of this text.

Monday, February 23

1. Show evidence of the planning you did before you began drafting your feature article. Include any comments that will help me understand your planning.

2. You should have a copy of the beginning draft of your feature article. Write and turn in a reflection that tells me about drafting and revising your feature article up to this point. Consider questions such as: How did you get started?

Did you revise a lot as you drafted, or did you get it down first and then go back through it? Has another writer given you feedback? Have you read it aloud to yourself? Have you tried any tools for revision that we've studied? How did your touchstone text help you? What are your plans for continuing work on this piece?

Friday, February 27
Class publication day. Have a finished copy of your feature article available and ready to turn in.

Due Monday, March 2
1. Turn in all evidence of drafting. Explain the thinking behind *three specific* decisions you made while working on drafting and revising your feature article. Be sure to show exactly where in the text you made the revision decisions. Please also note any specific crafting decisions you made that you think are particularly artful. You may use highlighters, sticky notes, keys, etc., to help document this work on your drafts. Pay special attention here to helping me see how you used what we learned in the study to help you write your piece.

2. Explain your process for editing (proofreading) your feature article. How did you make sure it was edited as well as it could be?

3. Reflect on what's most important in what you have learned about writing feature articles. What did you learn about yourself as a writer during this study?

FIGURE 8.2 *Sample Requirements and Expectations: Punctuation Study*

How Writers Use Punctuation in Interesting Ways to Craft Their Texts

Overview
Our study in writing workshop for the next three weeks will be a close look at *how writers use punctuation in interesting ways to craft their texts*. Using examples from excellent writing in a variety of genres, we'll focus our study around this single crafting issue in writing.

Expectations
By the end of the study, each student will be expected to publish one piece of writing on a topic and in a genre of his/her choosing. The piece must show clear evidence that the student has used the work of the study to strengthen the writing. As our study is only three weeks long, please choose a seed idea you can work on in this amount of time.

Each of you will be expected to participate in the inquiry part of this study and to use your writer's notebook to experiment with punctuation based on what you're learning from the study. The due dates for the process of your writing projects are outlined below.

As in every classwide unit of study, you may choose to work on "back-up" work during writing workshop after the work of the study has been completed.

(continues)

Wednesday, February 4 (three days into the study)

1. Describe the idea for the writing project you plan to finish during this study. Explain in as much detail as you can how and why you have chosen it. If you already know the genre you want to write, tell me about that decision.

2. Tell me about what material you already have in your notebook related to your idea. Then, write about the plans you have for the notebook work you want to do in the coming days to support this self-selected writing project.

Monday, February 9

1. Turn in a notebook chart that records and explains the work you have done in your notebook to develop your idea for this writing project.

2. Have an excerpt you have found from a published piece of writing ready to share with your classmates. The excerpt should be a good example of a writer using punctuation in an interesting way. Using our first week's inquiry as a model for how to talk about punctuation, write an explanation for how you think the writer is crafting with punctuation in the excerpt.

Monday, February 16

1. Drafts should be well underway. I'll expect to see them during writing conferences. Answer this question, in as much detail as you can: *What have you read that is like what you are trying to write?* Also answer this question: *What kind of person would be interested in reading what you are writing?*

2. Turn in a written reflection about how your drafting and revising is going up to this point. You might consider questions such as: How did you get started? Did you revise a lot as you drafted, or did you get it down first and then go back through it? Has another writer given you feedback? Have you read it aloud to yourself? Have you tried any tools for revision that we've studied? How did your touchstone text help you? What are your plans for continuing work on this piece?

Monday, February 23

1. Class publication day. Have a finished copy of your writing project available and ready to turn in. These may be handwritten or word processed.

2. Turn in all evidence of drafting and revising. Citing specific text, write about the single most important revision decision you made. Then, again citing specific text, write about *three* places in your piece where you used the work of our study to help you craft the writing with punctuation. Be ready to explain your decision making to your classmates.

3. Explain your process for editing (proofreading) your writing project. How did you make sure it was edited as well as it could be?

4. Reflect on what's most important in what you have learned during this study. What did you learn about yourself as a writer?

FIGURE 8.3 *Notebook Work: Developing an Idea for Writing (Be ready to show these entries in your writer's notebook)*

Writing Idea: Feature article—summer camp in the Adirondacks where grandparents go with their grandchildren

Short description of the entry	Length	Notes on how the entry came to be
List of questions about my topic	2 pages—12 questions	I decided to try this because I needed to think about what other people might think about my topic. I learned to do this—write questions—when we did our study on using our writers' notebooks better. I am still adding questions to the list when I think about them.
Quote from the news	Just the quote—then half a page thinking about it	I heard this thing on how email and cell phones are taking over people's lives and nobody really spends time together any more. I thought I might use it in my article.
A reflection entry where I answer one of my questions	A page and a half	I took one of my questions from my list and tried to think more about it. I thought about how my grandpa would do at camp. By the end of the entry I had a new thing I was thinking—that it might be pretty cool to have him there with me. I think the other kids would think he was funny.
Notes from interviews	Four pages!	I asked a whole bunch of other kids how they would like to go to camp with their grandparents and I wrote down what they said. I got some great stuff I can use. I need to interview some grandparents too.

spend a few days reading and enjoying the texts before we discuss requirements?" First, I don't see these as mutually exclusive. I suppose some students may have their spirits dampened if they know are they going to be required to do something, but I have seen many, many students who were excited by the prospect of writing something that would be *like* what they were reading in writing workshop. Some of it has to do with the selection of texts the teacher makes. If teachers take time to find high-interest, well-written texts to anchor their studies, then many of their students will probably think, "Cool . . . I want to write something like that!"

Second, the whole purpose of reading during *writing* workshop is taken away if students aren't reading with the sense of purpose that comes from expecting to write. Frank Smith (1988) says it so clearly: "[And] there is no reading like a writer when we have no expectation of writing the kind of written language we read. . . . We can and often do read simply like a reader, for whatever purpose we are reading. But to learn to write we must read like a writer" (25). Essentially, I believe it's important not to be half-hearted about your reasons for asking students to read the texts you've gathered during writing workshop. From the first encounter with the first text, help students start believing, "Soon, I'm going to write something like this."

Craft Pause

These two excerpts from Andrew Sullivan's essay "When Grace Arrives Unannounced" in the March 28, 2005 issue of *Time* magazine. The essay is about Ashley Smith, the woman in Georgia who talked her fugitive captor, an alleged rapist and murderer, into turning himself in to the authorities. First, the opening sentences of the essay:

> She went out for cigarettes.
>   That's my favorite detail of the story told by Ashley Smith. It was not a noble calling; it wasn't even a noble errand. But the craving for nicotine at 2 o'clock in the morning apparently led Smith into the loaded gun of one Brian Nichols, a man who was wanted for raping one woman and murdering another woman and three men.

And then this sentence much later in the essay, connecting itself back to this lead:

> One was a monster, the other a woman unable to care for her 5-year-old, looking for cigarettes in the dark.

INSIGHTS ABOUT CRAFT

What a compelling lead the writer crafts in this essay. Sullivan decides to take this one telling detail of the story and put it up front at the beginning of his journey of thought about the meaning of it all. Essays aren't always about the meaning of things that have happened, but when they are, this way of opening with a small, powerful detail from the story is very effective. He uses the pronoun *she* too, keeping it so simple, "She went out for cigarettes." The antecedent is in both the subtitle, "Tied up by a violent fugitive, Ashley Smith found a way to let the light in," and the sentence that follows the lead making it quite clear who "she" is. Referring to this detail again much later in the essay, the writer reminds the reader of how compelling he finds it. Reappearing details create a seamlessness across a text, a sense of everything adding up somehow.

Reading Immersion and Close Study

Once students have access to texts and know what they're studying, it's time to start reading, widely and deeply. When I think about reading immersion, I always think about hearing Ted Kooser, our National Poet Laureate, give this advice to aspiring writers, "Before you write one poem, you need to read at least 100." But when should those poems be read? If writing workshop is a place where students are supposed to do the work of writers, and if it's the work of writers to read, then it makes sense to me that this reading belongs in writing workshop. In other words, I don't think you are taking time away from students' writing when you have them do this kind of reading. Certainly, across a school year you want to keep in mind the balance of how students spend their time doing a writer's work, but I believe it's okay if some of that time belongs to reading. Look at the balance of time Ted Kooser is suggesting: 100 poems read for every one written.

The discomfort with this—students reading during writing workshop—is what has caused some teachers, I think, to try and figure out how to get the reading done at other times of the day. I don't think it's a good idea to ask students to use their independent reading time (during reading workshop) to do the immersion work for a study in writing. Most of the time, students haven't self-selected the texts they need to read for the study in writing; these texts have been assigned. Independent reading should be a time for students to follow their own intentions as readers. Certainly, in a perfect teaching world it would be wonderful if the texts you use to study writing could be texts students knew first for other reasons—in content area studies or from an earlier study of writing, for example. But that requires an enormous amount of long-range planning about how to piece together an entire year of studies in all content areas. If you can pull this off, go for it. But if not, I believe it's okay to use the writing workshop as the place of first encounter for texts. Remember, reading the kind of thing you're planning to write is part of a writer's work.

Reading Immersion

One guiding decision you'll have to make about time is whether you want to compress the immersion into just a couple of days or let it stretch out over more time. If it's compressed, students will likely spend two or three days basically just reading during writing workshop. If you stretch it out, there will be time for reading and other writing work during the immersion phase.

Guiding Questions for Immersion

As students are reading the gathered texts, you'll want them to begin making notes of things they are noticing in response to the questions guiding the study. If you are studying a particular writing issue, then your focus is quite narrow. You'll need to frame the issue into a guiding question (or questions) and ask students to read with this question in mind. For example, "How do writers use punctuation in powerful ways to craft their texts?" or "How do writers use the description effectively to enhance their texts?" If you are engaged in genre study, then the same three questions generally guide most any study:

1. *What kinds of topics do writers address with this genre and what kinds of things do they do with these topics?* This question helps students understand the human intentions this kind of writing serves in the world of writing.

2. *What kinds of work (research, gathering, reflecting, observing, etc.) does it seem like writers of this genre must do in order to produce this kind of writing?* This question helps students understand the preparation and process writers use to write in the genre.

3. *How do writers craft this genre so that it is compelling for readers?* This question helps students understand how writers do this kind of writing *well*.

As I discussed in Chapter 2, a big part of what you are teaching students is this line of questioning itself and how it can serve them throughout their lives whenever they want to learn about a particular kind of writing that's new to them. The content you'll develop from answering these questions about different kinds of writing is, in some ways, secondary to teaching students that these are important questions for writers to ask.

In addition to these general questions, specific genres often have specific big questions that are particular to the genre—where the main idea comes in an essay, for instance, or how much summarizing there is in a book or movie review. Studies of particular crafting issues also have specific kinds of questions driving them.

As students gain experience studying writing in this way, these guiding questions will become second nature to them. I have seen first graders who come to think in these ways about most new texts they encounter and often comment on these aspects of a writer's work around a text. But if this kind of study is new to your students, you'll need to introduce them to these questions early in the study and use shared texts from your stack to demonstrate how to think in these ways.

Here are some ways of working during reading immersion. Your goal, of course, is to have students read the gathered texts and to begin looking at them with an eye toward writing that kind of thing.

POSSIBILITY

Regardless of the age or experience of the writers you teach, reading some texts aloud is important during immersion. You can read short excerpts rather than whole texts, but students need to hear what the writing sounds like. If possible, you'll probably want students to look at the written texts as you read them aloud because so often, understanding why you are reading it the way you are has to do with how the writer has punctuated or formatted the writing on the page.

POSSIBILITY

Students can be reading from the gathered texts on their own, in partnerships, or in small groups during the independent work time of writing workshop.

POSSIBILITY

If you stretch the period of immersion out over time, you might have requirements for how much you expect students to read on their own each day, perhaps one new text and one rereading of a text they particularly like. Some students will spend most of the workshop time doing this required reading, but many will read what's required and still leave themselves time to develop their ideas in their writers' notebooks or work on other self-selected writing.

POSSIBILITY

Students can do some of the reading as homework. This is particularly useful for students in middle and high school where time for study is often much more compressed.

POSSIBILITY

Beginning writers will necessarily gain access to the texts through read-alouds. If the texts are new to the children, you'll probably read one each day. Remind the students what you are studying each time you read a new text so they can look and listen with the focus in mind. If the texts are new to the children, have them respond (with talk) as readers first.

POSSIBILITY

If a study is anchored in texts that students are already familiar with as readers, then the time for immersion can be tightened up and you can move to close study much more quickly. In this case, students simply need time to refamiliarize themselves a little with the texts you've gathered. The most likely scenario is that a study will be made up of some texts that are new to everyone and some that everyone—or at least some of the students—already know.

POSSIBILITY

During share time on some days, you might want to have choral readings when each student reads a favorite line from selected texts, or have students share favorite excerpts aloud that they've found on their own.

POSSIBILITY

You'll probably want to ask students to make notes about what they are noticing about the texts during reading immersion. Students can make these notes on the texts themselves, on sticky notes, or in their writers' notebooks.

POSSIBILITY

With the youngest writers, you might ask them about their first noticings after you read each text to them and chart some of what they say. You might also send them out with the books in groups of twos and threes and have them put sticky notes on pages where they think the writer or illustrator has done something interesting.

POSSIBILITY

You might use share time at the end of the workshop to simply talk about what students are noticing as they are reading the gathered texts. You may want to go ahead and chart some of this talk.

POSSIBILITY

If you've invited students to help you add texts to the ones you've gathered, you'll need to plan some time to look at what they are adding, read it, and talk about it. You may take a whole day to do this, or you might incorporate this right into the other ways you are working around the original texts you gathered.

In genre studies, particularly, it's a good idea to find out as much as you can about the people behind the texts you're reading and the kind of work they do to support their writing. If possible, you may find interviews with writers and either include them in the stack of texts for students to read, or in whole-class gatherings, you might highlight what you think are the important points from the interviews. Also, ask students to pay attention to any author's notes or information on book jackets that might provide insight into the writers and the work they do.

Moving on to Close Study

After reading deeply and widely in immersion, it's time to "dig in" with your students and become articulate about how writers craft this genre so that it is compelling for readers. With your students, you'll be looking very closely at how the texts are actually written, and you'll be using what you see to help students develop vision for the writing they will do.

Before I explain this phase of the inquiry, I should point out that even if you never went any further with the study than you are at this point, your students already know a lot more about writing than they did before they started a short while ago. All the reading they've been doing, combined with the expectation that they will write something that's *like* what they've been reading, has taught them quite a bit. They already have lots of vision and would almost certainly compose much better texts at this point than they would have before you started just because they've been reading like writers. The point of this next phase is simply to help them make explicit some of what they've learned vicariously (Smith 1988) from their reading, and for you as a class to develop some shared understandings and language to name the qualities of good writing you've seen in the texts.

You'll probably want to make a decision in advance about how long you will work at close study with your students. If you don't determine this in advance, it's easy to get stalled in this part of the study. And the problem is, you won't *feel* stalled; you'll feel a lot of energy because you're having these great conversations about how things are written and everyone, including you, will be learning a lot. But you have to remember: the point is to get students writing under the influence of the study. You can always come back after they've written, either right away or later in the year, study some more, and then write again. You'll also just have to grow comfortable with the notion of depth rather than coverage as a curricular understanding. You couldn't cover the topic if you tried, so dig in deep, learn a lot, and then move forward.

In truth, it's a little artificial for me to write about immersion and close study as if they were completely different work in inquiry. I've learned that it's not uncommon for some of the work of close study to happen very early in an inquiry when the class has just set out and started reading. This is particularly true in classrooms where students are very familiar with inquiry work and understand clearly why they're doing what they're doing. They can't help themselves. They start articulating what they're learning right away. As a matter of fact, the whole process of reading immersion and close study are likely to become intertwined in a natural progression of inquiry work over time in a classroom. When this is the case, the latter stages of the inquiry are more a process of refining the most interesting aspects of what you've learned along the way.

Ways of Working in Close Study

The important thing to remember is that if the process of close study hasn't begun on its own, you'll eventually need to turn students' attention in that direction and begin articulating some of what you've learned from reading the gathered texts. In the instructional repertoire that I know, there are three main ways of working at close study, each with different possibilities connected to them. In a single unit of study, it's likely that you might move among these different ways of working at different times, but I believe it's helpful to make a distinction between them and consider each one separately. The three ways are:

1. working from a whole-class list of student noticings across texts
2. returning to individual texts for close study
3. working with a specific question in mind

Working from a Whole-Class List of Student Noticings Across Texts

If you want to work in this way, I think it's helpful to take a full day of writing workshop and work together as a whole class. On this day your goal will be to make a big list of all the things students have noticed across the texts they've read. (Again, you may have already started this list during immersion.) You won't talk much about any of the things you add to the list on this day; just use the best language you can find to record what students have noticed. This list is helpful for you as a teacher because it lets you see the "lay of the land" (in terms of possibilities), and then you can make choices about which things you want to pursue as a whole class during close study in the days that follow. It requires an act of teaching faith at first, but you'll learn to trust that there will be so many possibilities for things you could study that you'll have to be selective about where you decide to dig in. The following are some possibilities for the work on this day.

POSSIBILITY

If you've asked students to make notes on their own during reading immersion, you might have them meet in small groups and make some decisions about the three or four things they think are most interesting that they'd like to contribute to a class list of noticings. These small groups can talk across all the texts they've read, or you might assign different groups specific texts to talk about. After the groups have had time to meet, pull everyone together and make a big master list of all their noticings like the one you see in Figure 9.1. This list was made during a study of feature articles in Jenifer Smith's fourth-grade writing workshop.

FIGURE 9.1 *Chart of noticings from Jenifer Smith's fourth-grade study of feature articles*

NOTICINGS FROM FEATURE ARTICLES

✦ has headings for different parts of the article
✦ has paragraphs
✦ several stories or examples that are different but fit the main topic
✦ has pronunciations for different words
✦ asks questions and then answers them
✦ uses parentheses to explain further
✦ has pictures to help you understand
✦ tells facts
✦ signals end with a symbol or author's name
✦ has a two-part headline—a big short one and a smaller longer one to explain
✦ uses dashes to continue, tell the meaning, and make you pause when you read
✦ uses italics to show thinking
✦ headline rhymes—they want to catch your attention—READ ME!
✦ uses sound words
✦ uses ellipses to make you pause
✦ uses thought bubbles
✦ has descriptive and specific vocabulary
✦ tells who wrote it
✦ has ending marks that help us read
✦ uses quotation marks
✦ uses commas

+ has photographs
+ has examples from well-known people
+ refers to the pictures in the writing
+ has drop caps
+ has quotes
+ uses exclamation marks to show excitement
+ charts examples on the side
+ contains captions
+ has photo credits
+ has different font for the titles
+ has a date
+ puts words in italics so the reader stresses them
+ explains the title in the article
+ has page numbers and the name of the magazine
+ puts pictures in different shapes
+ has maps
+ takes a common phrase and changes it a little—Lights, Animals, Action!
+ lists websites for more information
+ contains time elapsed photos
+ gives advice
+ gives facts that seem reliable
+ sounds like author knows what he is talking about
+ is about two pages long
+ tells who said quotes and why they are qualified to make them
+ uses new vocabulary specific to the topic and tells you what it means

POSSIBILITY

You can generate a class list like Figure 9.1 with the whole class gathered, calling on one child at a time. This is probably not the best option, however, because not as many children can engage at once, and there is no "filtering" work done to select the most interesting noticings as there is when small groups meet first.

POSSIBILITY

If you've made a list all along of things students have been noticing about the texts, you might simply look over that list on this day and add anything to it that you or the students would like to add.

If you teach the youngest writers and you haven't done it already (during immersion), you might send them out in groups of twos and threes and give each pair/group a book or two from your gathered texts. Have them put sticky notes on pages where they notice something about the craft of the writing or illustrating.

With a good list of possibilities in front of you, you have set up your teaching now for many days ahead in writing workshop. On these days you will choose one thing (or more than one if they seem to go together somehow) off the list or from the sticky notes to dig into each day, working in the time frame of a typical whole-class gathering in writing workshop.

Choosing What to Study from Students' Noticings

You really have two choices about how to decide what to talk about during the next days of inquiry-driven lessons: you can choose something or you can let your students choose something. I would probably recommend that you do some of both over the course of close study. You'll want to have some say in determining what seems to have the most potential on the list of possibilities, but you want to be sure that students' interests are honored, too. Of course, since the list is comprised mostly of their noticings, you really ensure that you are following their interests no matter who does the choosing.

When you think about which things to study from your possibilities, remember that there really is no "right" answer to what your students should learn in a particular study. I realize some instructional materials would make it seem otherwise, but the study of writing is always expansive, nuanced, and full of gray areas. I make this claim largely from my experiences as a writer rather than as a teacher. I have spent countless whole days of my life the last nine years writing, and I would say that I know lots about how this kind of writing comes to be. But much of what I know is more intuitive than operational, and what is implicit in my knowledge base about writing far exceeds what is explicit. I understand this as a writer, and it has made me comfortable as a teacher of writing knowing that a student's knowledge base will be comprised of both as well. The purpose of close study is to deepen both the implicit and the explicit knowledge base, not to "cover" the kind of writing you're studying.

Now, having said that, let me share some lines of thinking you might use to help you decide which possibilities to pursue. As you look over the list you've generated with your students, you might consider:

• *Which noticings seem most likely to lead you to genre-specific content and which ones seem to be more about the craft of writing in general?* In a genre study, you'll definitely want to spend most of your time on those things that seem specific to the genre; for example, how the factual information is presented in a feature article, where the main idea comes in a commentary or essay, how a memoir is focused, and so on. The very first thing on Jenifer's class list in Figure 9.1, for example, "Has headings for different parts of the article" would be a good one to explore because it is so typical of most feature articles.

• *Are there things on the list that you have noticed before, in other studies of writing?* The connections you make between studies can be very powerful (especially early on) in helping students understand that the craft of writing is actually more similar in different genres than it is different. In other words, they'll see writers of commentary doing the same things writers of short stories and movie reviews and feature articles do. On Jenifer's class list, for example, there are several references to different uses for punctuation in the articles. She might want to take a day and just lead a discussion about how punctuation is similar/different in memoir (or any other kind of writing they've studied) and in feature articles.

• *Is there anything on the list that seems really fresh and new and that could raise the level of everyone's thinking about writing?* Because you'll see so many things that are similar from one study to the next, the things that stand out as different will take on more significance because of their potential to stretch your students' thinking. The noticing, "Takes a common phrase and changes it a little—Lights, Animals, Action!" on Jenifer's list, for example, might lead to some very fresh and new thinking about the potential for word play that hasn't come up yet in other studies.

• *Do any of the noticings address areas of student need that you've noticed in your assessment?* If something students have noticed relates to something you know a lot of them struggle with as writers, while it may not be the most important thing to know about the topic of inquiry, you might choose to spend time on it anyway because it matches a need they have. On Jenifer's list, for example, she might decide to explore the idea of paragraphing (in feature articles) if she knows many of her students aren't as thoughtful about paragraphs (across their writing) as they might be.

Returning to Individual Texts for Close Study

Instead of moving into close study by pooling students' collective noticings across texts, you might decide instead to begin by revisiting a single text in the stack. If you go at it this way, you'll probably spend several days of whole-class work on a single text, so it needs to feel "teaching full" and like it can "carry the weight of constant talk and examination," as Isoke Nia says in her definition of a touchstone text (1999, 6).

You can work from what students notice about this text just as you would if you were asking them about what they noticed across all the texts. Basically, you want students to respond to the general, guiding question, *What do you notice the writer doing in this text that you think is interesting and makes this good writing?* Using the possibilities I outlined in the previous section, then, you work your way to content from your students' responses. If you teach the youngest writers in kindergarten and first grade, you might "walk through" the text, rereading it and stopping page by page to notice and talk, spending several days sometimes on a single book.

Choosing a single text as a touchstone for study doesn't mean, however, that you'll be talking only about that text. You'll be using that particular text as a touchstone, but you've still shared the others and your talk should move seamlessly among the touchstone text and the other texts you've shared.

For example, imagine a group of third graders involved in study of book reviews. They are looking closely at the *Kirkus* review (1993) of Patricia MacLachlan's book, *Baby*. One of the things they notice is that in the first sentence the writer refers to *Baby* as a "spare novel." To their teacher, it seems clear that their attention is drawn to this particular language because they're unfamiliar with this way of talking about a book. He helps them think about why the writer would refer to the novel as *spare*, and then wonders aloud with them about whether other writers of book reviews tend to label the books with words like this. At that moment, none of the students can remember anything like this in the other reviews they've read, but there are several possibilities for how they might pursue this wondering.

POSSIBILITY

If the teacher knows of another example like this off the top of his head, he may direct students' attention to it and let them talk it through while they're still gathered.

POSSIBILITY

While still gathered as a whole class, they might look at another review in the stack and see if they see similar language.

POSSIBILITY

While still gathered as a whole class, different students might skim different reviews and see if they can find similar language.

POSSIBILITY

Some or all of the students might agree to spend a little time that day during their independent work (or at home) looking for similar language in other reviews and then talk about what they find during share time or in the next day's whole-class gathering.

POSSIBILITY

The class might simply agree to keep an eye out for language used in this way as they carry on with their inquiry and add new examples to their chart as they find them. If they did, their chart might have phrases like these (from actual book reviews) on it after a while:

> "alternately hilarious and deeply moving novel"
> "in these precious hundred pages"
> "warm and winning book"
> "a dark novel"
> "lean yet lyrical narrative"

Choosing a few texts for deep study (and you'll only have time to study a few this way) can have several benefits. First, these texts that you linger with are the ones you and your students will talk most easily about because you both know them so well. When you are teaching students specific content in writing conferences, you can pull from your shared knowledge of these texts to give them examples that support the teaching. Touchstone texts are an invaluable resource in conferring for this reason, and not just in the studies where they're the touchstones. The more general aspects of craft you learn from these texts can continue to serve your conferring across the year.

Anchoring some of the inquiry in deep study of single texts limits the curriculum possibilities somewhat, but you'll feel a need for this at times when the possibilities for study across too many texts feels daunting. And, in genre study, particularly, the need to look at single texts as "wholes" is important to understanding representative examples of the genre.

Working with a Single Question in Mind

The third way of working in close study is to take a specific question about writing and study it across the texts students have read during immersion. You are already doing this if your study is of a particular writing issue, but you might choose to focus on specific questions as part of a genre study, too. The focus, in this case, is on the question, and the thinking you'll do together around a single question will probably stretch over several days of whole-class work. In addition to the general questions guiding any genre study (explained in the last chapter), here are some possibilities for other questions you might ask. I've separated them into ones you would discuss across several texts at once, and ones you would have to explore one text at a time.

Several-Texts Question Possibilities

• What kind of writing is this? How is it different than other kinds of writing in the world?

• What work does this kind of writing do in the world (topics, audiences, purposes)?

• What different approaches do people take to writing this kind of thing?

• How long, generally, is this kind of writing? Is it different lengths in different containers?

One-Text-at-a-Time Question Possibilities

• How is the piece organized? What are the "chunks" of it? How does the piece move from one chunk to the next? Does it move through time or through a list of ideas?

• Look closely at the lead and the ending—how does the writer manage these two critical parts of the piece?

• What particular language work is striking? What can we learn about language from studying these parts?

• How has the writer focused the piece? What's included, and what has likely been left out?

• What different modes of writing operate in the piece (description, exposition, narration, etc.)?

• Is there any interesting punctuation work in the piece?

• Are there any insights about how page-break (in picture books) or paragraph-break decisions were made?

• How do graphics, illustrations, layout, font, add to the meaning and the appeal of the piece?

• How does the title of the piece relate to the meaning? How was it likely chosen?

Questions like these might arise from the original class list of noticings, too. My point here is not so much the questions themselves; my point is that studying a single question across texts is one way to work during close study that might make sense for your inquiry.

Now you have three ways of working that move a class into close study of the writing in the gathered texts. One point I should make about this phase of the work is that over time, as students gain experience studying texts in this way, the lists of what they notice that they find interesting in texts should become shorter and more focused. This is because many of the crafting techniques they'll see writers using will be familiar to them from other studies is other genres. Students' growing knowledge base about the qualities of good writing will allow you to focus your study more on what is new and what stretches your students' current understandings about writing well across genres.

The next question in this work, then, is how do you work your way from general noticings to articulate curriculum? Exploring this question is the focus of the next chapter and the possibilities I'll suggest there are inextricably tied to the possibilities you've seen here, so please keep them in mind as you read forward.

Craft Pause

On August 12, 2002, *USA Today* published the first of a two-part special report on "the most radical action in aviation history," the decision to ground all aircraft on the morning of September 11, 2001. Seventh months of intense investigative research by Alan Levin, Marilyn Adams, and Blake Morrison led to the report, "Amid Terror, a Drastic Decision," truly one of the most powerful pieces of journalism I've ever read. Here's an excerpt:

> This is the story of the four most critical hours in aviation history—an ordeal that began at 8:15 A.M., when the first indication that something was wrong came during a telephone call to American Airlines.
>
> 8:15 A.M. ET
>
> 3,624 planes in the sky
>
> The call doesn't make any sense. Not at first.
>
> At American Airlines' operations center in Fort Worth, manager Craig Marquis talks to a reservations agent in North Carolina. The agent isn't sure what to do.
>
> On another line, the agent is speaking with a flight attendant who's in the air but can't reach the pilots on her jet. The agent wants to transfer the call to Marquis but the phone system won't let her. So she begins to relay messages coming from the back of American Flight 11, a Boeing 767 heading from Boston to Los Angeles.
>
> Aboard, flight attendant Betty Ong tells what's unfolding.
>
> Marquis, a blunt-spoken veteran, isn't sure what to make of the call. *Is the woman even a flight attendant?* he wonders. He checks his computer as he listens on the phone. There she is. Betty Ong. And she is on that flight.
>
> Ong can't contact the pilots, the agent says. That's why she's calling. *Why doesn't she just walk up to the cockpit and bang on the door?* But as he listens—as Ong, in hushed tones, tells of a passenger dead and a crewmember dying, of the jet's erratic path and intruders in the cockpit—Marquis realizes that Ong can do little.
>
> *The flight has been hijacked.*

Throughout the piece, the exact time and the exact number of planes in the air are updated at regular intervals, and the internal thoughts of people (in response to what's happening) are captured in italics.

This excerpt is from "Attack on Morrell Mountain," a chapter in *Fire in Their Eyes: Wildfires and the People Who Fight Them* by Karen Magnuson Beil (1999, 25).

> Deep in the rugged wilderness of Montana, a storm rumbles across the sky. Lightening flashes strike trees, igniting them like matches.
>
> It is two o'clock, Tuesday afternoon, August 2. Rowdy Ogden sits in a lookout tower, wondering when the fires will start showing up.
>
> Rowdy scans the horizon for "smokes," columns of smoke that reveal a fire. On a clear day, he can see one hundred miles all around. Today the sky is so hazy from recent fires that it is hard to spot smoke from new ones.

Through the haze Rowdy sees several gray shadows he suspects might be new smoke coming from Morrell Mountain. At 2:33 P.M. he radios Seeley Lake Ranger Station.

This excerpt is from Robert Burleigh's *Flight* (1991), the story of Charles Lindbergh's transatlantic flight.

The sun sets far behind the plane. Lindbergh flies over St. John's, Newfoundland, the last point of land in North America. Now he can no longer follow the land's edge for direction. He must chart his course carefully. The slightest movement could send him miles off course and risk the fuel supply.

He follows two compasses and the stars to navigate. As long as the sky is clear, he is safe. But he must stay awake. He writes: "Now I must cross not one, but two oceans: One of night and one of water."

Time passes slowly. It is almost 9:00 at night, Lindbergh's thirteenth hour in the air. He has completed one-third of the flight.

INSIGHTS ABOUT CRAFT

Recounting a story in present tense—as if it is happening as it's being read—is a very effective way to capture the tension and drama of unfolding events and to convey those feelings to readers. The addition of very specific data about what's happening (time, place, distance, numbers involved, etc.) adds to the feeling that readers are in the moment of the story being recounted. And capturing the internal thinking of those experiencing the story adds further intensity to the lived-through experience for readers.

Turning Talk into Text

The Language of Specific Curriculum

You're not using a *text*book to do this teaching, but you still need a *text* if you are going to have curriculum in a classroom. As I said in the last chapter, reading immersion will help students develop vision for writing whether you move on to close study or not. The purpose of close study is to help you articulate specific curriculum and for that, you need a text, you need something tangible you and others can read and say, "Here it is. This is what we studied." The three ways of working during close study—working from a whole-class list of student noticings, studying an individual text, or studying a specific question across texts—are really all about creating a text for teaching. To put it another way, you have gathered texts, and now your study of them will create a totally new text—a *text*book, if you will, written by you and your students about the subject you are studying. The container where you put your "textbook" may be a chart, a smart board screen, a computer file, a class notebook—wherever, just as long as you put it somewhere so there is a record of the teaching.

I hope I do not take liberties when I say I believe what you and your students create will truly be a *poem* in the transactional sense that Louise Rosenblatt helped us all understand in her seminal work, *The Reader, the Text, the Poem* (1978). The text you and your students write together, using your own words to capture your shared understandings about commentary or travel articles or short stories or how writers use punctuation in interesting ways or *whatever*, will be something only you could write. In other words, your understandings don't exist outside of how you experience them and come to understand them, and no textbook or set of lessons published far away from you could ever represent those same understandings in quite the same way that you will. As Rosenblatt (2005) says:

> The poem, then, must be thought of as an event in time. It is not an object or an ideal entity. It happens during a coming together, a copenetration, of a reader and a text. The reader brings to the text his past experiences and present

personality. Under the magnetism of the ordered symbols of the text, he marshals his resources and crystallizes out from the stuff of memory, thought, and feeling a new order, a new experience, which he sees as the poem. (29)

Rosenblatt is writing about single readers transacting with single texts here, but I believe what she's saying also applies to what happens when a group of readers transacts purposefully with a stack of texts in all the ways I've been describing throughout this book. The challenge of this teaching, of course, is to work together to create "a new order, a new experience" out of the somewhat chaotic noticing you've been doing.

Creating Text from Talk

One of the most fascinating teaching episodes I ever observed happened one morning in Lisa Cleaveland's first-grade writing workshop when a student commented on something he'd noticed in Karen Wallace's book *Gentle Giant Octopus* (1998). He said that on the first page of the book, it looks like the legs of the octopus are "protecting the words." On the two-page spread, the text is centered in a space between the octopus' eight wavy tentacles (three on top and five on bottom) in Mike Bostock's illustration. Ten minutes later, or so, the class had looked at other pages in the book, talked about the different placements of the text in relation to the illustrations, and come to a beginning understanding that *a writer should think a lot about the placement of text with illustrations because the relationship between the two can be meaningful for the reader*. Contained in their talk was also a beginning repertoire of techniques for *how* the text might be placed in relation to the illustrations.

What was Lisa's lesson plan for this day during their study of literary nonfiction? Her plan was to revisit this book with the children and work with their noticings to get at some specific content for their study. She didn't know what that content would be, but she was comfortable they would have no trouble finding something of interest to learn from Karen Wallace and Mike Bostock. And since all the children were working on writing their own literary nonfiction books at this time, Lisa also planned to move seamlessly from whatever thinking they did about *Gentle Giant Octopus* into thinking about their own work as writers.

You may remember in Chapter 2 as I described Lisa's teaching I said, "There was no content to her teaching until the children started talking." This was certainly true on this day. During close study, Lisa listens to her students and works with them to turn what they say into specific curriculum. And there is a turning that they have to do. The language of what students first notice about a text rarely emerges explicitly enough to be understood as curriculum, and as they should be, their first comments are also tied directly to the text at hand: "It looks like the legs are protecting the words." The teaching move is to help them untie their comments from the text at hand and state them as specific curriculum about writing in general: *A writer should think a lot about the placement of text with illustrations because the relationship between the two can be meaningful for the reader.*

Often, there is a good bit of talking and thinking that has to happen before a group can move to an explicit statement of curriculum like that one. Teachers like Lisa are comfortable engaging in conversation like this with their students, and with the tentative nature of the talk that is necessary before clarity is found. As I've studied this kind of conversation in classrooms, I've noticed that there are certain types of statements and questions teachers use over and over again to lead the way from noticing to understanding:

"What are you thinking?"
"What did you notice?"
"Tell me more."
"Can you explain what you're thinking?"
"Where, exactly, in the text are you talking about?"
"I don't know for sure, but my theory is . . . "
"Have you seen this kind of thing anywhere else?"
"Let's look in some other places and see if we see this."
"As a writer yourself, have you ever tried this? Can you imagine trying it?"

As I've said more than once in *Study Driven*, talk like this can't be scripted and used at another time in another place. Talk like this is, as Rosenblatt said, "an event in time" itself, and it happens completely in response to the given students interacting with the given texts for a given reason. And the thing is, I'm not sure exactly how to teach someone how to have this kind of conversation with students, or perhaps even more importantly, how to become comfortable having this kind of conversation. Knowing the questions to ask to get children talking is only half the challenge; knowing what to do with their responses is the other challenge.

I believe teachers who hold "big picture" understandings informing work like this know how to talk about what students notice in written texts and turn their noticings into specific writing curriculum. I believe these teachers also operate with a clear sense of where they are trying to move the talk. They understand what writing curriculum sounds like, in other words. They know they need to come to a place where they can articulate some understanding, strategy, or technique for writing that is specific enough to be helpful, yet general enough to be used in a variety of writing situations: *a writer should think a lot about the placement of text with illustrations because the relationship between the two can be meaningful for the reader.*

The purpose of the thirteen Craft Pauses scattered throughout *Study Driven* is to give you a clear sense of what writing curriculum sounds like when it comes from noticing what good writers have done in written texts. My hope is that these Craft Pauses, combined with all the possibilities I've offered to get children noticing what's happening in texts, have given you a sense of the beginning and ending points of this work. But in between, the conversations that must happen on particular days in particular classrooms with particular children necessarily depend on you making them happen.

To help you imagine how these conversations might go, I've created three short stories about inquiry showing teachers moving from what students notice to generating some specific curriculum statements. The stories aren't written in exhaustive detail. I've included just enough to help you get a feel for how this talk might unfold in your classroom. As you read through these stories, notice how the teachers use different questions and statements to steer the thinking.

Inquiry Story One: A Noticing About Memoir

In a study of memoir, students are reading from Kathi Appelt's beautiful, provocative vignette collection, *My Father's Summers—A Daughter's Memoir* (2004). One of the students reports that her group has noticed, "Some of them aren't really memoir." Curious, her teacher asks her to say more about what they mean by this. The group asks everyone to look at the vignette titled "Short Skirts" (77).

> At school, there was a rule about skirts. They had to touch the floor when you knelt on the ground. It must have been the same rule they had when my mother went to school eighteen years before me. In 1967 skirts were short. Very short. None of mine hit the floor. My favorite was yellow vinyl, no washing required. I simply had to wipe it off with a damp cloth, the same way I wiped off the kitchen table after dinner. I wore it with bright blue fishnet stockings and clunky black shoes. My leather purse with fringe on it hung lower than my skirt, swished against my legs when I walked, sang with every step. I learned to sashay. That's what my mother called it when I walked away from her, hips swinging from one side to the other, yellow skirt flashing down the halls.

Through conversation, the teacher realizes the students don't think this vignette is memoir because it doesn't tell a story. "It's just about a skirt," they say. This presents them with the question, "Does memoir have to tell a story?" They think together about other memoir they've read and whether any of it was nonnarrative. They're not sure, but agree to be on the lookout for it as they continue reading.

Someone discovers a short piece by Maira Kalman that is mostly a none-too-flattering description of her great aunt Tillie who was a dentist (*The Milestones Project*, 2004, 49), and they also find several other pieces in the Appelt collection that aren't stories either. With this evidence they conclude: *Memoir doesn't have to be a story. It can be your memory of an object, a person, or a place that holds meaning for you.* They write this on their chart, but they continue to think about it in subsequent conversations.

Since they've mostly seen memoir like this in collections, they wonder if nonnarrative memoir works best when it is part of a vignette collection where many of the vignettes *are* stories. Then their teacher finds a stand-alone memoir in a magazine and it's about cut-off blue jeans, nonnarrative, so they realize their theory won't hold.

A student shares that when he was reading Ralph Fletcher's *Marshfield Dreams*, he thought from the title that the chapter "First Pen" was going to be about an object, but then he realized there was a story connected to it. This pushed everyone's thinking as they remembered other writers who used the memory of an object to connect to a remembered story: Louise Erdrich in *The Range Eternal* and Eric Velasquez in *Grandma's Records*, for example. From this thinking they add more specific curriculum to their chart: *Sometimes the memory of an object, a person, or a place has a story connected to it that really shows why the memory of it matters.* They search their own memories for topic possibilities that might come from objects and people and places, and they write about these in their writers' notebooks.

Near the end of the study when they've learned all kinds of things about memoir, someone raises a question about an old favorite that brings them back to this earlier line of thinking. "I'm not really sure what *When I Was Young in the Mountains* is? I mean, it's kind of like a story, but not really. And it's not really about a thing or a person either." Since everyone knew this beloved Cynthia Rylant memoir so well already, the class had sort of taken it for granted and hadn't talked much about it, but in light of the new understandings about how memoir is sometimes not a story, a new question had arisen about an old favorite.

The class revisits the book and as they talk about it they realize in many ways, Rylant's classic picture book memoir is actually a vignette piece a lot like Fletcher's *Marshfield Dreams*, Appelt's *My Father's Summers*, Gary Soto's *Living up the Street* and others. The difference, of course, is that her vignettes are much, much shorter and they are woven together into a single text with the repeating line, "When I was young in the mountains." They realize their original statement about nonnarrative memoir needed to include *a time in your life* along with an object, a person, and a place.

Inquiry Story Two: "Hey! It's like you're the cow!"

Early in the year in a study of where writers get ideas, a primary teacher has chosen several books to share with her students to help them understand that writers often write about everyday things they know a lot about. On this particular day she is reading the picture book *Cow* by Malachy Doyle to the children. To these children of rural America, cows are quite an everyday sort of topic, and her plan is to talk with them when she's finished reading about other everyday topic possibilities they might consider. But in a pause as she is turning a page, someone says quite spontaneously, "Hey! It's like you're the cow!" She has just read these words: "You tear the grass and chew the cud, rolling your mouth from side to side, pushing the food with your thick, wet tongue, over and over for hours."

There is a quiet moment as everyone considers this, and then a bit of a giggle as they think of themselves as cows chewing the cud. The teacher says, "You know, it is like that," and she rereads the page and invites the children to really be the cow as the author has invited them to be. Mouths move from side to side and wet tongues wag. They continue reading the book "being the cow," having quite a time, and even rereading some of the earlier pages they read before they realized they needed to be the cow.

When things settle down a bit and they're back to being children again, the teacher asks them, "What did you think about that?" And of course they say, "It was fun!" telling her what they feel, not what they think. At this point the teacher decides to abandon her plan to talk about choosing everyday topics. That's not where the energy is and she decides instead to follow the energy. "Let me ask you something," she says, "Why do you think Malachy Doyle decided to write it this way? To write it so you could be the cow? Why do you think he did that?" She is asking them to shift from feeling responses to thinking responses.

One child suggests, tentatively, that perhaps Doyle did this because he likes cows. The teacher thinks out loud about this, letting the children hear her train of thought. "Hmm, I think you're right. He must like cows, but I'm still wondering *why* he wrote it so it seemed like we were the cow. He could have just written something like, 'Cows like to eat grass and their mouths move a lot.' Something like that. But why did he write it so we could be the cow?"

"So it would be more fun?" a child says.

"Tell me more."

"So we could do the cow-stuff and have more fun when we read it."

The teacher takes this idea and makes it bigger, saying the student might be on to something because writers often think about their readers and how what they write will suit them. She asks the children if they ever think about the people who will read their books and whether they will have fun reading them.

There is a little talk around this, but for the most part it seems the children haven't thought much about this before. The day's session ends with the teacher suggesting this is something worth thinking a little more about—how writers think about their readers and make books more fun to read.

The next day when the class gathers, the teacher has three books in her lap: *Night Is Coming* by W. Nikola-Lisa, *Earthdance* by Joanne Ryder, and *Dream Weaver*, by Jonathan London. She tells the children that she couldn't stop thinking about what they talked about the day before and how Malachy Doyle had written his book so they could be the cow when they read it. She explains that her curiosity sent her looking for other books like this, and that she has found three more where writers have done the same thing. She reads a little of each one (not the whole texts) so the children can see how they are similar to *Cow*. For example, from *Dream Weaver* she reads, "Nestled in the soft earth beside the path, you see a little yellow spider. If you're quiet and listen, maybe you can hear its feet on the sparkling web." As she reads the different excerpts, she makes sure the children are attending to the *you* stance in the text. She asks, "Can you see it? The little spider? Do you hear its feet?"

After they've looked at these books, they talk about how all these writers helped the reader be in the book, and the children realize it's the word *you* doing that work for the writers, helping them make the book fun for the reader. The teacher helps them say this clearly, and in doing so, writes important curriculum with her very young students: *one way to write a book is to use the word* you *a lot so people who read it feel like they're in the book doing stuff.*

The next day, they follow through on their mini-inquiry one more time and together they use this new technique to write a few pages of a book about an everyday thing they all know a lot about (the original intention of the teaching): the class guinea pig. When they're sent out to write that day, the children are told they're welcome to try this in their own writing if they'd like and if it suits their intentions, and if not, to keep it in mind for future writing. They also agree to be on the lookout for other ways writers make their books more interesting for readers so they can learn other techniques for this.

Inquiry Story Three: A Noticing About an Interesting Punctuation Decision

In a study of how writers use punctuation in interesting ways to craft their texts, a student has written "one-word sentence" in the margin of a Leonard Pitts piece about the tragic aftermath of Hurricane Katrina (*The Miami Herald*, 9/4/05). While this type of crafting is very common across many types of writing, this particular class has very little experience looking at what writers actually do in texts and they've not considered this kind of punctuation work before this day. The teacher writes the passage from the Pitts piece on the overhead so everyone can look at it together:

> When the going got tough, the privileged got going. And the poor were left where they always are. Behind.

Notice that the teacher also wrote the sentences just before it, pulling from a knowledge base that tells him that to understand the one-word sentence, they will have to look at the sentences around it. The teacher first comments on the word play connected to the cliché about what happens when the going gets tough, and he thinks aloud about the crafting intention of taking a cliché and changing it in a surprising way. Next, he asks the student who has brought this sentence work to their attention to read it aloud the way he thinks Pitts would have wanted the reader to "hear" it.

The teacher asks the students what they think of the punctuation decisions Pitts has made in the passage, and someone comments that having it there by itself brings more attention to the word *behind*. Someone else says that it's almost like the word has been left behind too, all by itself in the sentence. They seem to agree that having it like this makes the idea of the word much stronger.

Next, the teacher nudges them to figure out how this word can work by itself as a sentence and not be a fragment. "What completes it?" he asks. "What is the subject and verb of this sentence?" This is clearly new territory for the students and no one really knows what to say, so after a long pause the teacher decides to show them. He knows they will get better at understanding this kind of sentence work over time. He explains that you understand from the sentence before it that the subject is *they*, meaning the poor, and the verb is *were left*: "They were left behind."

Next he asks the students to think about other punctuation decisions Pitts might have made in these three sentences. Thinking aloud, they consider a number of different possibilities involving different marks and sentence combinations. Finally, the teacher asks them why they think Pitts settled on this way of punctuating the sentences. They return to their original idea that having the word there by itself has a powerful impact and kind of visually shows the meaning of the word. The teacher also shares his thinking that it sort of matches the way a person talks when he or she is passionate about something, the pause and separation between words adding impact. He reads it aloud to them again so they can hear what he means.

In the end, they decide to write down three things they've learned from studying this sentence:

- Punctuating a single word as a sentence is a powerful way to bring attention to the word (if it needs attention for some reason).
- Sometimes punctuation decisions are made to make the writing sound like someone talking.
- The subject and verb of a sentence like this must be clearly understood from the sentences around it for it not to be a fragment.

They do a couple of quick try-its together on the overhead, writing sentences such as, "Maria felt the way she always did at the end of the school day. Tired." And then they follow the same lines of thinking they used to study the Pitts sentence, identifying the subject and verb of *tired* and looking at other options for how the sentence might be written. The teacher asks students to play around with this kind of punctuation work in the writing they do that day, and he makes a plan to talk about what they've learned from trying it during share time.

Together they also make a plan to be on the lookout for other writers making similar punctuation decisions, and they leave a space in their class notebook for students to add other examples. By the end of the study the students and their teacher have added many sentences to the notebook, some found in the texts gathered for the study, but a good many of them coming from their reading outside writer's workshop. It seems once they had this conversation, they began noticing sentences punctuated like this all over the place. Here are few that have been added:

> And my grandfather put on his coat and watched me walk off into the dark morning. Sometimes there were other children to walk with. Sometimes not.
>
> (Cynthia Rylant, "On Beginning School," in *The Milestones Project*, 43)

> They all should be pulling out the checkbooks soon. The NFL. The NCAA. All of them. Giving millions. When has the term "disaster relief" ever meant more to this country?
>
> (Mike Lopresti, "Superdome's Past Glory Hard to Imagine Now," Gannett News Service, September 2, 2005)

> People say things about me. Bad Things.
>
> (Sharon Flake, "So I Ain't No Good Girl," in *Who Am I Without Him?: Short Stories About Girls and the Boys in Their Lives*, 1)

This story begins within the walls of a castle with the birth of a mouse. A small mouse. The last mouse born to his parents and the only one of his litter to be born alive.

(Katie DiCamillo, *The Tale of Despereaux*, 11)

What will the first female president of the U.S. be like? Very tall. Thus predicts ABC, which cast six-footer Geena Davis as Mackenzie Allen, a Vice President who comes to power when the President dies of a stroke, in the drama *Commander in Chief*, debuting Sept. 27.

(James Poniewozik, "Hail to the She," *Time*, September 26, 2005)

With each addition to the list, the thinking about punctuating in this way is rounded out a little more, and before the study is over students have to revisit more than once what they've written about punctuating in this way and add new curriculum statements to account for their new understandings. They add:

Some sentences can't stand alone outside of texts. They are fragments without the surrounding sentences there to complete them.
Sometimes these sentences are understood to be an answer to a question that's been posed. (Poniewozik)

Sometimes these sentences say more about an idea that ended the last sentence. (Flake, DiCamillo)

Sometimes several sentences in a row can share the same understood verb. (Lopresti)

Craft Pause

NOTICE

Here are three endings to three different memoirs.

From "Close Encounters" by Dan Berry in the "Lives" section of the *New York Times Magazine*, April 25, 2004. The piece is a memoir about growing up as the child of parents who searched for U.F.O.'s.

The U.F.O.'s never came to the Wanaque Reservoire. At least not that night. At least as far as I know. After a while, my brother fell asleep, and then so did I. But before I closed my eyes, I took in the wonder of it all: the taste of powdered sugar, the warmth of my siblings beside me and the sight of my parents staring into the Jersey darkness, peering with hope, peering up.

From *My Father's Summers—A Daughter's Memoir* by Kathi Appelt.

I have a photograph of my father, his blonde hair combed to the side. He's standing in the sun without a shirt, holding me, a toddler, in his arms. He's very thin and his pants are very baggy. He looks like a boy, too young to be a father, and he was too, only nineteen. He's looking at me looking out, looking toward the camera. His face is shining, his smile is sweet. It's clear he's happy to be holding me, hanging on to me. Despite everything, that was always clear.

From the picture book, *The Range Eternal*, by Louise Erdrich.

Now I sit by the stove on cold winter afternoons. Sometimes, as the dusk lowers, I do not switch on the lights. I watch flames pull shadows down the walls. I teach my son to enter the pictures, the way I used to do.

Even here in the city, I show my husband and son how the animals race back and forth, across the walls to the horizon, beneath a deep and darkening sky. I keep the fire going. Together, we see again the old range, the vast range, the living range restored.

I keep The Range Eternal.

INSIGHT ABOUT CRAFT

These three memoir endings, crafted to evoke a sense of calm and peace with the memories they shared, have so much in common. Read each one aloud and listen to how the phrasing catches the starting and stopping sound of someone remembering. Close your eyes and see the small scene each one paints: the family in the car on a dark night, the photograph of the smiling father holding his baby, the mother and son huddled together in front of the warm old range, entering the pictures. Hear the beautiful echo of repetition in each one: peering, looking, the old range, the vast range, the living range. Understand the older person looking back on each memory, finding some gentle perspective on it all.

Writing Under the Influence in All Phases of Study

Writing workshops include significant stretches of time each day when students work independently as writers. This time generally follows the whole-class teaching sessions for which I've been outlining possibilities in the last three chapters. Your unit of study will certainly influence some of what's happening during independent work time, but there should still be a range of options from which students can make independent decisions about how they will manage their work during this time. The purpose of this chapter is to think about what some of those possibilities might be during each phase of inquiry.

To write about these possibilities, I first need to address those of you who teach the youngest writers in grades K and 1, and even in grade 2 if your students haven't had a lot of experience with writing workshops. In truth, most of this chapter doesn't apply to you because the process of writing just looks different when very beginning writers engage in it. An entire chapter of my book with Lisa Cleaveland, *About the Authors: Writing Workshop with Our Youngest Writers* (2004), is devoted to understanding these differences in process. I don't really have the space in this book to go into all that thinking, but if the work you've read about in *Study Driven* is something you'd like to try in your workshop, I highly recommend that book and the corresponding DVD, *The Teaching Behind* About the Authors (2005), as companions to this one.

For the purposes of this book, I'd like to make one main point about writing under the influence in grades K and 1. If you teach the youngest writers, you should probably go ahead and invite them to start trying the work of the study right from the start, even in genre study. This means, of course, that some of them may write several pieces under the influence of the study while it lasts, and that their vision for the writing will grow across those pieces. Other children may need to be reminded and helped to try some of the work of the study if time passes and they haven't initiated trying anything on their own. The bottom line is, it's just not really developmentally appropriate to ask children this age to wait to start until you've gotten further along in your study.

With more experienced writers, though, you don't want them to begin the drafts that will show what they've learned in the study until you've done the work to help them develop vision for the writing. I believe it's helpful to set a date that marks when students can begin their actual drafts. This is so you don't have the overachieving child come in on the second day of the study and say, "I wrote mine last night. I'm finished." There's not much point in carrying out the study if you don't hold off on the writing.

The question then, is, what is the writing work in the early stages of an inquiry before drafts are started? And then much later in the study, what is the writing work for students who finish the requirements of the study before others? Before reading forward, take a look again at one of the outlines of study requirements you first saw in Chapter 8 (Figures 8.1 and 8.2). As you look them over, imagine when and how in the context of a writing workshop students might accomplish the required work outlined for them on the handout. (See Figure 11.1.)

FIGURE 11.1 *Sample Requirements and Expectations: Feature Article Study*

Feature Article Genre Study

Overview
Our study in writing workshop for the month of February will be *how to write a feature article*. Using good examples of feature articles from magazines and newspapers to guide us, we'll focus our study around these guiding questions:

✦ What kinds of topics are appropriate for feature articles?

✦ What kinds of prewriting work do writers of feature articles do?

✦ How are feature articles *crafted* in ways that make them compelling for readers?

Expectations
By the end of the study, each student will be expected to publish one feature article on a topic of his/her choosing. In addition, each of you will be expected to participate in the inquiry part of the study during writing workshop, and to turn in all the reflective writing about process and evidence of work along the way (outlined below). During writing conferences, please remember that I will ask to see evidence that you are trying the work of the minilessons on a regular basis.

As in every classwide unit of study, you may choose to work on "back-up" work during writing workshop after the work of the study has been completed.

Monday, February 9
1. Describe the topic you have chosen for your feature article. Explain in as much detail as you can how and why you have chosen this topic for this feature article project.

2. Tell me about what material you already have in your writer's notebook related to your topic. Then, write about the plans you have for the notebook work you want to do in the coming days to support you in writing your feature article.

Monday, February 16

1. Show evidence of all the notebook work you have done with your seed idea up until this point. Tell a little about how each separate entry of this work came to be. You may use the big sticky notes to do this if you'd like. You may photocopy your entries or turn in your notebook to me. If you turn your notebook in, I'll be sure you have it to work with during writing workshop.

2. Provide a copy of the feature article you are using as a touchstone text for your writing. Explain why you admire the writing and selected it as a touchstone text, and detail three specific things you have learned about crafting a feature article from the writer of this text.

Monday, February 23

1. Show evidence of the planning you did before you began drafting your feature article. Include any comments that will help me understand your planning.

2. You should have a copy of the beginning draft of your feature article. Write and turn in a reflection that tells me about drafting and revising your feature article up to this point. Consider questions such as: How did you get started? Did you revise a lot as you drafted, or did you get it down first and then go back through it? Has another writer given you feedback? Have you read it aloud to yourself? Have you tried any tools for revision that we've studied? How did your touchstone text help you? What are your plans for continuing work on this piece?

Friday, February 27

Class publication day. Have a finished copy of your feature article available and ready to turn in.

Due Monday, March 2

1. Turn in all evidence of drafting. Explain the thinking behind *three specific decisions* you made while working on drafting and revising your feature article. Be sure to show exactly where in the text you made the revision decisions. Please also note any specific crafting decisions you made that you think are particularly artful. You may use highlighters, sticky notes, keys, and so on to help document this work on your drafts. Pay special attention here to helping me see how you used what we learned in the study to help you write your piece.

2. Explain your process for editing (proofreading) your feature article. How did you make sure it was edited as well as it could be?

3. Reflect on what's most important in what you have learned about writing feature articles. What did you learn about yourself as a writer during this study?

Before I consider possibilities for writing work that might be happening in each phase of a study, I need to define what I mean by "back-up" work as you see in Figure 11.1. The idea of back-up work is an important one.

On the Importance of Back-up Work

For a long time the only answer many teachers (including me) had to what students might do in the down time before they started or after they finished the required writing in a study was "write in their notebooks." And certainly working on ideas in writer's notebooks should always be an option in a workshop. The problem is, though, for many students there is not a lot of energy in writing still more notebook entries. The energy for writing in notebooks is something writers experience more away from their desks than at them. Just like professional writers (and just like me), these students wanted to spend their desk time *making* something with writing. And many of them were making something even when it looked like they were writing notebook entries. How many notebooks have you peeked into and seen "Chapter Four" written at the top of a page? Recognizing this issue and rethinking some of my own understandings about the role a notebook plays in a writing life has helped me realize a writing workshop also needs a place for what I'll call "back-up" work.

One option for what students might work on during independent work time, at any phase of a study, is self-selected back-up work. Some of my writing friends and I have decided back-up work is the best management tool we know for writing workshops. What is back-up work? It's something or some several-things that students are working on all on their own. Kid-sponsored, often recklessly wonderful writing work that may not be very good but is something students have chosen to work on because the idea of writing it gives them energy. For example, imagine a writing workshop in a third- or fifth- or eighth-grade class where in their back-up work students are making:

- a choose-your-own-adventure novel
- a play that is passed among four writers who each add scenes to it
- a series of short chapter books about a girl who flies airplanes
- a fashion magazine
- a comic book
- a cookbook of family recipes with stories attached to each one (to give to family members for Christmas)
- an historical novel based on an uncle's stories about time in Vietnam

- a poetry anthology of sports poems that go with pictures cut from magazines
- an ABC picture book about trains (to give to a three-year-old brother)
- lyrics for original songs a band can sing in their sessions after school
- words for cheers (the motions choreographed at recess)
- a science fiction novel about a group of teenagers lost on a strange planet
- a series of guides for players of various video games

Notice that all these "things" students are making have the energy of vision backing them. All the students making these things can answer the question, *what have I read that is like what you are trying to write?*

Back-up work is anything students can imagine they'd like to write, and the bigger the better. I often tell teachers, "Hope all your students start a novel when you invite them to get involved in back-up work. This way they always have something they can go to when it's time to write." You also hope students have several different projects going in their back-up work. Why? So they can do as Jane Yolen says she does in an interview posted on the Scholastic website: "I never get writer's block because I write on a number of things at the same time. So that if one thing is not going well, I turn to another" (n.d.).

To put it simply, if students have some things they are working on all on their own, they always have something to do during independent writing time and you are freed from worrying about how they will fill that time. One of the reasons I've always liked to refer to this writing as back-up work is because of the message those words send to teachers. You should feel like those words let you off the hook. You don't have to do anything more with this writing than support the fact that it is there. Just let them work on it. Let it be okay for this writing not to be any good. If anyone outside asks you about it, you can always say, "Oh, it's just back-up work." Be sure to flip your hand a little when you say it.

You know, so many writers tell us some version of, "You have to do a lot of bad writing before you do any good writing." If writing workshops are places where students are learning how to write, then some of that ought to be bad writing! And as long as you are balancing that with regular expectations for finished writing that does show evidence of deep engagement with the process, then you don't need to worry about the somewhat lower (okay, maybe a lot lower) quality of the back-up writing.

As I suggest possibilities for what students will be working on during independent work time, then, I'll assume they have writing folders with some ongoing back-up work in them, writer's notebooks that they use both in class and out of class to gather and grow ideas for writing, and at some point, a draft they are working on that will show what they have learned in the unit of study (this draft is probably in the same folder as the drafts of back-up work).

When Back-up Work Becomes THE Work

I can promise you that a fair number of your students will come to a place where they would much rather work on their back-up writing than on the drafts sanctioned by the study in the room. This is a nice problem to have, and across the school year, it's not always a problem. In any study that is not tied to genre, there is no reason why something a student is working on in back-up work can't become the work for the study. A chapter from the science fiction novel about teenagers lost on a strange planet can be revised and edited to reflect the learning in a study of how writers use punctuation in interesting ways to craft their texts. An article from the fashion magazine could be submitted to show the learning from a study of how to make thoughtful paragraphing decisions. The ABC picture book could be revised to reflect the work of a study of how to write accurate, engaging descriptions.

Even in genre study, students can sometimes be helped to see how to shape some of the intentions of their back-up work into the genre under study. The student who is writing historical fiction about the uncle in Vietnam might choose to write commentary about how war veterans are treated by others when they return home. The play passed among four students might become a piece of short fiction. The song lyrics might become a poetry anthology.

Having defined the idea of back-up work, now I'd like to think about the independent work time during each phase of an inquiry study. As Figure 11.1 suggests, I recommend students show evidence of the process of their work—from notebooks to finished drafts—over the course of the study. It's a given, then, that some of their independent work time will be spent fulfilling the requirements of the study and reporting on their process along the way.

Independent Work Time: Reading Immersion

Obviously, students are spending some of their independent work time reading during the immersion phase of an inquiry. Here are some possibilities for what their other work might look like during this time.

POSSIBILITY

In their writer's notebooks, students are developing an idea—or possibly several ideas so they have options—for the writing they will eventually do under the influence of the study. You want there to be a feeling in the room of "living toward a draft." This idea development might include things like:

- writing entries where the student is thinking through the idea
- rereading the notebook looking for connected ideas
- doing secondary research to develop the idea: reading and taking notes, interviewing experts, and so on
- doing primary research to develop the idea: observations, surveys, interviews, experiments, and so on
- writing lists of possibilities connected to the idea
- playing around with writing parts that might be included in the draft: scenes, leads, descriptions, and so on

As you see in Figure 11.1, I recommend you ask students to show evidence of the notebook work they have done to develop ideas for the writing they will turn in for the study.

POSSIBILITY

You'll want to find opportunities for students to be talking with others about the ideas they are developing for the writing they'll eventually do. Students need to become known in the room as "The person who is working on. . . ." By the time they actually do begin a draft, they should have talked through their ideas as many times as possible.

POSSIBILITY

You may want to make a chart announcing each child's commitment to a topic for the writing and encourage them to help each other with the thinking and collecting around these ideas.

POSSIBILITY

Students might simply be writing randomly in their notebooks if they have collected ideas that interest them but don't connect to the study in any way.

POSSIBILITY

During the immersion phase, students can work on any self-selected back-up writing they have going—as long as they have also done the work to develop the idea for the piece they'll do in the study.

Independent Work Time: Close Study

Certainly at some point during close study you want students to start their drafts, but when, exactly, is a tricky question because there is no right answer to it. I usually recommend several days of close study before drafts are started, and then this study can continue as students are composing their drafts. I would recommend that at the onset of close study, students have settled on a topic for their writing and have used their writers' notebooks to grow this idea in meaningful ways.

Back-up work, further notebook work, and sometimes even continued reading may all be happening during independent work time in this phase of the study. Here are a few other possibilities for what might be happening.

POSSIBILITY

Students may spend some of this time following up on a question or idea that has come up in whole-class close study. You may remember in the stories of inquiry in the last chapter that students went in search of other examples of non-narrative memoir and sentences with understood subjects and verbs. Some of this searching may be happening during independent work time.

POSSIBILITY

You may ask students to use some of their work time to try things in their notebooks or think about things you've discussed. Pulling again from the stories of inquiry in the last chapter as examples, the students studying memoir might be asked to reread their notebook entries and see if they find any possibilities for memoir that could be connected to objects or people or places. The students in the punctuation study might be asked to try and write or rewrite a few passages in their writers' notebooks or drafts of back-up work and punctuate them the same way Pitts did.

POSSIBILITY

Depending on the kind of writing students will be required to do, they may use some of their time to plan and organize their ideas for drafts. Writers of feature articles, for example, may outline or make a web of what their sections will be, or writers of short stories may flesh out ideas for characters or scenes. If you've focused on some aspect of the writing such as leads, you may ask students to try writing several leads in their notebooks. Any prewriting that makes sense to prepare for a draft should happen during this time.

POSSIBILITY

Once drafting is officially underway, the bulk of independent work time, of course, is spent composing drafts. If you ask students to try things from the close study once the drafts are underway, they might still try them in their writers' notebooks first and then decide if they want to include the try-its in their drafts.

Independent Work Time: Writing Under the Influence

As the study nears its end, the attention will turn to revising and editing drafts and making the writing the best that it can be. This time doesn't need to be long—a week is usually plenty of time since students have drafts in hand and have been drafting and making revision decisions under the influence of close study all along. The whole-class sessions as students are finishing their drafts will be short and will likely focus on issues you are seeing as you confer with students in the final stages of their drafting.

POSSIBILITY

Students will need some time to get feedback on their drafts from peers. This will happen during independent work time.

POSSIBILITY

Depending on how fancy you want the finished work to be, students will spend some of their independent work time embellishing the finished work. And the thing to remember is, the fancier the work, the longer this takes. My recommendation would be to have just a couple of requirements for truly fancy publications in a school year and let the rest of the writing in studies be finished in a not-so-fancy way. If students want to add publishing embellishments to finished writing (and they often do—especially when they are going to give the writing to someone) this can become their future back-up work during writing workshop, but the class as a whole can move forward instead of stalling everyone for this work.

You'll need at least one day and perhaps more than one day to sit back and process what you have learned from your study. Sharing the stories of process and the new thinking students were able to do as a result of the study is just as important as the finished writing itself, so you'll want some time to have whole-class and perhaps small-group conversations about what students learned from the process of writing. Here are a few possibilities for how you might share the writing itself that students do during a study.

POSSIBILITY

You might have a choral reading with each student contributing a passage of twenty words or less from his or her piece.

POSSIBILITY

Students might share their entire pieces, either aloud (if they're short) or silently by passing them around, with a small group of other students. You might spend more than one day sharing in this way and reconfigure the groups each day.

POSSIBILITY

You might create a class anthology, magazine, or newspaper (depending on the type of writing) of pieces and present everyone with a copy.

POSSIBILITY

You might share in pairs or small groups with people from outside your classroom.

POSSIBILITY

The fancy-finished, embellished writing could be placed in the class library for use during independent reading.

Evaluating Student Work During a Study

As you think about finishing work in a unit of study, remember Lucy Calkins' sage advice that your job is to teach the writer, not the writing. If you have required students to account for their process along the way, you should be able to look at the evidence they've provided and the thinking they've done and see whether you've taught the writers anything. The writing students finish won't be perfect, after all it was finished by eight-year-olds and eleven-year-olds and seventeen-year-olds, but perfect writing isn't the goal of the teaching. Deep, lasting learning for writers is the goal.

And if you must give grades for writing, what then? My opinion, and clearly it is an opinion, is that if you have faith in the work you are asking students to do, if you believe this work will help them get better at writing, then grades should come mostly from an honest evaluation of students' investment in the work you've asked them to do. For example, you might evaluate students' investment in some or all of the following areas.

Working Through the Process
- evidence the writer used workshop time wisely
- evidence the writer regularly tried the work of the study
- attention to minding due dates and turn-in times
- attention to quality and depth in writing reflections about the process

Choosing and Growing an Idea for Writing
- evidence of thoughtful and deliberate topic selection
- evidence the writer's notebook was used as a tool to grow thinking

- evidence the writer engaged in the necessary work (research, gathering, talking, etc.) to support the kind of writing s/he was doing

Drafting and Revision
- evidence of thoughtful and decisive planning for drafting (could range from a detailed outline to just starting and seeing where it goes—and all kinds of planning in between, but the *reason* for doing the planning is thoughtful and decisive)
- evidence the student engaged in strategic revision: rereading often, reading the piece aloud, reading to get feedback, trying things out, and so on
- evidence of revision *decisions* that resulted in changes in the text
- evidence the writer used the teaching during the study to raise the level of the writing
- evidence the writer made decisions during drafting and revision that show an attention to the *craft* of the writing

Finishing
- evidence the writer paid careful and strategic attention to editing and proofreading the piece for errors in spelling and usage
- evidence the writer paid careful attention to "presentation" and the finished look of the piece

For diagnostic purposes (rather than evaluative ones) I do believe it is valuable from time to time to do a close analysis of actual pieces of writing. If students will be required to write as part of a mandated assessment, you'll want to be very familiar with how the assessment will be scored or evaluated and use this as a lens to study your students' writing. If students won't be taking a mandated writing assessment, you might consider using a traits-based model to study writing samples and plan further instruction for both individual students and whole-class studies. If you use some sort of rubric to "score" pieces of writing, you (and perhaps you and your teaching colleagues) will have to decide whether the scores should be considered when giving children grades in writing.

I believe it's also important to have students do a close analysis of both their process and their products at the end of a study. You might want to look back in Chapter 6 at the examples of questions that help students account for and reflect on the process of writing. These questions are generic and selected ones of them could be used again and again across studies to help students analyze their process of writing.

In addition to these, however, you'll also want students to reflect on the qualities of writing that are specific to whatever you've been studying. Students studying the development of setting in fiction, for example, should be asked to explain the decisions they made while crafting setting in the pieces they finish for the study. Students studying how writers use punctuation in interesting ways to craft their texts should be asked to reflect on three or four interesting ways they used punctuation to craft their texts.

Sometimes you might not know what you want students to comment on in their finished writing until *after* you've gone through close study. When this is the case, it's usually because your attention has been drawn to a quality of writing you weren't expecting to study so closely. On the flip side of this, there may be some questions you ask students to respond to each time they finish a piece of writing regardless of the study. For example, I think it's important to ask students frequently (if not every time) to explain how a finished piece of writing is organized. I want the writer to be able to name the "chunks" of the piece and explain why they are ordered the way they are ordered. Organization is such an important quality of good writing, and I believe the best way to help students understand this is to teach them that they are expected to answer this question each time they write.

When students are writing under the influence of study, you should expect they will write better than they would if the study hadn't happened. There will still be a range of quality in the finished writing that is connected to the range of development in the room, but the work in the study should raise the level of everyone's writing.

Craft Pause

NOTICE

This is an excerpt from Jacqueline Woodson's picture book *Show Way* (2005).

> In South Carolina, Big Mama raised Soonie's
>   great-grandma.
> Raised most of the slave children on that
>   large patch of land.
>
> At night, Big Mama told the children stories.
> Stories she'd tell in a whisper about children
>   growing up and getting themselves free.
> And the children leaned in.
> And listened real hard.

This is an excerpt from Nancy Hundal's picture book *Camping* (2002).

> Evenings around the fire, wrapped to my
>   ears in a blanket.
> Bug guard, chill guard, both try to sneak past
>   my skin.
> Hot chocolate warms lips, throat, stomach,
>   hands.
> We sing old songs, new songs, camp songs,
>   Gramp songs.
> More chips, more sun, less TV, less washing.
> More time, less o'clock.

This is the lead to a personal essay I clipped from the *Chicago Tribune* on August 23, 2000 and have kept in my blue notebook ever since.

It's by Mary Beth Sammons and it's titled, "Mommy, I knew that if you just let go, you could fly." It's about a mother and daughter experience trying their hands at a trapeze.

> The rush of fear grips, paralyzes, as I climb
> the ladder, step by step. My toes are perched
> over the edge of the steel platform. My heart
> is pounding. I am petrified. Terrified. Of
> heights. Of recent transition. My trembling is
> making the platform swoon.

INSIGHTS ABOUT CRAFT

I'd suggest you read each of these excerpts aloud and listen to how similar they sound. I believe what these writers show in two picture book texts and a personal essay is a faith in phrasing. The human voice, when it is telling a story, relies on all sorts of understood connections between words and sentences and their relationship to the whole of the story. The stops and starts of the voice telling a story are old and familiar language patterns to us as both listeners and tellers. When writers choose to write in this phrased way, they create a very real sense of that familiar story-telling voice readers know so well.

The Predictable Rhythm of Process Studies in Writing Workshop

From behind my video camera I watch as Lucas, a first grader in Lisa Cleaveland's writing workshop, explains to his classmates some of his process thinking as he is finishing his memoir about his beloved dog Sassy. "Sassy's New House," as it is titled at this point, is a simple text, but the thinking behind it is anything but simple. Because he is in a room where he and his classmates have been asked to explain their thinking all year long, Lucas shows a complexity of thinking about process that is characteristic of a much more sophisticated writer. In Figure 12.1, you see each page of his memoir and underneath it an explanation of what Lucas told us he was thinking about.

Learning the Process by Living the Process

Lucas and his classmates don't think of the "writing process" as a set of steps they follow, as a *procedure*, in other words. As a matter of fact, at the beginning of the year there is no real talk about the process of writing until everyone gets started writing. The process doesn't exist outside of how the children are using it to get their writing done, and Lucas and his classmates come to think of the writing process as the stories they tell about how their writing is going. From the first days when they've been engaged as writers, they've been asked to respond to some form of the question, "Tell me about your process. What decisions are you making in this piece of writing?" Over time they come to think of themselves as the kinds of people who ought to be able to answer these questions.

The main way that any writer learns about the process of moving from an idea to a finished piece of writing is to live through that process many times. The more pieces of writing you've finished, the more strategic you are in your future work toward that goal. And as I said in Chapter 6, writing workshops, by design, are meant to be places where students learn about the process of writing by engaging in it on a regular basis.

When writers share their stories of having written with one another, the strategic pool of process possibilities in a workshop is deep. Knowing this, you'll want to find as many opportunities as you can for students to tell their stories of having written in all your studies across the year. Writing conferences are probably the best forum for individual writers to be asked to explain their processes. When you go out and "catch them in the act" of writing you'll ask them, "Tell me about what you're doing right now as a writer." Share time, that coming-back-together-time many teachers have at the close of writing workshop is a great time to have selected students tell their stories of process. Many of the teachers I know actually use share time as the main vehicle for whole-class teaching about the process of writing. And of course older students can be asked to account for their writing process as a standard routine for finished work (see Figure 6.2 on page 82 in Chapter 6).

The writing that students will finish to serve the kinds of studies I've written about so far in this book, as well as their self-selected back-up work, will deepen their understandings about process in many ways. Sometimes, however, you might want to dig in and think deeply with your students about some aspect of process in a unit of study. Units of study in process might include issues such as:

- where writers get ideas and how they decide which ideas to pursue
- using a writer's notebook as a tool to make your writing better
- a writer's work *other* than writing (research, reading, talking, etc.)
- different ways writers plan and organize before drafting
- what writers think about and do during drafting and revision
- using talk as a tool to make your writing better
- the process of trying to get something published
- dealing with predictable problems (writer's block, organizing stuff, committing time to writing, etc.)
- strategies and tools for editing and proofreading

In addition to being studies by themselves, any one of these issues might also be an overlay of inquiry for a few days in a product-based study.

The instructional framework I've been writing about up to this point in *Study Driven* is a framework for studying any aspect of products in writing, the actual texts themselves. But there is a similar, predictable way you might go about carrying out a unit of study in process as well. Once you have decided which aspect

FIGURE 12.1 *Lucas' Memoir About His Dog Sassy*

Page One: *Sassy's New House*
Lucas explained that he needed to go back and change this title because he realized when he wrote it, he was thinking about when Sassy came to live with him and his family. But in truth, Sassy's new home is in heaven, "dog heaven," he explained, so he wanted to change this title.

Page Two: *Written and illustrated by Lucas.*
I dedicate this to Sassy.

Page Three: *Sassy was a good dog. She was a daschaund. She died in 2004.*
Lucas explained that this page was not in the original draft of the text. The memoir originally started with the next page and Lucas said no one knew for sure who "she" was, so he added this page to "set us [the readers] up."

Page Four: *Me and Sassy watch television.*

me and sientse play to govn thene.

me and sittet tkenaber.

Page Five: *Me and Sassy play together.*
Lucas pointed out that he needed to go back and change the speech bubble in the bottom left corner of this page because you can't tell what it says.

Page Six: *Me and Sassy take a bath.*
Lucas explained that this page is related to the page before. He and Sassy had gotten wet (see the raindrops on the previous page) and sweaty and so he needed to give her a bath.

me and sietr gong to spes.

my mom kir whn she seen sit ae leag thene. she knw it wsd the leagt she wood see hne.

Page Seven: *Me and Sassy watch go to sleep.*

Page Fight: *My mom cried when she seen Sassy laying there.*
She knew it was the last time she would see her.
This page was not the original last page of the book. The first ending that Lucas wrote said, "Me and Momma and Daddy and Sassy are taking a bath." One of his classmates asked Lucas how this page fit as an ending for the rest of the book. At first Lucas tried to explain how it fit, but in the midst of his explanation, he realized, in fact, that it didn't fit as an ending. This page was thrown away and the new ending written. Lucas explained that he was going to "stand on Anna's [another student in the class] shoulders" to write the new ending. In Anna's memoir about going to Disney World she had said that when they first walked into the park and saw all the characters, "My mom cried tears. Happy tears." Lucas said his mom was going to "cry sad tears."

of process you'd like to study and approximately how long you'd like to spend studying it, then your work is really quite simple:

Immersion	You and your students will spend time talking and listening to people who write and you'll find out how they do what they do.
Close Study	Together you'll chart the understandings and strategies about process that you are learning from what these writers say. You'll probably try some of the strategies out, when it makes sense to, in your work as writers.
Writing Under the Influence	Students will finish a piece of writing (in any genre they choose) and will be asked to be very articulate about the particular aspect of process you've been studying and how it influenced their writing.

Just as with product studies, you'll want students to find this teaching familiar, so a study of any aspect of process will basically follow this same predictable pattern for developing curriculum. The goals of a study like this are severalfold. First, you want to heighten students' awareness of some aspect of process in their work as writers, broaden their repertoire of strategic possibilities for getting that work accomplished, and deepen their understandings about what it means to be a writer engaged in the process. But you also want students to become part of the language community that has words to talk about the process of writing. To do this, students need to be immersed in that talk, they need to hear what it sounds like when good writers talk about process. Immersion in talk about process is what will help them talk, and hence *think*, in smarter ways about their own writing.

Now as we have in previous chapters, let's consider some possibilities for this work in each phase of a process study.

Immersion in Talk About Process

When you first looked at the previous framework, you may have been thinking, "How am I going to get access to writers for my students to talk with about process?" But you don't have to have writers "in the flesh" in order to listen to what they have to say about process. I remember asking Eloise Greenfield once who her writing mentors were as a child and she replied, "I didn't know any writers as a child." Clearly, Eloise and I were operating with different definitions of what it means to be a writing mentor. Regrettably, I've never met or even spoken with lots of the people I consider to be my writing mentors: Cynthia Rylant, Jacqueline Woodson, Anne Lamott, Gary Paulsen (though I was in a crowded elevator with Gary once at an NCTE conference). But despite having never met them, not only do I know lots about the actual texts these writers have published, I also know a good bit about what each of them has to say about the process of writing. They mentor me in that way, too.

To launch a study of process, you'll need a good collection of things writers have said about the aspect of process you'd like to study. Here are possibilities for finding out what writers have to say about process.

POSSIBILITY

First of all, remember that there are a bunch of writers "in the flesh" sitting right in front of you! What your students have to say about how they go about writing can be an important curriculum resource. You'll want to get them talking about the aspect of process you are studying, chart some of this talk, and use it to develop understandings and strategies for the study.

POSSIBILITY

Students may need to revisit old writer's notebooks or writing they have finished in the past (even in past years of school) in order to contribute thoughtfully to the aspect of process you are studying. For example, in a study of where writers get ideas, students might need to look at their portfolios of finished work and think about where they have been getting their ideas. In a revision study, students might need to study changes they have made in past drafts of things. Any way that it makes sense for students to look back at how they have engaged in the process in the past may lead to rich thinking for the present study.

POSSIBILITY

Your own experiences with writing are an important curriculum resource for this study as well. Over time you'll want to save your own stories of having written so you can share them in studies of process right along with those of your students.

POSSIBILITY

Certainly if you do have access to either professional writers or people who write a lot as part of another profession, you can bring them in and let your students interview them about the particular aspect of process you are studying. It's probably a good idea to let these writers know in advance what you are studying because they might be able to bring along examples of notebooks or drafts that can help them show how they do their work as they are explaining it.

POSSIBILITY

Students might interview writers in other writing workshops in your school about the aspect of process you are studying and bring their insights into the "gathering of talk" you are creating.

POSSIBILITY

Author's notes are often wonderful sources of information for process studies. One of the main purposes of an author's note is to tell something about how the piece of writing came to be, so there is usually lots of good information about this in them. Similarly, you can often find really good quotes from writers about where ideas came from in the author's "blurbs" on book jackets and sometimes even in dedications.

POSSIBILITY

Many authors now have websites and there is a wide range of information found on these sites. A lot of it is not very helpful for a study of writing process, but sometimes you do find writers who include some kind of information about how they do their work. Also, running an author's name in a search engine will often take you to other sites where an author has been interviewed or studied in some way and you'll sometimes happen across great material for a process study here as well. You might invite students in on the search of authors' websites and send them looking for any quotes they can find about the process of writing.

POSSIBILITY

Writing about writing is a popular genre these days, and most bookstores have a section of books on how to write. These books can be treasure troves when it comes to process studies as they are really all about the process of writing. Some of these books are written by just one person, and some of them are collections of what different writers have to say about process.

Close Study

Pulling from these possibilities, once you have gathered a good collection of what writers have to say about the aspect of process you're studying, you'll move into a predictable teaching rhythm where you'll pull one or two ideas from writers to talk about each day with your students. You'll probably have more possibilities than you need for the amount of time you've decided to devote to the study, so you'll need to select those that seem most ripe for good talk around them, and as with product studies, let the energy of one day's talk lead you to what you select on subsequent days. There is no sense of coverage or of scope and sequence to a study of process. Your goal is just to dig in and find depth in your conversations with students about the topic you are studying.

Sometimes the ideas you share with students will be more strategy based, meaning a writer is making a very specific suggestion for how something might get done in writing. For more strategy-based teaching about process, I turn to books like Georgia Heard's *The Revision Toolbox* (2002), Ralph Fletcher's *How Writers Work* (2000), and William Zinsser's *On Writing Well 25th Anniversary Edition* (2001). The "how-to" sections on writing in bookstores are filled with books like these, as well as a fair number of professional books written for teachers of writing.

On days when you're considering strategy-based lessons from writers, you might have students try the strategy either together or independently or both, if it makes sense to do so. For example, in *The Revision Toolbox*, Georgia Heard recommends that writers look at drafts and ask themselves, "What am I really trying to say?" You might read some of the section on this strategy right from Georgia's book (2002, p.77), and then demonstrate asking this question on a working draft of your own, noting your thoughts in the margin. And if it seems practical, you might ask students to try this in their drafts during independent writing that day, too. The key is to maintain a healthy balance of things you are asking everyone to try and things you are leaving as optional invitations for students to decide to use when they make sense in their work.

Many of the ideas from writers you'll want to share during a process study might not be strategies at all. These ideas will be more about the understandings writers have that help them live and think their way through the journey of process. They aren't things to do, in other words, they are just things to understand about how this work gets done. Since these are the quotes that really induct students into the language of process, you'll want to think a lot about the language writers are using to represent their understandings and whether it might be good language for students to have (because it might help them think new thoughts about writing).

To illustrate this, I've selected five days of teaching anchored in quotes that I might use in a study of what writers think about during drafting and revision. For each one, I'll explain ways I might talk about these quotes with students in order to make them more curriculum specific, and I'll highlight language I think is important in each one. One predictable question I'd ask often is whether any of the students have thought this same thing about writing or worked in this same way. The particular way we would chart what we'd learned from these quotes would depend on the language we used to talk about it and what emerged as significant in our talk around each one. These are in no particular order, as ordering them thoughtfully would require me to be engaged in an ongoing conversation of teaching and learning with a group of writers.

POSSIBILITY

I might put two quotes side by side, one from Sharon Creech and one from Liz Rosenberg:

> If I think a story is not going well, I will put it aside for weeks or months, and then come back to it and I can usually figure out what's wrong with it and make it work. I feel that if the beginning of a story has come to me, there's a good reason why it has come and I know if I just give it time, it will evolve into something better. (From an interview with Sharon Creech posted on www.scholastic.com)

> Let's say you write something you don't altogether love at first. Maybe there's something you forgot to say in the poem, or said the wrong way, and you just don't like the music of the poem. (Never forget the music of the poem! Poetry isn't prose chopped into shorter lines.) Put it aside for a few days—hide it from yourself. I tuck mine behind my typewriter, or lay it face down on my desk, or under a pile of other poems. When you look at it after a few days, or a week, or a few weeks, it will seem almost new to you, at least for the first minute you glance at it. That's a good time to revise. (From Liz Rosenberg in Janeczko 2002, 99)

Ways I might talk with students:

- I'd likely tell students that I have had this same experience writing professional books and articles, and that since Sharon Creech is talking about revising fiction and Liz Rosenberg about revising poetry, then this must be a good revision strategy that is not specific to the writing of a particular genre.

- I'd want to get the idea of "seeing with new eyes" in the room and I might try and help students imagine this experience in a context other than writing. Perhaps discovering a toy they haven't seen in a long time, or finding a book they used to love when they were younger. We'd use this thinking to deepen our understanding of this possibility in writing.

- We might imagine ways in our own workshop (with respect to finishing expectations) that we could put things away for a period of time and come back to them later. Perhaps even doing this on purpose with a piece of writing for a later revision study, or going back to something we wrote several years ago in another workshop.

POSSIBILITY

I might share this quote from Bruce Brooks, one of my favorites about revision:

> I think "revision" is badly named. The "re" prefix implies that you are going back over something you've already done. But you're not going back. You are going on with the writing process. It's all a part of getting it right. A friend of mine who played basketball once said that he envied me because he had just missed a foul shot that would have tied the score at the end of an important game. He said, "But you can write that foul shot until you make it." He was right. I write a first draft that I know is going to be partly good, partly bad. I may go over a manuscript three or four times before I'm satisfied. (Marcus 2000, 14)

Ways I might talk with students:

- I love the metaphorical language in this quote of "writing that foul shot until you make it" and can imagine a group of students finding deep meaning in it. I'd certainly want to highlight it and see what students think about.

- I'd probably talk to students about how this is true of the difference between *talking* and *writing* as well as shooting a ball and writing. So often when talking we say the wrong thing, we miss the shot, and it's hard to take it back because it's already been said. The beauty of writing is we can stay with it until we've said the right thing.

- The idea of going on with the writing process, I think, is an important one that I'd like to talk about with students. Perhaps they would have more energy for this aspect of the work of a writer if they thought of it as going *on* instead of going *back*.

- Since Brooks highlights the idea that "re" is a prefix, I might use this as an opportunity to open up the idea of the root of the word, *vision*. I'm sure I would have talked to students a lot about having a vision before they write, but this might be a good opportunity to think about the role of vision after they've drafted.

POSSIBILITY

Eve Bunting says:

> I always read my work aloud, making myself aware of how it sounds. Do the words flow pleasantly? Do they evoke vibrant images? I check for over-writing. Does the dialogue sound real? I have written, "I know I am well loved." I, the author, might say that. But would my protagonist, the one who is speaking in

my book? He's a fourteen-year-old boy. Come on, Eve. Get Real! (McClure and Kristo 1996, 224–25)

Ways I might talk with students:

• Clearly, I'd talk about reading our writing aloud during revision. I'd ask students to think with me about how we could do this more often in our workshop—perhaps even ritualizing this revision tool in some way.

• I love Bunting's idea of *overwriting* and I would hope this word would help students think about this more specifically in their writing. I'd want to crack this word open with talk.

• I might share with students my own revision story about writing about my mother once. I had written, "She wanted the house to smell of cookies when we got home from school." I kept reading that sentence, knowing something was not right, but it took me a while to figure out it was the word *of*. I would never say it like that. I would say, "She wanted the house to smell *like* cookies when we got home from school." The person "saying" the words is important—the words need to sound like what that person would say.

• On the next day, I might follow the conversation about this quote with a demonstration where we look at part of a draft that I suspect has some over-writing in it and think together about how to revise it.

POSSIBILITY

Linda Sue Park says:

> I think of poetry as language at its purest. I wrote poetry for many years before I tried my hand at fiction. There's no doubt in my mind that my experience with poetry contributes invaluably to my fiction work, because in addition to the Big Picture, the story itself, I am fascinated by words. I work as hard at sentence level as I do at story level—with imagery and sound and trying to make sure that every single word is the best one possible. The challenge is to make it whole, seamless, so that story and language aren't separate concerns, but work together to en- hance each other. (from the WHO files on the *Time for Kids* website)

Ways I might talk with students:

• What I really like in this quote is simply the idea of "sentence level" and "story level." I think this is such an important understanding about revision, that writers have to be thinking about how both are working, apart and together, all the time.

- I'd probably suggest that we substitute the words *whole text* for *story* and I would explain to students that I think at both these levels too when I'm writing chapters and articles—so they don't think it is just about stories.

- We might use the metaphor of a zoom lens on a camera to help us deepen our understanding of what Park is saying.

- This conversation, like the one from Bunting's quote, might lend itself to a follow-up day where we look at a draft and identify the kinds of things we'd be thinking about at the "whole text level" and at the "sentence level."

POSSIBILITY

And believe it or not, I might even include these two quotes from a single interview with my beloved mentor Cynthia Rylant. Speaking of her collection of poems *Waiting to Waltz*:

> Poems didn't trickle out one at a time over a period of three or four years; I simply sat down and wrote the book in a couple of mornings. Everything just flowed together.

> It's not that I write very often. I haven't actually written in about seven months now. But when I do sit down to write, I can do a book in a day if the magic is there. For me, writing happens in a very magical way; I just have to wait and have faith that it will happen again. (both quotes from Copeland and Copeland 1994, 25, 31)

Ways I might talk with students:

- First, I'd probably just ask students, "What do you think of this?" and see what they think.

- I might have a conversation about the word *magic* and wonder aloud about its sometime role in the writing process.

- I might talk about something I really believe is true of writing: the end justifies the means. If Cynthia Rylant is able to just sit down and write really, really well the first time, then I don't think she needs to revise just for the sake of keeping her moral character in tact!

- I'd probably engage students in thinking about how we could keep ourselves honest as writers with regards to magic. Who could we count on to let us know when the magic is not there, even when we may think it is?

- I'd certainly explain that if we are going to study the true process of drafting and revision from writers, we can't ignore one of our favorites and most accomplished. This is how she says she gets her drafts written.

- And just in case anyone thought she or he might have a style similar to Rylant's, one that only finds the "magic" to write well every seven months or so, I'd be ready with another quote. I'd say, "That's fine, but in the seven months while you are waiting on your magic, remember J.K. Rowling's wise words, 'Resign yourself to the fact that you're going to write a lot of rubbish before you write something really good' " (Campbell and Collison 2002, 27). Writing workshop is a place where you can write the rubbish while you wait on the magic.

As you talk with students about what writers say about particular aspects of process, remember that you'll need to move seamlessly from thinking about the quotes into thinking about the students and their writing. The whole point of sharing these quotes is to use them as new ways to talk and think about the work students are doing in writing workshop.

Remember, too, that this kind of work is richer if you take an inquiry stance to the development of curriculum from what writers say just as you do in product study. When doing this teaching, it's tempting to think, "I know exactly what I want students to learn from this" and to write it in your lesson plans ahead of time because you've obviously pulled the quotes purposefully. But sometimes students take the thinking around what writers say in very interesting directions that you may not expect. For this reason, I'd recommend you not chart what you've learned from the talk around the quotes ahead of time. Let what you state as specific curriculum come from the talk.

Writing Under the Influence

Writing under the influence of process study is really quite simple: you'll want students to finish a piece of writing (self-selected topic and genre) and report on the aspect of process you have studied. The youngest writers may report with just talk, but with more experienced writers it's probably a good idea to give them some sort of handout at the beginning—much like the ones suggested for product studies in Chapter 8—detailing your expectations for their work. These students can use writing and artifacts to tell you about how they used the work of the study in their own process, and you may get some of your best quotes for future studies from what these writers say in these assessments.

Why Study Process in This Way?

Studying the process of writing by looking closely at what people who write actually do ensures the teaching around process will be grounded. There is a great deal of "myth curriculum" floating around out there about process, ideas that just don't bear out when you look closely at what successful writers really say they do. I believe a lot of this myth curriculum comes from attempts to oversimplify what teachers teach students about process because it feels more manageable that way. But invariably, oversimplifying process *changes* the very nature of the thing you are trying to teach, so my advice is to try and get comfortable with the complicated and sometimes contradictory thinking you'll need to do with students around how a piece of writing comes to be.

Finally, the study of process as I've outlined it has another benefit in a writing workshop that I haven't mentioned yet. In addition to the deeper thinking about process that students do out of a study like this, a study of process also affords students an opportunity to work on absolutely any kind of writing they'd like to do, on any topic, and still be working in the unit of study with the rest of the class. For this reason, if for no other, I believe a few well-placed studies of process during the year are a healthy thing for a writing workshop.

Craft Pause

NOTICE

This is the lead to an article in the May/June 2005 issue of *American Girl* magazine (16). The article, "All Fired Up," is about a girls' jump rope team.

> Imagine spinning a jump rope so quickly that the crowd can barely see it. Imagine holding a rope for someone else to jump while you're jumping a rope yourself. Imagine jumping not just on your feet but on your knees, your tummy, and your backside.

This is the lead to Nicola Davies' picture book *Surprising Sharks* (2003, 6):

> You're swimming in the warm blue sea. What's the one word that turns your dream into a nightmare? What's the one word that makes you think of a giant man-eating killer? Shaaaaarrrkk!

This is the lead to an angry (justifiably, in my opinion) Leonard Pitts commentary posted on September 4, 2005, in *The Miami Herald* in the aftermath of the Hurricane Katrina disaster.

> Maybe if Terri Schiavo had been caught in the hurricane?
> You think that would have done it?
> Think maybe that would have moved federal officials off, to paraphrase the frustrated Mayor of New Orleans, their posteriors a little faster?

And then just a little further into the commentary he writes more series of questions, including (but not limited to):

> Do you think Schiavo would have been left there to die, not from the storm, but from neglect, and have her wheelchair pushed ignominiously against a wall?
> Do you think maybe somebody failed to see the sanctity in these lives?

INSIGHTS ABOUT CRAFT

The need to engage the reader is present and immediate in all types of nonfiction, and one of the most common ways writers do this is to engage them very directly as you see in these excerpts. The first issues a friendly command to the reader, "Imagine." Pitts uses a series of very provocative, in-your-face questions to engage his readers.

Commands and questions invoke the most basic verbal instinct we have as humans and that is to respond in some way when we hear our names called, so to speak. Even if we chose not to respond, that in itself is a form of response. In other words, it's hard to be intellectually passive when someone is asking you a question, and that's what makes this engaging way of crafting so effective.

The Tension of Time, the Promise of Depth

When was the last time you were in the middle of a moment with your students and you thought to yourself, "I wish someone else could hear this. This is so incredible—what's happening here." When was the last time you came home from school and said to anyone who would listen, "You won't believe what we talked about in my class today."

I hope you had one of those moments just the other day, or today, and that you can look forward to another one tomorrow. But as I talk to teachers in a wide variety of settings, I find, sadly, that moments like this are becoming harder and harder to find. As counterintuitive as it may seem, the "standards" climate in schools has crowded out time for rigorous, intellectual work. It's no wonder no one comes home from school anymore to share something wonderful and insightful a student has said. There is no time for wonderful and insightful. And as Ellin Keene (2005) has said, "You can't get good thinking done quickly. The tension of moving too quickly leads to, at best, superficial responses."

What a precious, precious commodity, this thing called *time*. If we only had more of it, but of course, we don't get more. It is what it is.

If you've read this far in *Study Driven* you know that the stance of this book with regards to time is fairly clear: I believe good teaching takes time and good writing takes time and students need time for both. Some readers of this book might have thrown their hands up chapters ago, stopped reading, and thought, "There's just no way I would ever have time to do any teaching like this." But if you've stayed with it, perhaps it's because the promise of this work appeals to you. The promise of deep, interesting conversations with your students, with plenty of room for you to learn and grow, too. The promise of authentic, life- and voice-filled writing that comes from the clarity of vision. The promise of newfound purposefulness and energy in your teaching.

But all that promise still doesn't give you any more time.

Teaching—Without All the Time in the World

What I have attempted to do in this book is to write about this teaching work in its fullest, richest sense, as if there was all the time in the world in which to do it. I did that in large part to give you vision for the work, not because I believe you have all the time in the world. Much as the fifth graders wrote with a vision of Pulitzer prize–winning commentary guiding them, I'm hoping the vision I've given you here can help guide you in your teaching. But I also know that for all of us, teaching is always an approximation of our richest vision of what it might be. I hope that you will value your own approximations of this teaching, many of them brought about by the complex issue of time. What I'd like to consider here are some ways of dealing with time in the less-than-perfect world where teaching really happens.

Whenever I think about dealing with time, the first thing I think about is what I must absolutely, positively make time for no matter what. It's sort of like the thinking I do when I'm going somewhere wonderful on vacation but I can't do everything I might want to do in the time I'm there. Let's see, the Eiffel Tower or the Louvre? Tower of Terror or the Rockin' Roller Coaster? A balloon ride or (yet another) wine tasting? You get the point. When it comes to the teaching of writing, what *must* I do?

Of everything you've read about in this book, in my thinking there are three things that I just couldn't give up—no way, no how—in the teaching of writing. One of them is time for students to write. I would give up teaching any whole-class lessons about writing if it meant students weren't left with any time to write. And if I didn't have time for both, I'd rather students spend their time doing lots of bad writing than spend all their time listening to me talk about how to write well. I know that I haven't written much about that part of the workshop in this book because my focus here has been on whole-class teaching, but time for student writing is an absolute must in my mind. And in truth, any time devoted to students "just writing" actually is valuable teaching time too because that's when conferences happen. So there is really no way—in terms of time—that I could not have time for both writing and teaching; it just wouldn't be whole-class teaching.

The second thing I just couldn't give up would be talk. I would have to find ways for students to be talking about what they're writing about and how they're going about writing it. The talk about what they're writing about is where such important idea work happens. Ideas and thinking grow as writers talk them through with others, and the words writers need to say what they want to say often come more easily if they've had the chance to talk ideas through some before writing them. The talk about how students are writing things—the processes they are using—is where all the important teaching about process happens. When students share their stories of having written, they become more articulate about their processes, and therefore more thoughtful and reflective about how they're writing, and everyone who is listening to the stories can learn from them. Talk is just essential to a writing workshop.

The other thing that I couldn't walk away from in any way is the role of vision in writing. If I truly didn't have any time for whole-class teaching and only had time for students to write, if I simply pushed the issue of vision on them, required that they be able to tell me what they have read that is like what they are trying to write, I would be doing *huge* work in terms of helping them write well. I just don't believe good writing is possible without clarity of vision. There is no way I could be in a room full of students, be charged with teaching them to write, and not have the idea of vision be a driving force in our work together.

With those three essentials in place, I'd like to consider the teaching work you've read about in this book and how you might make some decisions that could help you deal with time. Actually, all along the way as you read about different options for how the work might happen in a study, you've seen alternatives that take more and less time. Hopefully this range of options has already helped you think about how you might deal with some time issues. Following the same menu format I've used in earlier chapters, now I'd like to offer a few "big picture" possibilities for dealing with time.

What I hope comes across in these possibilities is the idea that just because you might not be able to do everything doesn't mean you can't do anything. I don't see these possibilities as ways to give up; I see them as ways to make things happen. If the idea of study with students makes sense to you, there are a few entry points you can find to help you do this work.

POSSIBILITY

In a year of teaching in a writing workshop, you might create a balance of units of study and units of preplanned lessons on topics. In other words, some of your curriculum during the year might come from units that are totally study driven (as you've read about in this book), but at other times you might deliver a series of lessons on a topic in a more direct way. In units of lessons, I would still encourage you to keep them grounded. Lessons about process should come from what people who write say they do, and lessons about how things are written should be matched with real-world text examples.

POSSIBILITY

In a single unit, some of the curriculum might be generated through study with students and some of it might be more teacher directed. It doesn't have to be all one or the other.

POSSIBILITY

I'd actually recommend that you plan a little downtime in between studies during the year when students are just writing whatever they want and you are conferring each day. Let all of your whole-class teaching during these times come directly from what you are seeing in your conferring. These downtimes give you a chance to catch your breath from the intensity of study and they let students catch their breath too.

POSSIBILITY

While I mentioned this in earlier chapters, it's worth saying again here. It's a good idea to plan how much time you are going to spend in each phase of a study and stick to it. And if you must, tighten this time as much as you need to in order to still be studying. If you need to limit the number of texts you consider during close study you can do this to buy some time, too.

POSSIBILITY

If you now have separate times for teaching vocabulary, spelling, handwriting, and grammar, in addition to your time for teaching writing, you might want to reconsider the necessity of this. Spelling and handwriting have always been inextricable from students' work in writing, and so minding the thinking around them is something that can easily be layered into the work you do with students in writing. But what I hope has become clear from reading about the kind of study I've suggested is how rich vocabulary and grammar talk can be when students are spending a lot of time talking about well-written texts. Take a look back at the Leonard Pitts commentary in Chapter 7, or for that matter, any of the other texts shown or books recommended in the later resource sections. The vocabulary in them is sophisticated and wonderfully crafted, in the grammatical sense, making the potential for teaching and learning in these areas during a study easily apparent.

Each of these possibilities is really for decision making at the classroom level. What I'd like to suggest next, however, is that some of the most influential decision making, in terms of the time it affords teachers for rigorous study, happens at the whole-school level.

Whole-School Efforts to Deepen the Teaching of Writing

I sat down recently for a conference with a third grader and I asked her to tell me about the writing she was doing. "This is something I started in second grade," was the first thing she said. I loved this answer. I loved that she was engaged in writing work that was spanning two years of her life in school. I loved that when she moved from second grade to third grade, she found a familiar time and space for writing.

In the past few years I've been fortunate to consult with a few schools whose teachers were thinking about the teaching of writing in whole-school ways. "How can we grow this work across the years so that students are doing deeper and deeper work in writing as they grow older in school?" As we've worked together to think about this question, one thing we've realized is that depth in writing work is made possible more by what stays the same year after year than by what is different from grade level to grade level. When students encounter whole new ways of doing things every year, whole new stances to teaching and learning, whole new notions of what writing means and what writing is supposed to be when it's good, it takes a long time to get to anything very meaningful or deep because there is so much time spent wallowing in the newness of it all.

Whenever I think about this, I can't help but picture scenes from the book and movie *Holes* where you can see the young boys surrounded by all their shallow holes. There is no way for the boys to dig deep, to dig, say, to China, because every day they have to start digging a new hole. I think this is what is happening to a lot of children in schools. Every year they start digging a different hole in a different classroom with a different agenda, so they can only get so far before they have to start all over again. Imagine how different it would be if each year, students could continue digging into the same "hole" they dug into the year before? Imagine the depth they would find in their work as the years of digging deeper went by. The challenge, of course, is for whole schools of teachers to agree on what hole should be dug.

Okay, enough of the hole metaphor, but the challenge remains. Is it possible to agree on some basic beliefs about the teaching of writing and on how, in essence, those beliefs should be manifested in practice? Is it reasonable to suggest that teachers might agree on what students should recognize and find familiar in the teaching of writing across grade levels? And even if such agreement can be found, is it possible to find it without robbing individual teachers of their decision-making powers and stylistic ways of being in their own classrooms?

I actually believe it is both challenging and possible. I also realize that different communities of teachers could reach different agreed-upon beliefs and practices, even when pulling from essentially the same body of professional resources to inform their consensus. What I would like to share with you here is my thinking about what should be consistent in the teaching of writing across grade levels. If this consistency did exist, if students in third and fourth and fifth and eighth grades just expected these kinds of things to happen at school when someone said, "It's writing time," their teachers could truly dig deeper with them in far, far less time. So, what should students expect from year to year when someone says, "It's time for writing"?

Year after year, students should expect to have:

- the empathy of a teacher who knows what it is like to do what she is asking her students to do. The empathy of a teacher who writes.
- healthy stretches of time to sit and write on a regular basis
- choices, much of the time, about what they will write about and how they will go about writing it
- time to share their writing with others and share in the writing of others
- a teacher who understands and values the role of approximation in learning
- individual, honest conversations with their teacher about their writing
- a portfolio of finished writing that gets fatter with each passing year, and the opportunity to revisit, rework, or continue pieces of writing in subsequent years
- a curriculum that is grounded. Process teaching matches what people really do when they write. Product teaching matches how things are actually written in the world outside school.
- only the best mentors for writing: Newbery medalists, Pulitzer prize winners, Nobel laureates

I believe there is strong support for these essentials in the wide body of professional resources we have available on the teaching of writing—resources created from research, theory, and practice (see Appendix A). And I do believe these essentials leave plenty of room for different teachers to bring themselves to this teaching in different ways, as none of them imply *stylistic* ways of teaching, only principled givens that students should recognize and expect across classrooms.

So much time could be saved if there was simply some consistency in teaching across time for children. I have used this metaphor before (Ray 2001), but it seems useful to employ it again here. I really believe that if writing workshops could operate in schools with the consistency that lunchtime operates, particularly in terms of how things are happening from day to day, then truly rigorous, intellectual work of very high standards could take place because the structure to support that work would already be in place.

Standards and Testing

I have honestly never been involved in a study in a classroom where the curriculum that was being generated from that study, and the quality of student thinking and reflection in the study were not far higher in terms of a "standard" of work than any curriculum documents I've ever seen. As a matter of fact, I believe it's difficult to engage in much study with students around well-written texts and not come to a place where you feel most curriculum documents actually underserve students in terms of both content and expectations for their work. There is no challenge to try and somehow infuse a study with high standards; if you're studying good stuff, high standards are already there. The challenge is to make sure the curriculum from the study is clearly articulated so that you can be accountable to anyone who wants to know the content of your teaching.

The other challenge is to make sure you can communicate with others clearly about what students are doing in the writing that comes from a study. Because this writing is bound to be more challenging and students are expected to carry the weight of decision making, there will be approximations (in terms of process and craft) in the writing that wouldn't be there if you just spelled out for students how to write things and made everything simpler. I think it's so important to be clear about the fact that approximation is often evidence that students are doing much harder work in writing. You'll also need to highlight in very visible ways the parts of students' writing where they are trying the work of the study so the focus is on that high standard work they are trying to do.

And what about testing? To do well on tests, I believe students need four key "ingredients." While tests vary from state to state, I'll assume the most common test scenario is a piece of writing written in response to a prompt in a single sitting. To do well on such a test, I believe students need:

- to be very comfortable with the task of writing, the whole idea of it; something they've done so often that it's no big deal
- the stamina to sit and work on a piece of writing for a long stretch of time
- to know what good writing is and how to craft it well
- some experience with the weird process of going from an idea they've never seen to a finished piece of writing in a single sitting

The writing workshop itself is where students will acquire the first two ingredients, and the studies you plan will support the third, especially if you tie some of the studies to the kinds of writing students will have to produce on the test and some of them to general crafting interests that will help them write well in any genre.

I actually believe these first three ingredients are the most important three. Why do I say this? Because I believe that if someone walked in right now and gave me a writing test I would do fine on it because I have these first three firmly in place. I've actually had very little experience writing to prompts in a single sitting, and most other writers I know haven't either, but we could *handle* it if we had to handle it because writing is just second nature to us. Interestingly enough, in schools, it's the last ingredient (practicing prompts) that gets the most "air time" even though most everyone agrees the first three are more important.

I do believe students should have some experience going from a prompt they've never seen to a finished piece of writing in a single sitting before they have to do this on a test. The only way I know to get experience with this weird process is just to practice it from time to time. You might consider spreading this practice out across the year, having students do a practice writing prompt once a month, or in between studies, for example. Or you might want to do a short study of testing where students practice this and you teach into that practice. Study what they do when they're in this situation and study what they're producing out of it to inform this teaching.

I want to be clear about one thing. A study of testing should be a study of *process*, not of *product*. The process students are asked to use to produce writing on tests is not the same process people who write things often use. But the kind of writing students are expected to produce should be real, quality writing, and that's what you'll be studying all year long. This shouldn't change for tests. If students are being asked to produce a kind of writing that does not exist in the known world of writing outside school (making it impossible to study), then students, parents, and teachers need to be marching on the statehouse steps in protest. In my thinking this is equivalent to a math test that would ask students to answer that $2 + 2 = 3$. Having said that, I've actually never seen a description or a rubric for a writing test that said students needed to write a formulaic, unreal kind of writing in order to do well on it, even though myths abound that this is true.

As Randy Bomer so thoughtfully reminded us in his wonderful book *Time for Meaning*, nobody gets more time. There isn't any *more* time. You have what you have, and for all the different lines of reasoning I've set out in this book, my hope is that you'll spend as much time as you can on the promise of deep study.

section
THREE

Resource
Sections

Introduction

As I write this, it is December and the holiday season is full upon us. I can't help but travel back in my mind to the late sixties when I was a little girl. Sometime in October every year, the Sears toy catalogue would arrive at our house. For the next eight weeks or so, my sister and I would look at the pages in that catalogue over and over and over, wishing. Each toy represented a possibility for a better kind of life, we thought, if we just had it. An Easy Bake oven. A Red Cowgirl outfit. A track with miniature race cars. A new Barbie enthroned in a pink convertible. Eventually, we had to make decisions about which lives we wanted, and which toys would best make that living possible. By the time Christmas actually arrived, the glossy, smooth pages of the catalogue were stained and dog-eared and torn in places where we'd tussled to have a look.

What you will find in these resource sections are ideas for different ways to gather texts for product studies. My hope is that as you read through them, you will feel a little like my sister and I felt with the Sears catalogue, each one of these possibilities offering the promise of a rich study that might happen in your classroom. I hope each one of them becomes a possibility you might suggest to an individual writer in a conference to help him find just the right vision he needs to make his idea come to life. I hope that whole-school faculties might be able to use these sections to imagine vertical study that grows and yields more sophisticated curriculum as students grow older and more experienced as writers.

I must confess that assembling these resource sections makes me a little nervous. There is so much gray area in trying to classify different kinds of writing in the world in ways that make sense for teaching. I'm often not quite sure which words are the right words to describe different kinds of writing in the world, and publishing my own in this way forces me to freeze my thinking about them and frankly, that makes me nervous. I know that by the time this book actually is published a year or so from now, I'll wish I could rewrite parts of this.

Added to this, whenever I start to put this thinking down, I always feel like I'm not nearly well-read enough to be doing this. I know way more than a single reader ought to know about Rick Reilly and Cynthia Rylant, and not nearly enough about the writers Lee Gutkind mentions in her books about creative nonfiction or William Zinsser mentions in his writing about memoir. I have a few writers I've come to love and trust and, as a teacher of writing, I come back to their work over and over to anchor my teaching.

At some point I have realized, however, that my own nervousness about writing these resource sections is precisely why I should write them. If someone like me—who does nothing in her professional life but think about the teaching of writing—feels the challenge of this thinking, then I might as well lead the way in saying, "Okay, it's messy, imprecise work we're doing here, but let's get on with it anyway." I hope you will see my thinking here as a demonstration of the kind of thinking that's possible more than as definitive explanations that need no examination. Please, examine them. And then add your own thinking to mine to round out your understandings.

Many of the possibilities you'll find here are for genre studies, looking at different kinds of writing in the world. And I won't try and cover the whole world of writing, just the kinds I believe might be most helpful for your planning. But remember, if you can gather it, you can study it, so any kind of writing in the world could become a study: brochures, guides, comic books, plays, speeches, song lyrics, catalogues, and so on. I also have included some possibilities for product studies *other* than genre in the final eight sections. These studies, along with the process study possibilities I suggested in Chapter 12, are important because they allow students to choose their own genres as they show the work of the study in their finished writing. All together, these possibilities for studies of both process and product should be helpful as you begin to think about a whole year of study in a writing workshop.

While it was quite a challenge to do so, each section has been written very tightly and with great focus. The only purpose of these sections is to suggest study possibilities; from there I'll trust the studies themselves to teach you what you need to know. That has, after all, been the whole point of this book, and I really do trust *study*. I hope you do, too.

You'll find a few basic kinds of information in each section. First, a brief explanation of the genre or writing issue I'm suggesting for study. And while whole books have been written on many of these genres and writing issues, my self-imposed limit on my explanations was a single page (think Sears catalogue). On these single pages I'll try to say just enough to help you think, "Okay, I know what she's talking about." In most cases of genre, I'll consider the intentions a particular kind of writing serves in the world as part of the explanation because, as I've explained earlier in the book, I think this language of intention is so important. Please know that I'm not trying to define anything in any complex way; again, that's the point of the study. And also know that there is *lots* of gray area in all this. You'll see some of it in my attempts to explain how kinds of writing are different, and you'll find even more gray areas when you actually engage in study. Gray areas and overlapping complexity are the very nature of what you are studying. There's just no way to make it simple.

If the kinds of writing I'm suggesting have widely used and accepted labels, labels you can walk into a bookstore and use to help you find them, I'll use them. If they don't, or if I'm making a particular distinction that sets something apart from a label, I'll use other words.

Next, each section will consider the "containers" where you find different kinds of writing and whether they will serve the suggested study: newspapers, magazines, picture books, collections, excerpts from chapter books (if it makes sense for the study), and the Internet. I will only address the Internet as a container if I know of specific websites that are really excellent for locating example texts. Otherwise, I'll assume two things. One is that you realize most all magazines and newspapers are archived and you can get to all kinds of writing using these archives, and two, that you know you can take any key words, put them into a search engine, and see what you come up with. *Memoir*, for example, or *short stories*, can yield all sorts of interesting sites.

If the kind of writing can be found in books, I'll suggest just three to five titles I know that fit the study. I consider these to be "starter stacks" and I labored over the decision to keep the lists short. In most studies, I could list so many more, but as I always say, "It's not these particular titles that matter. It's the kind of writing in them that matters and lots of other books have this same kind of writing in them." But if I say that, and then list twenty to thirty books, it doesn't seem like I really mean it. Well, I do mean it, so I'm not doing that. My hope is that if you don't know the books I'm listing already, you can get your hands on just a couple of them to see the kind of writing I'm talking about, and then you and your students can find other texts where writers seem to have the same intentions. In some cases, I've actually included whole text examples of various kinds of writing from newspapers and magazines to give you an idea of the potential in these containers.

And finally, because I have tried to show how the same study might happen across a wide range of grade levels, the content in some books (especially collections) is more mature and is probably most appropriate for middle school and beyond. I would not recommend that you order books without previewing them first. I should point out, however, that in collections of shorts stories, essays, poems, and so on, there are often some selections that aren't content-appropriate for the students you teach, but many others in the collection are, so teaching discretion is needed to make these text selections.

My greatest hope for these sections is that they will help you get excited about the possibility of study with your students. The world is full of fascinating, wonderful writing, and filling your classroom with it can bring new life and energy to your teaching of writing.

STUDY POSSIBILITY
Memoir

Memoir is a type of autobiographical nonfiction where a writer takes a reflective stance in looking back on a particular time in his or her life. The time may be connected to a particular event that happened during that time, or to a person, a place, or an object from that time that is particularly vivid. Memoir is most often written in first person, in the past tense, and generally has some quality of reflection attached to it. In other words, readers don't just get the memory, they also get a sense of the person who is remembering. Sometimes personal essays fulfill the intentions of memoir.

There is some gray area in the distinction between autobiography and memoir. Generally, something referred to as a memoir is more focused and doesn't try to faithfully recount the chronology of a life in the way an autobiography does. Also generally, autobiography is more the domain of those whose lives have been made famous in some way and people want to know about the life because of that fame. Famous people might also write more focused memoir, but very few nonfamous people write the whole stories of their lives (autobiography) and have them published. Nonfamous people write memoir all the time, however, and people like to read it just because they like to hear the stories of other people's lives.

NEWSPAPERS

Sometimes newspapers will have special feature sections that have memoir in them. My local paper, the *Asheville Citizen-Times*, has a weekly column called "Our Stories." Readers submit pieces for publication in this column, and they are usually memoir. Sometimes around the holidays, newspapers will have story contests and these submissions are often memoir, too. And from time to time, columnists in the "Life" or "Family" sections of papers will write memoir. You have to be on the lookout for these—the column won't have a different label or title on it to alert you that it's memoir.

MAGAZINES

I get some of my best examples of memoir from magazines, most often women's magazines. For some reason, the memoir is often found on the back page columns, as it is in my beloved monthly *Southern Living*. The "Lives" column in the *New York Times Magazine* is often memoir as well. One of my favorites from there is a column written by Nicole Keeter in the May 5, 2005 issue. Ketter writes about her experiences as the only black child living in a small Iowa town in the early 80s, and how everything changed when another black child arrived at the school. It's beautifully written, and it has a prized place in the memoir section of my fat blue notebook.

PICTURE BOOKS

Memoir is found in picture books. Before I place a book in this stack, I like to find some communication from the writer (in either an author's note or dedication) that the book is a work of memoir. Sometimes I can make this judgment on my own if I know a lot about the writer's life. Here's a short starter stack to get you started searching.

Calling the Doves/El canto de las palomas	Juan Felipe Herrera
Christmas in the Country	Cynthia Rylant
Saturdays and Teacakes	Lester Laminack
The Trip Back Home	Janet S. Wong
Two Mrs. Gibsons	Toyomi Igus

COLLECTIONS

There are actually several different kinds of collected memoir, so I'll make those distinctions in these starter stacks.

Collections of Memoir Vignettes by Different Authors

I Thought My Father Was God and Other True Tales from NPR's National Story Telling Project	Paul Austere, editor
Linda Brown, You Are Not Alone: The Brown v. Board of Education Decision	Joyce Carol Thomas, editor
The Milestones Project: Celebrating Childhood Around the World	Richard and Michele Steckel, editors

Guys Write for Guys Read (*Most selections are memoir*)	Jon Scieszka, editor

Collections of Memoir Vignettes by Single Authors

The Circuit: Stories from the Life of a Migrant Child	Francisco Jiménez
Marshfield Dreams	Ralph Fletcher
My Father's Summers—A Daughter's Memoir	Kathi Appelt
Somehow Form a Family: Stories That Are Mostly True	Tony Early
A Summer Life	Gary Soto

Collections of Personal Essays, Some with Memoir Intentions

Dress Your Family in Corduroy and Denim	David Sedaris
Me Talk Pretty One Day	David Sedaris
Never in a Hurry: Essays on People and Places	Naomi Shihab Nye
Plan B: Further Thoughts on Faith	Anne Lamott

EXCERPTS

Because they are written episodically, memoirs that are chapter book in length often have stand-alone excerpts that could go in a stack of memoir. Here's a starter stack of books rich with stand-alone excerpts.

26 Fairmont Avenue	Tomie dePaola
Bad Boy	Walter Dean Myers
Breaking Through	Francisco Jiménez
Caught by the Sea: My Life on Boats	Gary Paulsen
Knots in My Yo-Yo String: The Autobiography of a Kid	Jerry Spinelli

"Culture Comes to Pearl Street"
Cheryl Hiers

Southern Living, August 2002

Our street in a small Florida town ran straight and flat as a ruler. No hills. No curves. You could stand at one end and see what was coming from the other. One bright summer Saturday, a white car appeared at the far end of our street and glided toward us. We stopped pedaling and straddled our bikes. A new family was arriving.

A mother and father and two slender young girls emerged from the car. They all had skin the color of a pecan shell. Short and plump, the father was the most ordinary looking of the group. We learned later that Ravi Singh was a doctor, but at the moment he seemed a chauffeur of the exotic.

Clad in a vaporous tunic and pants of sky blue cloth, Mrs. Singh stood before us like a character from *The Thousand and One Nights*. A small dot marked her forehead, and she wore silver bracelets on her wrists. She seemed a figure impossibly glamorous for our palmettoed Pearl Street.

The girls—slim, lovely beings—wore everyday shorts and blouses and flip-flops, just as we did. Each carried a drawstring purse embedded with bits of mirrors that caught the summer sun and broke it into glints of spangling white. We were hypnotized with envy.

The strangeness of the new family quailed us. We were a street of Southern Baptists and Methodists. We had never encountered Hindus. We stared impolitely, not knowing what to do.

The Singh's elegant old greyhound, Nanda, broke the ice. She was the last to emerge, uncurling her long legs and sauntering out of the car like a stiff ballerina. Our own dogs spied the comely newcomer and barreled across the street to investigate. We hollered, dropping our bikes to run after them.

To meet her, Mac smacked his front paws on the ground in a play bow. Nanda bowed back. The she began to run—running our street faster than any dog I'd ever seen. Mac and Bullet chugged behind, comically outclassed.

"Nanda!" Dr. Singh called, and she came immediately, like a good dog.

"Good Nanda," he said, rubbing his hand along her lovely backbone. When she wasn't running, she moved with the languid gait of a sleepwalker.

Thanks to the opening Nanda had given us, we learned many things that day about our new neighbors. Mrs. Singh delighted in citrus fruit, particularly kumquats. The painted red dot on her forehead was called a *bindi*. Her ravishing blue pantsuit, which she permitted us to touch, was a "Punjabi." The girls were Pari and Habiba, names meaning "fairy" and "beloved." They showed us their small change purses, shaped like fish and covered in sequins.

That night we lay in bed, saying aloud the names of our new friends. Habiba, Pari, Nanda. The greyhound, we agreed, was a wise and wonderful creature. Earlier that day, Dr. Singh had revealed the meaning of her name.

"Nanda," he said, "means 'joyful.' A good name, yes?" he asked.

Tongue-tied and shy, we nodded vigorously. Not in all the world could we think of a better one.

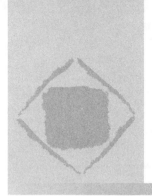

STUDY POSSIBILITY
Short Stories of Realistic Fiction

W riters are drawn to fiction for lots of reasons. One is, as humans, we are simply drawn to stories. We love to tell our own, over and over, but with fiction, a writer faces the possibility that anything might happen in the telling. Writing fiction is about exploring possible realities for the characters writers create. Sometimes life informs fiction in fairly direct ways, but the basic stance the fiction writer takes is to say, "I am making this up." Fiction has certain required elements, and short stories must contain these elements too, though in a very compressed format compared to a novel. The elements of story are plot, setting, character, change, and movement through time. (See Janet Angelillo's *Making Revision Matter* [2005, 80–81] for a good discussion of these elements.)

NEWSPAPERS

To my knowledge, most newspapers do not contain short stories of realistic fiction (or any other kind of fiction). If they did, I believe they would be in very special feature sections or perhaps as published winners from story contests the paper has sponsored.

MAGAZINES

Many magazines for both adults and children publish either original short stories or stories reprinted from collections. Children's magazines such as *Ladybug*, *Cricket*, and *Jack & Jill* are actually great resources for realistic short stories for beginning writers. *American Girl* and *Boy's Life*, as well as *Stone Soup* often have short fiction in them as well.

PICTURE BOOKS

Many picture books contain realistic fiction. My preference when selecting picture books for this study is to find ones with limited dialogue, clear story elements, and text structures that are more subtle than obvious. (Saving ones with obvious structures—*Wilfrid Gordon McDonald Partridge* by Mem Fox, for example—for studies of text structures that are obviously crafted.) If students are new to the study of realistic fiction, I also prefer to start with more examples written in third person than first. This is simply to help create some distance from the first-person writing students have likely used often as writers before this study. But these are all just my personal teaching preferences. Here's a starter list of picture books that contain short realistic fiction.

Ish	Peter Reynolds
"Let's Get a Pup!" Said Kate	Bob Graham
Moe McTooth	Eileen Spinelli
See the Ocean	Estelle Condra
The Ticky-Tacky Doll	Cynthia Rylant

COLLECTIONS

The most obvious, easiest, absolute best place to get examples of short stories. Here's a starter stack.

Collections Written by Different Authors

No Easy Answers: Short Stories About Teenagers Making Tough Choices	Donald R. Gallo, editor
On Her Way: Stories and Poems About Growing Up	Sandy Asher, editor
Places I Never Meant to Be: Original Stories by Censored Writers	Judy Blume, editor
Every Man for Himself: Ten Short Stories About Being a Guy	Nancy E. Mercado, editor

Collections Written by a Single Author

Gone from Home: Short Takes	Angela Johnson
Kissing Tennessee and Other Stories from the Stardust Dance	Kathi Appelt
Past Perfect, Present Tense: New and Collected Stories	Richard Peck
Local News	Gary Soto
Who Am I Without Him? Short Stories About Girls and the Boys in Their Lives	Sharon Flake

EXCERPTS

In this study, excerpts from novels would best be used to show how writers deal with elements of story or some particular aspect of crafting fiction such as writing good description or dialogue. You're not likely to find stand-alone excerpts in novels that can represent a short story in the "whole text" sense.

INTERNET

You might be surprised at the number of sites that pop up when you put the key words *short stories*, *realistic fiction* into your search engine. Here are two you might want to check out.

www.eastoftheweb.com   aboutteens.org/fiction

STUDY POSSIBILITY
Historical Fiction

Just as is true with short realistic fiction, historical fiction must contain all the elements of story: plot, setting, characters, change, and movement through time. The particular time period in history in which the story is set must impact both the characters and events in the story in ways that are true to that period. The story is an act of the writer's imagination; this is what makes it *fiction*. But the backdrop of history in which the story takes place must be as true as the writer can possibly make it; this is what makes it *historical*.

I actually make two stacks when I look at my picture books of historical fiction, admittedly creating some real gray area but making what I think is an important distinction. In one stack I place books where writing good fiction seems to be the writer's intention: the characters and the story matter most and the historical setting functions as it does in other kinds of fiction, as a backdrop to the story. In the other stack I place books where the setting in history seems to matter more and the "characters" living through it, as portrayed in the book, are rather stock so that the historical events can take center stage. The events that happen in these books seem more designed to represent history than to allow readers to live through a fictional character's story. They are slightly different writing intentions that lead to equally wonderful ways of bringing history alive through well-crafted literature.

Teachers often try and connect the study of historical fiction to another content area by assigning the time period where the story must be set. I'd like to suggest two things to think about if you're considering this. First, in the writing workshop, the study of this kind of writing is of the writing itself. If it is tied to a period of history, the curriculum probably won't be general in the way it needs to be general to be a study of the *genre* of historical fiction. Second, if you study what writers of this genre say about how they get their ideas, it is usually because they have become fascinated with some period of history for some reason. Students may or may not be fascinated with the time period you are studying in social studies or history, so they may not get to experience the real intentions of the genre at all if it's tied to what you are studying.

MAGAZINES

Cobblestone (American) and *Calliope* (World) are two children's magazines devoted to history and both of them have pieces of short historical fiction in them from time to time.

PICTURE BOOKS WHERE THE DEVELOPMENT OF CHARACTER AND STORY REALLY MATTER

Baseball Saved Us	Ken Mochizuki
Freedom Summer	Deborah Wiles
Paperboy	Mary Kay Kroeger and Louise Borden
True Heart	Marissa Moss

PICTURE BOOKS WHERE THE SETTING IN HISTORY MATTERS MORE

The Little Ships: The Heroic Rescue at Dunkirk in World War II	Louise Borden
Patrol: An American Soldier in Vietnam	Walter Dean Myers
Players in Pigtails	Shana Corey
Sunsets of the West	Tony Johnston

STUDY POSSIBILITY
True Stories from History

Historical Narrative

Writers sometimes take an actual story from history, research to learn as much of the true detail of the story as they can, and then craft the story into a piece of literature. These aren't articles or books *about* an event in history; they are written as the actual story of what happened. The primary difference in this writing and historical fiction, of course, is that the basic story elements are all true: plot, characters, setting, movement through time, and change. The challenge in this kind of writing is to round out the bits and pieces of the story that the writer knows and craft them so the piece reads as a full-blown, engaging story.

MAGAZINES

Cobblestone (American) and *Calliope* (World) are two children's magazines devoted to history and frequently have this kind of writing in them.

PICTURE BOOKS

Flight	Robert Burleigh
The Librarian of Basra: A True Story from Iraq	Jeanette Winter

(very recent history, but from the same writing intentions)

The Man Who Walked Between the Towers	Mordicai Gerstein
Black Cowboy, Wild Horses: A True Story	Julius Lester
Rosa	Nikki Giovanni

(not in the biographical sketch stack because it is so focused on the particular story of Rosa Parks' refusal to give up her seat on the bus [rather than a broader look at her life])

COLLECTIONS

Great Moments in Baseball History   Matt Christopher

EXCERPTS

This text is a little longer than what you expect students to write, but it has some excellent stand-alone excerpts.

The Journey That Saved Curious George: Louise Borden
    The True Wartime Escape of Margaret
    and H.A. Rey

STUDY POSSIBILITY
Crafting Family Stories into Literature

Sometimes writers will take a family story or memory that has been passed on to them orally and craft that story into a piece of literature. Reading the author's notes and dedications in books like these, you realize that often a big part of the motivation for this writing seems to be to pay tribute to the people who lived the story. This kind of writing seems a lot like memoir, it's often found in the same places as memoir, and sometimes even under the label *memoir*, but actually the writer's intentions are a bit different. The ideas for the writing come from a very different place than memoir: the writers aren't writing about their own lived-through experiences, they're writing about someone else's.

NEWSPAPERS

Same notes as memoir study. Read to see whether what the author is writing about is from his or her memory, or a family story that was passed on.

MAGAZINES

Same notes as memoir study. Read to see whether what the author is writing about is from his or her memory, or a family story that was passed on.

PICTURE BOOKS

All the picture books in this starter list have some communication from the author that the writing comes from a family story or memory that was passed on to the writers.

Good-bye, 382 Shin Dang Dong	Frances Park and Ginger Park
Miz Berlin Walks	Jane Yolen
Quinnie Blue	Dinah Johnson
Show Way	Jacqueline Woodson
Those Building Men	Angela Johnson

COLLECTIONS

In any collection of memoir, it's possible that some selections may represent writers crafting family stories they remember rather than writing from their own experiences. This is because the distinction I'm making here isn't made for readers of these collections; it's a distinction writers need. Always be on the lookout for this stance as you're reading a collection of memoir. Here are two more collections to add to this stack. They have selections written by a variety of writers.

Grand Fathers: Reminiscences, Poems, Recipes, and Photos of the Keepers of Our Traditions   Nikki Giovanni, editor

Grand Mothers: Poems, Reminiscences, and Short Stories About the Keepers of Our Traditions   Nikki Giovanni, editor

EXCERPTS

I do know some chapter-length books that are based on family stories. Pam Muñoz Ryan's *Esperanza Rising*, for example, was crafted from the stories of experiences of her maternal grandmother. Just as with fiction, however, it's difficult to find stand-alone excerpts in chapter books like this that can stand on their own as an example of the genre.

STUDY POSSIBILITY
Poetry

One of my all-time favorite definitions for poetry I found on a publicity flyer for Jacqueline Woodson's picture book, *We Had a Picnic This Sunday Past*. On it Jacqueline was quoted as saying, "When I first sat down to write [this book], it was because I wanted to write a poem. I wanted to experiment with joy and urgency in tiny spaces. I had done this in other genres and wanted to see how much was possible in this new space."

Joy and urgency in tiny spaces. I love that.

Poetry is both a form and a genre, clearly evidenced by the fact that many writers use the form of poetry to write memoir, fiction, essay, and to serve all manner of intentions associated with various other genres.

For studies of poetry as a genre itself, I'm clearly partial to studying collections of poems written by one poet on a topic. In a study like this, I want students to understand the work of poetry *as a genre* and that it can serve a topic they love and help them write a lot about that topic. In other words, I don't want them to think of poetry in the single-poem sense. Collections of this kind are listed later in the starter stacks.

I also have starter stacks listed that show poets using the form of poetry to fulfill the intentions of other genres (refer to other resource sections for how I'm defining these intentions). There's some gray area in stacking this way, but I believe the distinctions are useful for teachers of writing. In terms of study, you'll have to decide whether you want to look at all kinds of poetry and have students decide what intentions they have for their collections, or whether you'll study them separately. You might also want to include the poetry collections that do the work of other genres (memoir, essay, fiction, etc.) in those particular genre studies, showing students a form other than prose for fulfilling those intentions.

In addition to the titles you see listed here, I have multiple collections of poems written by many of the poets on these lists. Please consider this a recommendation of the poets themselves, and look for other titles by each of them.

Picture Book Collections

Fireflies at Midnight	Marilyn Singer
Hoop Queens and Hoop Kings	Charles R. Smith, Jr.
A Humble Life: Plain Poems	Linda Oatman High
Fold Me a Poem	Kristine O'Connell George
Under the Christmas Tree	Nikki Grimes

Nonpicture Book Collections

19 Varieties of Gazelle: Poems of the Middle East	Naomi Shihab Nye
Delights and Shadows	Ted Kooser
Neighborhood Odes	Gary Soto
Ordinary Things	Ralph Fletcher
The Trouble with Poetry and Other Poems	Billy Collins

Poetry Fulfilling the Intentions of Memoir

Baseball, Snakes and Summer Squash	Donald Graves
Been to Yesterdays	Lee Bennett Hopkins
From the Bellybutton of the Moon/Del ombligo de la luna	Francisco X. Alarcón
The Other Side: Shorter Poems	Angela Johnson
Waiting to Waltz: A Childhood	Cynthia Rylant

Poetry Fulfilling the Intentions of Crafting a Family Story into Literature

Becoming Joe DiMaggio	Maria Testa

Poetry Fulfilling the Intentions of Short Fiction

Amber Was Brave, Essie Was Smart	Vera B. Williams
Nathaniel Talking	Eloise Greenfield
Running Back to Ludie	Angela Johnson
Under the Pear Tree	Brenda Seabrooke
The Way a Door Closes	Hope Anita Smith

Poetry Fulfilling the Intentions of Longer Fiction (Novels)

Bronx Masquerade (actually poetry and prose combined)	Nikki Grimes
Locomotion	Jacqueline Woodson
Love That Dog	Sharon Creech
Make Lemonade	Virginia E. Wolff

Poetry Fulfilling the Intentions of Feature Articles

Cactus Poems	Frank Asch and Ted Levin
Hummingbird Nest: A Journal of Poems	Kristine O'Connell George
I See Rhythm	Toyomi Igus
Least Things: Poems About Small Natures	Jane Yolen
Sacred Places	Jane Yolen

Poetry Fulfilling the Intentions of Short Biography

All by Herself	Ann Whitford Paul
Carver: A Life in Poems	Marilyn Nelson
Cool Melons—Turn to Frogs: The Life and Poems of Issa	Matthew Golub
(translated poems and prose combined)	
Heroes and She-roes: Poems of Amazing and Everyday Heroes	J. Patrick Lewis
Love to Langston	Tony Medina

Poetry Fulfilling the Intentions of Historical Fiction

Almost Forever	Maria Testa
Mississippi Mud: Three Prairie Journals	Ann Turner
Out of the Dust	Karen Hesse
Voices of the Alamo	Sherry Garland
Witness	Karen Hesse

Poetry Fulfilling the Intentions of Historical Essay

Fortune's Bones: The Manumission Requiem	Marilyn Nelson
A Wreath for Emmett Till	Marilyn Nelson

Poetry Fulfilling the Intentions of Personal Essay

Boris	Cynthia Rylant
Come with Me: Poems for a Journey	Naomi Shihab Nye
A Dime a Dozen	Nikki Grimes
(see author's note on this book)	
God Went to Beauty School	Cynthia Rylant

Poetry Fulfilling the Intentions of Photo Essay

Here in Harlem: Poems in Many Voices	Walter Dean Myers
Horizons: Poems as Far as the Eye Can See	Jane Yolen
Perfect Harmony: A Musical Tour with the Boys Choir of Harlem	Charles R. Smith, Jr.

STUDY POSSIBILITY
Journeys of Thought: The Essay

As I've said before, I like Randy Bomer's (1995) definition of an essay better than any I've ever seen. He says that in an essay the writer takes the reader on a journey of thought as she or he (the writer) tries out an idea. In fact, the French verb *essayer* means "to try." The world is full of wonderful essays and they are easy to gather. While essays are essentially expository in mode (I'm using this in the sense that they move through a list of ideas as you journey along), you will find lots of first-person narrative in them because writers often use life stories as a way to illustrate ideas in essays.

While some are easy to stack, I actually find a fair amount of gray area when distinguishing some essays from other kinds of writing. This is because, of course, of the overlapping intentions of different genres: personal essays and memoir, for example, or commentary and essay, or the distinction between literary essay and literary critique. To help with this sorting, I look for several characteristics, not the least of which is the label *essay* on the piece of writing. But since I can't always count on the label, I also look for the journeylike quality of the thinking in the writing. Because of this quality, the main idea of the piece is sometimes not revealed until near the very end (the reader has to go on the journey to get there). Also because of this quality, in an essay the writer's *thinking* about a topic is actually more important to the piece than the topic itself.

While an essay can address any topic at all, essays are sometimes distinguished by the kinds of topics they address: personal, historical, literary, political, cultural, media, nature, travel—even culinary essays! (See the *Time* article on page 210.)

NEWSPAPERS

I mostly clip essays in the form of commentary from the newspaper, and because the work of commentary is so specific, I like to include it in its own separate stack (it has its own resource section in this book). I sometimes find personal

"Free the Children: Summer Should Be a Time When Rules Can Be Bent and Boredom Is a State of Grace"

Nancy Gibbs

Time magazine, July 14, 2003

My daughters are upstairs shrieking. And thumping. Nothing sounds broken, so I am leaving them alone to savor the outlaw feeling of playing hooky from the afternoon session of camp. They know absences don't count against them on some Permanent Record somewhere.

I long for them to have a whole summer that doesn't matter. When they can read for fun, even books that don't appear on the officially sanctioned summer reading list. When even the outfielders get to play first base sometimes because the game doesn't count. When they can ruin their brand-new sneakers because they found a great new creek. When a rule can be bent, if only to test its strength, and they can play all they want, without playing for keeps.

I want summer not to count because what happens as a result counts for so much. Maybe we adults idealize our own red-rover days, the hot afternoons spent playing games that required no coaches, eating foods that involved no nutrition, getting dirty in whole new ways and rarely glancing in the direction of a screen of any kind. Ask friends about the people and places that shaped them, and summer springs up quickly when they tell their first story: their first kiss, first beer, first job that changed everything. The best summer moments were stretchy enough to carry us all through the year, which is why it's worth listening to all the warnings from social scientists about our Hurried Children who for the rest of the year wear their schedules like clothes that are too tight.

The experts have long charted the growing stress and disappearing downtime of modern children; now they say the trend extends across class and region. The combination of double shifts, shrinking vacations, fear of boredom and competitive instincts conspires to clog our kids' summer just as much as the rest of the year. Even camp isn't likely to be about s'mores and spud anymore: there is math camp and weight camp and leadership camp, as though summer were about perfecting ourselves, when in fact the opposite may be true.

That's because summer should be a season of grace—not of excuses but of exceptions, ice cream an hour before dinner just because it's so hot out, bedtimes missed in honor of meteor showers, weekdays and weekends that melt together because nothing feels like work. It's not just about relaxing; it's about rehearsing. All our efforts to guard and guide our children may just get in the way of the one thing they need most from us: to be deeply loved yet left alone so they can try a new skill, new slang, new style, new flip-flops. So they can trip a few times, make mistakes, cross them out, try again, with no one keeping score.

This may require some re-education, a kind of summer school of play that teaches kids not to expect to be entertained every moment, to adjust to days measured out not in periods or practices but in large chunks of opportunity called Morning and Afternoon. Go build a fort. Use every single art supply in the house to make something big. Be bored and see where it takes you, because the imagination's dusty wilderness is worth crossing if you want to sculpt your soul.

Giving children some summer privacy and freedom takes nerve, and not just because this is also precious time to be together as a family. Last summer, the Amber Alert summer, who could take their eyes off their kids in the front yard? When my 7-year-old was half an hour late coming home one afternoon and the lifeguards and counselors started asking me what she looked like, what she was wearing, I couldn't get enough air in my lungs to tell them, the fear was so strangling.

But when we finally found her, happily engrossed near Dead Man's Cave catching frogs with a friend, I had to take a deep breath and remember that maybe I had neglected to teach her to call home if she was going to be late, because I had never needed to. She is shuttled from school to playdate to soccer to chess, and only in the summer does she control her own time and whereabouts at all. Do I punish her for savoring liberty the first time she ever tasted it? So we had a long talk while sitting under a tree before I grounded her for a day.

We are bombarded with reasons to stay inside: we're afraid of mosquitoes because of West Nile and grass because of pesticides and sun because of cancer and sunscreen because of vitamin-D deficiency. Ours is the generation that knows too much, including what other kids are doing in the summer to get a head start in the marathon that ends with a fat envelope from a top school. So apart from the challenge of trusting our kids, there is the challenge of trusting ourselves, steering by the stars of instinct and memory rather than parent peer pressure or all those guidebooks on how to raise a Successful Child.

I send my girls out to play in the hope that by summer's end I will see the gifts that freedom brings. Kids seem four inches taller in September than in June, whether they've grown any or not. And the measuring stick is marked off in bruises healed and flags captured, friends lost and found, goals achieved without anyone's help. I hope for the discipline not to discipline them too much, because that's how I will learn how strong they have become.

essays in the writing by columnists in the "Family and Living" sections, but for the most part, magazines offer me lots more essays than newspapers.

MAGAZINES

The back pages of two major news magazines, *Time* and *Newsweek*, publish essays each week on a range of topics. *Newsweek* also has the regular column "My Turn," which is almost always a personal essay written by "at large" contributors from all walks of life. Of high interest to many young people, especially teenagers, both these magazines also regularly publish essays and critiques about our media culture: television, music, movies, and literature. I have a range of these in my blue notebook including one about why "old" guys like Rod Stewart (imagine that) and Tony Bennett are raging onto the pop music scene, and another on America's fascination with the losers on the television show *American Idol*.

The "Outdoors" feature in my *Southern Living* magazine is sometimes an essay about nature, and the back page "Southern Journal," when it's not memoir, is often a personal essay about some topic of interest to those who live in the South. Whatever magazines you know best, look for essays in them that can support your teaching.

I don't find a lot of what I would categorize as essay in children's magazines, but keep your eyes peeled for them. You never know where you might find a writer going on a journey of thought.

PICTURE BOOKS

I do believe that the writers of some picture books seem to be taking readers on a journey of thought about a topic, and I think these books can help the youngest writers understand this intention in writing whether you refer to it as an essay or not. You may simply say to children, "Sometimes writers write about an *idea* they want their readers to think about."

Here's a starter list of picture books that seem to fulfill the intentions of essays.

I Want to Be	Thylias Moss
Let's Talk About Race	Julius Lester
A Quiet Place	Douglas Wood
What You Know First	Patricia MacLachlan
Who Was the Woman Who Wore the Hat?	Nancy Patz

"Much Too Soon, a Teen Mother Joins the Club"
Kathleen O'Brien

Newhouse News Service, May 16, 2005

She's a new mother, so she hadn't yet realized it is easier to do your food shopping by placing the baby in the grocery cart.

Instead, she was slowly maneuvering her balky stroller through the produce section.

Yes, I'd heard the rumors around town. Knew this high-schooler was pregnant. Knew there'd been a baby shower. Heard she had come to health class to talk about the perils of teen pregnancy.

I was out of the loop for the birth, apparently, yet here was clear evidence that it had occurred.

And now, too quickly, the moment was upon me: What to say to a childhood friend of my daughter's upon greeting her and her new baby? I admit to being weighted down by caution. After all, we wouldn't want to imply approval of giving birth during one's junior year of high school.

Yet there was no avoiding the encounter, awkward though it promised to be. She and my daughter had been casual friends until the swirls of middle-school social circles saw them drift apart.

It was just a few short years ago that they were on the same softball team, and I remember spending one sunny afternoon on the sidelines with her dad. He clearly hoped her softball days would continue. His daughter, out in left field, signaled with her body posture of extreme boredom that they would not.

In the three seconds' warning granted me there among the grapes and broccoli, I had one cogent thought: The baby's here. Regardless of the circumstances of its birth, a new person is among us and deserves to be greeted with enthusiasm.

So I smiled and peeked into the stroller at the baby dressed in pastel green footsie pajamas. No help there in the gender department, so I had to fake it. I oohed and ahhed. The baby stared, wide-eyed, at its mother.

"Only has eyes for Mom!" I chirped, adeptly avoiding any reference to "he" or "she."

We exchanged a few more pleasantries about the baby, and then I bailed.

On the drive home, a small section of my brain buzzed with static, vague discontent. I found myself unsettled, bothered by something I couldn't name.

A year ago I would've said she and I had nothing more in common than our zip code. Now, however, we share one huge similarity: We both belong to the grand club that is motherhood.

And she is not just a mother, but that most vulnerable (and tired) version: the new mother.

With shame I realized she had deserved a more gracious welcome.

Like it or not, she is a fully functioning woman. She might not be legally allowed to drink, buy cigarettes or drive a car past midnight, but in sheer biological terms, she is a woman. Without anyone's permission, she has crossed a threshold.

I'd been chary with my encouragement, stingy with my kindness. Sure, I greeted the baby. But I didn't actually greet her.

While it makes sense for society as a whole to disapprove of teen pregnancies in general, when the baby lies before you right there in the supermarket, disapproval is a moot point. And not particularly helpful.

I'll do better when I see her next. I'll say the things I always say, the things she deserves to hear.

Don't try too much, I'll say.

Take care of yourself, I'll say.

And sleep when the baby sleeps.

COLLECTIONS

Feasting the Heart: Fifty-two Commentaries for the Air	Reynolds Price

(*Though the title labels them "commentaries," they are not the op-ed type of commentary. They are personal essays Reynolds read on* All Things Considered.)

Going to Ground: Simple Life on a Georgia Pond	Amy Blackmarr
Never in a Hurry: Essays on People and Places	Naomi Shihab Nye
Small Wonder: Essays	Barbara Kingsolver
Thinking Out Loud: On the Personal, the Political, the Public and the Private	Anna Quindlen

(*The "political and public" essays tend more toward the work of commentary.*)

COLLECTIONS OF ESSAYS *ABOUT* READING AND WRITING

The Faith of a Writer: Life, Craft, Art	Joyce Carol Oates
How Reading Changed My Life	Anna Quindlen
Rereadings: Seventeen Writers Revisit Books They Love	Anne Fadiman, editor
Take Joy: A Book for Writers	Jane Yolen
Telling Time—Angels, Ancestors and Stories: Essays on Writing	Nancy Willard

INTERNET

When it comes to finding good essays, I have become a big fan of *Slate*, the online magazine found on the MSN website. That particular kind of essay so necessary it seems to school, the literary essay/critique, can be found in the "Arts and Life" section of *Slate*, as well as essays about other popular media like movies and music. The "Travel and Food" and "Style and Shopping" sections of *Slate* have great essays on all sorts of topics related to those general categories.

"Harry Potter: Pampered Jock, Patsy, Fraud"
Chris Suellentrop

Posted on *Slate*, November 8, 2002. www.slate.com

Like most heroes, Harry Potter possesses the requisite Boy Scout virtues: trustworthy, loyal, helpful, friendly, courteous, kind, obedient, cheerful, thrifty, brave, clean, and reverent. But so do lots of boys and girls, and they don't get books and movies named after them. Why isn't the movie that comes out next week titled *Ron Weasley and the Chamber of Secrets*? Why isn't its sequel dubbed *Hermione Granger and the Prisoner of Azkaban*? Why Harry? What makes him so special?

Simple: He's a glory hog who unfairly receives credit for the accomplishments of others and who skates through school by taking advantage of his inherited wealth and his establishment connections. Harry Potter is no braver than his best friend, Ron Weasely, just richer and better-connected. Harry's other good friend, Hermione Granger, is smarter and a better student. The one thing Harry excels at is the sport of Quidditch, and his pampered-jock status allows him to slide in his studies, as long as he brings the school glory on the playing field. But as Charles Barkley long ago noted, being a good athlete doesn't make you a role model.

Harry Potter is a fraud, and the cult that has risen around him is based on a lie. Potter's claim to fame, his central accomplishment in life, is surviving a curse placed on him as an infant by the evil wizard Voldemort. As a result, the wizarding world celebrates the young Harry as "The Boy Who Lived." It's a curiously passive accomplishment, akin to "The Boy Who Showed Up," or "The Boy Who Never Took a Sick Day." And sure enough, just as none of us do anything special by slogging through yet another day, the infant Harry didn't do anything special by living. It was his *mother* who saved him, sacrificing her life for his.

Did your mom love you? Good, maybe you deserve to be a hero, too. The love of Harry's mother saves his life not once but twice in *Harry Potter and the Sorcerer's Stone*. Not only that, but her love for Harry sends Voldemort into hiding for 13 years, saving countless other lives in the process. The book and the movie should be named after *Lily* Potter. But thanks to the revisionist histories of J.K. Rowling, Lily's son is remembered as the world's savior.

What Harry has achieved on his own, without his mother, stems mostly from luck and, more often, inheritance. He's a trust-fund kid whose success at his school, Hogwarts, is largely attributable to the gifts his friends and relatives lavish upon him. (Coming soon: Frank Bruni's book, *Ambling into Hogwarts: The Unlikely Odyssey of Harry Potter*.) A few examples: an enchanted map (made in part by his father), an invisibility cloak (his father's), and a state-of-the-art magical broom (a gift from his godfather) that is the equivalent of a Lexus in a high-school parking lot.

Harry's other achievements can generally be chalked up to the fact that he regularly plays the role of someone's patsy. Almost all Harry's deeds in the first book take place under the watchful eye of Hogwarts headmaster Dumbledore, who saves Harry from certain death at the end of the book. In *Chamber of Secrets*, the evil Voldemort successfully manipulates the unsuspecting Harry, who must once again be rescued. In *Goblet of Fire*, everything Harry accomplishes—including winning the Triwizard Tournament—takes place because he is the unwitting pawn of one of Voldemort's minions.

Even Harry's greatest moment—his climactic face-off with Voldemort in *Goblet of Fire*—isn't too much to crow about. Pure happenstance is the only reason Voldemort is unable to kill Harry: Both their magic wands were made with feathers from the same bird. And even with his lucky wand, Harry still needs his mom's ghost to bail him out by telling him what to do. Once again, Lily Potter proves to be twice the man her son is.

Harry's one undisputed talent is his skill with a broom, which makes him one of the most successful Quidditch players in Hogwarts history. As Rowling puts it the first time Harry takes off on a broom, "in a rush of fierce joy he realized he'd found something he could do without being taught." Harry's talent is so natural as to be virtually involuntary. Admiring Harry for his flying skill is like admiring a cheetah for running fast. It's beautiful, but it's not an accomplishment.

In fact, Harry rarely puts hard work or effort into anything. He is a "natural." Time and again, Harry is celebrated for his instinctual gifts. When he learns that he is a Parselmouth, or someone who can speak the language of snakes, Rowling writes, "He wasn't even aware of deciding to do it." (In fact, when Harry *tries* to speak this language, he can't do it. He can only do it instinctively.) When Harry stabs a basilisk in *Chamber of Secrets*, Rowling writes that he did it "without thinking, without considering, as though he had meant to do it all along." In *Goblet of Fire*, during Harry's battle with Voldemort, Rowling writes that "Harry didn't understand why he was doing it, didn't know what it might achieve. . . . "

Being a wizard is something innate, something you are born to, not something you can achieve. As a result, Harry lives an effortless life. Although Dumbledore insists, "It is our choices, Harry, that show what we truly are, far more than our abilities," the school that Dumbledore runs values native gifts above all else. That's why Harry is such a hero in wizard culture—he has the most talent, even if he hasn't done much with it. Hogwarts is nothing more than a magical Mensa meeting.

STUDY POSSIBILITY
Feature Articles and Literary Nonfiction

R andy Bomer's (1995) definition of a feature article is that it is something written "to inform readers about something they never realized could be so complex and interesting." Not the top news article, interesting to read because it's *news*, not the straight facts-only information found in encyclopedias and reference books, the feature article is *literary* nonfiction, interesting to read because the writer has deliberately crafted it to engage the reader's attention while including all sorts of interesting information.

I love Randy's definition and believe it covers the intentions of a wide range of nonfiction writing that's found in every imaginable container in a wide variety of forms and formats. For the purpose of discussion, I'm going to use the label *literary nonfiction* to refer to any nonfiction writing in any container that does the work of informing and engaging.

In magazines and newspapers, and on the bookshelves in a library or bookstore, this kind of writing is generally grouped by topic, but to keep the focus on the work of the genre itself, it probably makes sense not to make topic distinctions in a study of this kind of writing. Instead, you might want to look at the different kinds of information found in this kind of writing. For example, texts

> that provide a variety of information on a topic (this is a big, wide category);
> that give advice;
> that are designed to teach a reader how to do something;
> that inform readers about how something is done;
> that are based on interviews;
> that are biographical sketches or profiles of people; or
> that present a list of possibilities.

Your study might be an overview of these possibilities where students choose the kind of writing they'd like to do, or it might be a study of a specific kind of literary nonfiction. I'll actually consider these separately in the sections that follow this one because I believe each one represents a different potential for study. The

"Atlantis: Did This Lost City Really Exist?"
Michael N. Smith and Debora L. Smith

National Geographic Kids, March 2005, 26–27

Ηow in the big, wide, wacky world do you find a sunken city? Not easily! But explorer Robert Sarmast claims he has discovered the long-lost city of Atlantis at the bottom of the Mediterranean Sea.

Think something sounds a little fishy? Many experts say Atlantis is about as real as SpongeBob's pineapple. But we want you to slap on your flippers, dive into the controversy, and judge for yourself.

Living Large in Atlantis
Atlantis was an ancient paradise island—or so the story goes. When Greek philosopher Plato first wrote the tale of Atlantis around 360 B.C., he described an idyllic island that may have been located near the Straits of Gibraltar—a waterway that separates Europe and Africa (see map).

The Atlanteans were supposedly fat cats, ruling the richest empire in the world. Three sparkling moats of water encircled a metropolis of posh palaces, with a silver-and-gold temple towering above the city's center.

Elephants and other wild animals roamed the island, and food was so plentiful that every night was like an all-you-can-eat buffet.

Shake, Rattle, and Roll
Legend has it that Atlanteans soon grew so spoiled and lazy that the Greek gods literally blew their tops! They set off earthquakes, raised the seas, and sank the city faster than you can say *blub, blub, blub*. But did Atlantis every really exist?

YES!
Explorers claim to have discovered Atlantis everywhere from Ireland to Brazil to Antarctica. So how is Sarmast's recent discovery different? He says images of an underwater island near Cyprus (see map) show evidence of walls, canals, and a temple hill that fit Plato's description perfectly. "Atlantis matches the maps of this island so closely," Sarmast says. "It just can't be coincidence."

NO!
You'd have to have seaweed for brains to believe Atlantis was real, according to some historians. "So far not a single piece of solid evidence has emerged," says Atlantis expert Richard Ellis. Others point out that Plato dated the island in the Stone Age—long before a sophisticated city could have existed. To these doubters, Atlantis is just a fable, reminding people not to be greedy and selfish—or else!

Did Atlantis really get swallowed by the sea? Who knows? But one thing's for sure: The mystery of this famous city will stay afloat for years to come.

---

first possibility, then, is to look at texts that provide a variety of information on a topic.

NEWSPAPERS

Newspapers, of course, are filled with feature articles of this type, usually grouped by broad, general topics based on the daily section divisions of the paper. The key is to get off the front-page news stories that are really *reported* more than they are researched and crafted because the news, whatever it is, just happened. The writers of feature articles find their topics; the writers of the day's top news stories are found by theirs.

MAGAZINES

Magazines of all kinds and for all audiences are filled almost exclusively with this kind of writing. The key is to start the youngest writers out with very short articles from great children's magazines like *Ranger Rick* or *American Girl*, and then move up in sophistication as students get more experience across grade levels.

PICTURE BOOKS

Perhaps because the intended audience is children and writers work hard to engage this audience, there is a true abundance of picture books that have this kind of writing inside them. There is a wide range of sophistication in them too, making the picture book container a possible anchor for studies of literary nonfiction even in middle and high school. Perhaps the hardest list for me to make as I have over a hundred of these in my personal library, here's a starter stack of a few favorites.

Titles

Bread Comes to Life: A Garden of Wheat and a Loaf to Eat	George Levenson
Gentle, Giant Octopus	Karen Wallace
On Earth	G. Brian Karas
Penny: The Forgotten Coin	Denise Brennan-Nelson
A Handful of Dirt	Raymond Bial

COLLECTIONS

Beyond the Game: The Collected Sportswriting of Gary Smith (longer pieces, mostly profiles)	Gary Smith
Girls Think of Everything: Stories of Ingenious Inventions by Women	Catherine Thimmesh
The Kid Who Invented the Trampoline: More Surprising Stories About Inventions	Don L. Wulffson
Time for Kids Almanac 2006 (a collection of all kinds of things from Time for Kids, including many short articles)	*Time for Kids*, editors
Toys! Amazing Stories Behind Some Great Inventions	Don L. Wulffson

You can find a plethora of articles about a wide range of topics by searching around on the Internet. I always scan the day's offerings on MSN when I log on and often print off short, high-interest articles to add to my file. I also check in regularly to see what the online magazine *Slate* has to offer. You can put a topic into a search engine and be taken to a variety of sites that, if they're reputable, might offer excellent articles on the topic. The trick is to make sure they look like the writer has worked to engage the reader's interest in the topic. You're not looking for online encyclopedia entries with just straight facts.

"The Truth Behind the New Movie *Shark Tale*"
Adrienne Mason

National Geographic Kids, October 2004, 28–30

So you're just a little cleaner fish minding your own business when *bam!* An anchor comes out of nowhere and squashes a great white named Frankie, the son of a grisly gangster shark. Suddenly you're a hero because everyone thinks *you're* the reason the coral reef is rid of such a big baddie.

That's what happens to Oscar in the new movie *Shark Tale*. In real life a cleaner fish, which isn't much longer than a great white shark's tooth, would *never* take on such a powerful predator. What else is a whopper of a tale in the movie? *National Geographic Kids* reels in the truth.

Table for One

Head gangster Lino likes to dine with other great white sharks in a swanky seafood restaurant. Swordfish waiters pile their plates with shrimp, oysters, salmon, and seaweed salad. But in real life these incredible hunting machines prefer to dine—and hunt—alone. And a great white's "catch of the day" would be something a bit more filling, such as a tasty seal of sea lion.

Dance Moves

Swaying her long fins that look like hair, Angie the angelfish boogies alone on her balcony. In real life an angelfish's fins are small and stubby. Instead of making the fish look cool on the dance floor, the fins help propel, steer, and brake these colorful beauties around the reef.

Wash, Wax . . . and Nibble?

Oscar makes his bucks at the Whale Wash spa, where he darts into a whale's gaping mouth to apply a tooth flossing and an under-the-tongue vacuum. Fish like Oscar, who is a bluestreak cleaner wrasse,

don't do whales, but they do help clean big fish such as eels. Fishy customers literally line up at "cleaning stations" and allow cleaner wrasses to groom them. The cleaners nibble parasites off skin and inside mouths. *Yum!*

Swell Guy

When Oscar messes up at work, watch out! His boss, Sykes the porcupine fish, can barely control his anger. "When Sykes is upset, his blood pressure rises, and he puffs out," director Vicky Jensen says. Real porcupine fish (a kind of pufferfish) do inflate two to three times their normal size, but only when they're threatened—not out of anger. The power to puff happens when the fish swallows water, which causes tiny spines to stick out of its body. It's like a floating pincushion!

What a Shocker

When jellyfish Ernie and Bernie are sent to find Oscar, the duo sneakily greets him with an electrifying *zap!* Real jellyfish do sting, but they don't use electricity. Instead, they use special cells packed with ammunition. Like tiny coiled harpoons, nematocysts fire out of the cells to sting and stun prey.

Agent Octopus

Luca the octopus slinks around corners and glides into rooms, secretly gathering information about Oscar. Real octopuses would make great spies. They sneak around rocks and crevices in search of prey. They're also masters of disguise. The skin of octopuses contains special cells called chromatophores, which are filled with different colors. An octopus can change color by contracting the muscles around the chromatophores, making the cells expand over the skin.

STUDY POSSIBILITY
Practical How-to Writing

Consider this lead to the article "Your Own Snow Village in 3 Easy Steps" in the December 2005 issue of *Southern Living*:

> Miniature houses make popular decorations this time of year, and with only a few materials, it's easy to fashion your own. Just give ready-made wooden birdhouses a quick paint-and-glitter treatment to add sparkle and shine to your home this season. It couldn't be simpler. (116)

The photograph of these lovely little houses with the caption, "One inexpensive trip to the crafts store, and you can create this display," all conspire to make me read on and see exactly how I might make a little village like this of my very own.

How-to writing does two main kinds of work. The heart of the work is to walk readers through a set of steps and show them exactly how to do something, with the expectation that they should be able to do it from the procedure that's explained. The work around that is to convince readers that they would like to know how to do this. You can find how-to's that don't do that second part of the work, but my preference for this study is to find writers who are doing both and are writing about the project in an engaging, interesting way.

NEWSPAPERS

My local paper actually has a whole how-to section on Tuesdays, and on other days I cut lots of these out of the living, home and garden sections of the paper. Just recently there was a long article on some of the history of gift wrapping and then several insets showing you how to wrap gifts in interesting ways. Look for how-to's in children's sections of newspapers, too.

MAGAZINES

Children's magazines are one of the best resources for finding short, high-interest how-to articles. *Ranger Rick*, for example, has either an advice or a how-to in it every month. Craft magazines are full of how-to articles, but they sometimes don't work as hard to engage readers and make them think the projects are interesting because people who buy craft magazines already have a built-in interest.

PICTURE BOOKS

Lots of picture books have how-to writing in them making this a great study for even the youngest writers.

Caring for My Horse	Toni Webber
Loo-Loo, Boo and Art You Can Do	Denis Roche
Making Music: 6 Instruments You Can Create	Eddie Herschel Oates
The Most Excellent *Book of How to Be a Juggler*	Mitch Mitchelson
The Usborne Book of Hair Braiding	Fiona Watt and Lisa Miles

(*Usborne actually publishes a whole series of how-to books.*)

COLLECTIONS

Crafts for Kids: Fancy Dress Book	Tessa Brown

(Crafts for Kids *is a whole series.*)

Making Faces: A Complete Guide to Face Painting	Sian Ellis-Thomas
Sneaky Uses for Everyday Things	Cy Tymony

EXCERPTS

Ultimate Kids' Money Book	Neale S. Godfrey

(*has advice, how-to, and how things are done pieces in it*)

STUDY POSSIBILITY
Informative How-to Writing

I once read a fascinating article that explained the entire process of cloning and how it happens. There was no expectation (thank goodness) that readers of this article could go off and clone for themselves after reading it; the purpose was simply to be informative and engaging.

The article about cloning represents a particular type of literary nonfiction, not a "how-to do it" (yourself) but a "how-it's-done" (so you'll know about it) kind of article. Sometimes the substance of the writer's intention is to help readers understand how something happens or how something works. The writing is fairly procedural in nature, moving through the process in an organized way, but the writer isn't trying to teach readers how to do it. For example, in this section of my notebook I have an article about how vacuum cleaners work that, believe it or not, I clipped from an airline magazine, an article about how maple syrup is harvested from trees from a Vermont travel magazine, and two articles from one issue (May/June 2002) of *Click* magazine, one explaining how guitars are made and one showing the process of silk making—from moths to weaving!

NEWSPAPERS

Feature articles in newspapers are sometimes written with this intention. Perhaps one of the most provocative, engaging articles I ever read was a *USA Today* piece that explained the process for shutting down the airspace over the United States on the morning of September 11, 2001.

MAGAZINES

Magazines are my resource for most examples of this kind of writing, and children's magazines are especially rich with them. Both *Click* and *Muse* (published by the same group who does the *Smithsonian*) are good resources for finding this kind of article.

PICTURE BOOKS (ABOUT HOW THINGS ARE MADE)

Cookies	William Jaspersohn
From Head to Toe: How a Doll Is Made	Susan Kuklin
Mosque	David Macaulay
(*Macaulay has numerous books that show how things are constructed.*)	
Pasta Factory	Hana Machotka

PICTURE BOOKS (ABOUT HOW THINGS HAPPEN)

Cow	Jules Older
Celebrating Ramadan	Diane Hoyt-Goldsmith
Fire Fighters	Norma Simon
Going to My Ballet Class	Susan Kuklin
Mail Carriers	Dee Ready
(*a whole series of these called "Community Helpers" by Capstone Press*)	

EXCERPTS

Longer works of literary nonfiction on a wide range of topics often have stand-alone excerpts that inform readers about the how something is done. For example, in the chapter length *Fire in Their Eyes: Wildfires and the People Who Fight Them* (1999) by Karen Magnuson Beil, there's a section on how a controlled burn is carried out that could stand by itself as an example of this kind of writing. Use the index and table of contents in books like this to look for topics that might have this kind of writing in them.

A Beekeeper's Year	Sylvia A. Johnson
Ultimate Kids' Money Book	Neale S. Godfrey
(*has advice, how-to, and how things are done pieces in it*)	

INTERNET

In yet another plug of the MSN website, I have to mention that I often find articles of this kind on this site.

STUDY POSSIBILITY
Advice Writing

An important subcategory of literary nonfiction is writing that gives readers advice on a topic while engaging them in thinking the topic is worth being advised about. Lots of articles and books are written with this intention. Three recent additions to my blue notebook were articles that give advice on various topics: one is on how *not* to gain weight over the holidays, one is about what to look for when buying a new sofa, and the third was on how to make a family road trip more enjoyable (i.e., bearable).

Probably the only gray area in this distinction is between writing that gives advice and writing that is designed to show how to do something, which I've called practical how-to writing. Writing that goes in my advice stack often has some recommendations about what to do or how to do something, but they are provided more as a range of options for how you might accomplish something. Notice these in the "Does Your Pet Come with Papers?" piece on page 226. They're not steps to be followed, in other words, they're more like guidelines to follow. In my how-to stack I actually have writing that's designed to teach you how to do something very specific, step by step, *and* make you think it would be a great thing to do (that's the engaging part). You might decide to lump these two kinds of writing together in a study or keep them separate.

NEWSPAPERS

All three of these recent additions to my blue notebook mentioned came from the newspaper. I usually find them in the family, life, or travel sections, though they occasionally pop up in other sections as well.

MAGAZINES

A magazine is a container rich with articles that offer advice on a wide range of topics depending on the readership of the magazine. Children's magazines frequently have this kind of article in them as well. The *Ranger Rick* article "Backyard Campout" reprinted in Chapter 6 would go in the stack of advice writing.

PICTURE BOOKS

Home Safety	Nancy Loewen
How to Be a Friend	Laurie Kransy Brown and Marc Brown
When a Pet Dies	Fred Rogers

EXCERPTS

Ultimate Kids' Money Book	Neale S. Godfrey

(*has advice, how-to, and how things are done pieces in it*)

INTERNET

By entering a topic into a search engine, you can find links to a variety of articles that give advice (make sure they're from reputable sites). As with other kinds of articles, I find lots of these on MSN and *Slate*, a recent favorite addition to my notebook being an article I found on MSN about what to do if you are attacked by a shark (hope I don't ever need that advice, but I thought it might be of interest to students).

"Does Your Pet Come with Papers? Pet Resumes Newest Trend in Lease Negotiations"
Helene Lesel

houseandhome.msn.com

Natalie Youn is in love. Her darling Maltese puppy has silky white hair and big brown eyes, whose hobbies include long walks in the park, playing fetch and chewing on slippers. What should Natalie do if she wants to have her true love, a Golden Retriever, move into her apartment?

Depends on her landlord and the rental situation. What type of pet is best? If the lease specifies "no pets" what's the best way to convince the landlord to let a dog join the household? What are the rights of the elderly and disabled?

Before picking a dog, get a collar on personality types. Every breed is known for its temperament, some more calm, others more energetic. For example, Dalmatians and Golden Retrievers love running, being high-energy sorts, and are not usually suggested as apartment dwellers. Maltese dogs, a small fluffy puff of white usually weighing less than 10 pounds, are considered by many as fine apartment dogs. A good resource for information can be found at www.dogbreedinfo.com or through your local humane society.

In San Francisco, The Open Door Program was created to foster greater acceptance and understanding of pets by landlords. A branch of The Society for the Prevention of Cruelty to Animals, the program offers the following suggestions, plus from other sources:

- **Write up a pet resume.** Include the pet's age, activity level and breed traits, preferably highlighting a history of good behavior. If the pet has been obedience trained or has special training, include that information. Include something outstanding about your pet, such as unlikely to shed (like a poodle) or slow to bark. If the pet is spayed or neutered, include that information, too.
- **Exercise.** Detail how often, when and where you will take the dog out for outdoor entertainment and relief activities. If there's a nearby park, all the better.
- **Has the pet lived in an apartment already?** If so, perhaps a letter from a previous landlord would notch up your chances.
- **Specify who your vet is and how often your pet is groomed and taken for shots.** Detail how fleas will be kept controlled. If it's a cat, mention if it is indoor only. Explain that cleanup is a priority of its litter, and is always placed in a sealed bag.
- **Include a photo of your pet, along with its name.** Seeing a picture of little Max or Sassy may just win their hearts. Mention how and why you obtained the pet if the story is particularly heartwarming. One tenant explained she was single and wanting kids—but a dog would do the trick to assuage her maternal yearnings until the right fellow came along.

Landlords may appreciate that pet owners are more familiar with the neighbors and neighborhood, and creating a sense of community. Tenants working at home, or close to home, may find that a plus when convincing landlords. Letting in the plumber is less of an issue if the tenant is available, since some tradesmen won't enter premises with a dog. Cats seem harmless, but can slip out the door and be lost. Who will have the responsibility if a pet runs away? If asked, be ready to explain.

Offer to sign a pet agreement, and provide extra deposit funds to cover any pet damage. Most state and local laws limit security deposits taken, even with the added pet deposit. Pet agreements are handy; since they supply written proof the pet owner will tend the animal as agreed. Information highlighting the name, age and breed of the pet is also included, along with date of the rental agreement. Other concerns addressed by the agreement, such as having sufficient liability insurance, are also often detailed.

For the elderly or disabled, a special place for pets is found in the Federal Housing and Urban/Rural Recovery Act, Section 227. "As a condition of tenancy or otherwise, no owner may prohibit or prevent any tenant in federally assisted housing from owning common household pets living in the dwelling accommodations."

Assistance dogs, such as dogs for the blind, have a special set of laws in many states. Refusing to rent to a person with a guide, hearing or service dog is prohibited in more than 30 states, including California, Louisiana and New York. Non-profits groups, such as Canine Companions and the Delta Society, may provide further information for those with assistance dog needs.

Above all, don't sneak in a pet and hope no one notices. Breaking a no-pet rule may be grounds for eviction, and leave you in the doghouse—with no place to call home.

STUDY POSSIBILITY
Feature Articles Based on Interviews

"Have you read the interview with Heath Ledger in *People* magazine this week? Wow, he rocks!"

If you hear something like that, then someone has been reading this kind of writing and they'll probably refer to it simply as an *interview*. Now, I suppose technically it's the interaction itself that is the *interview*, but if the person says she *read* the interview, then a writer has taken the interaction and crafted it into a piece of writing that stands alone (on paper). Written interviews are based on an actual conversation and their texts are filled with long quotes from the person who was interviewed. The writer of an interview must ask questions to get the subject to say clever and interesting things, because whatever is said is what he or she must write about. Of course, selection from *all* that is said in an oral interview down to what will be included in the article based on the interview is the central challenge of this kind of writing. From all that is said, the writer must think about what will be engaging for readers and also what will support the angle she or he wants to take in portraying the interviewee.

There is a range of sophistication in how interviews are presented in writing, from the basic question and answer format, to writers establishing setting and mode and tone for the interview ("In a noisy, crowded restaurant I saw Heath Ledger come rushing in late for our appointment, seemingly oblivious to the fact that every head was turning his way, the faded jeans and nondescript tee shirt not helping him fade at all . . . "), to a fair amount of the writer's own commentary and reflection about what is being said wrapped around the quotes from the interviewee.

As you gather texts for this study, make sure you're not gathering straight *transcripts* of interviews (and yes, sadly, this includes transcripts of Terry Gross' wonderful interviews on *Fresh Air*). You're looking for texts where writers clearly intended to craft the interview as a piece of writing itself.

NEWSPAPERS

You will find interviews published in newspapers (in special sections for children and teenagers, too), often as feature pieces highlighting political, sports, and entertainment personalities, but also, sometimes, everyday people touched by triumph or tragedy. Here's a starter stack of places to find written interviews.

• Janis Campbell and Cathy Collison regularly write great articles based on interviews with children's authors for "Yak's Corner" in *The Detroit Free Press*. Find them at www.freep.com. The link to Yak's Corner is at the very bottom of the homepage.

• In the Kids Scoops section of *Time for Kids* you can find interviews conducted and then written up by children. The writing isn't as sophisticated as it is in articles written by adults, but they're still good starters. Check out www.timeforkids.com.

MAGAZINES

Magazines (of all kinds, those for adults and those for children) are the main sources where I find interviews as they are a very common kind of feature piece in these containers. The entertainment sections of *Time*, for example, often contain quite wonderful, sophisticated write-ups of interviews. I have one on Jamie Foxx in my blue notebook that I clipped from the October 18, 2004, issue.

PICTURE BOOKS

I don't know of any interviews published in the container of picture books. I wouldn't be surprised to find one there, but I've never actually seen it.

COLLECTIONS

There are collections of articles based on interviews. Perhaps because of my own interests as a teacher of writing, my stack of these is heavy on collections of interviews with writers. Here's a short starter stack.

Authors by Request	Janis Campbell and Cathy Collison
Author Talk	Leonard S. Marcus
The Book of Changes: A Collection of Interviews	Kristine McKenna
Talking with Artists, Vols. 1–3	Pat Cummings

While there are lots of interviews available online (Scholastic's website publishes wonderful interviews with authors who write for children), many of them are simply transcripts of interviews and there's been no attempt to craft them as pieces of writing.

STUDY POSSIBILITY
Exploring Possibilities

List Articles

20 Quick Family Getaways. A Roundup of Hot DVDs for Children This Holiday Season. Eight Books to Carry You Through the Snow Days. Seven Reasons to Be Thankful in the Thanksgiving Season. 5 Video Games Worth Sore Thumbs.

You know these kinds of articles; they're very, very common. In them, writers present readers with a list of possibilities inside a particular category of possibilities. Part of the writer's work is to cull the list of possibilities down to the few she or he decides to write about. With a lead designed to convince readers they need to consider these possibilities, the writer then moves through the list in an almost minireview sort of way, the challenge being to help readers understand why this particular item made it to the list while other possibilities did not. Sometimes there is some compare and contrast work between the different possibilities, but often not. Often they are presented simply as separate, distinct options.

The only real gray area for me around this kind of writing was whether to include it in the resource sections on genre or with study possibilities other than genre (it would go with a study of text structure if I put it there). I decided to put it here because, while writers can fulfill all sorts of intentions with writing like this, the nature of this kind of article is so distinct in the world of articles. Readers know this kind of writing and expect certain things from it, making it almost a genre unto itself.

You will have to decide whether you want to study this particular kind of article by itself or look at it simply as one possibility for how literary nonfiction can be written.

NEWSPAPERS

I find these kinds of articles in the feature sections of newspapers all the time.

MAGAZINES

Hardly a magazine is published that doesn't have at least one of these in it somewhere.

INTERNET

Lots and lots of these on the online news magazines and websites.

STUDY POSSIBILITY
Biographical Sketches and Profiles

If you're wondering why I don't just call this *biography*, it's because if you go into a bookstore and ask for *biography*, the clerk will take you to a section of very long chapter books. I don't think that's what you want your students to write. Is there a kind of writing in the world that comes from biographical research but is much shorter and more focused? Yes. The picture book biography is a popular genre, and lots of news magazines will run short biographical sketches, sometimes called profiles, of prominent people from time to time as well. The central challenge of this kind of writing is to look at a theme or an idea *across* a person's life, but to do it in a very focused way in a limited space of text.

Often, teachers will select this kind of writing as a study thinking, "Well, we already do reports on famous people, so this is really the same thing." It's not, actually, the same thing. It's not even close, really. Picture book biographies and short biographical sketches in newspapers and magazines are highly engaging to read because they are filled with anecdotes that illustrate important themes in a person's life. Most school reports on famous people are fact driven, not anecdote driven, and often students don't even have access to the kind of research that will lead them to the anecdotal evidence they'll need to do this kind of writing well.

And what about the intentions of this kind of writing? Most of the time, writers are drawn to biographical research because they have a fascination with a person's life. You see this intention reiterated time and again if you read the author's notes that accompany these texts. If students are going to do this kind of writing, it's probably a good idea for them to find those same intentions for themselves and be allowed to choose someone who truly fascinates them and is researchable. Too often when students are asked to do this kind of writing, they are forced to choose from famous scientists, inventors, statesmen, or, you name it, whatever has been studied in another content area. If you want the writing to be really good, let them find the intention from their own fascination with a person.

NEWSPAPERS

In the feature sections of newspapers you often find biographical sketches. I recently cut one out of the October 13, 2005 *Asheville Citizen-Times* and added it to my blue notebook. The short piece is about Popcorn Sutton, a self-proclaimed moonshiner who lives nearby in Maggie Valley, and it highlights his life from the time he took his first taste of "likker" at age six to the present when he is gathering notes for a second book he wants to write about his life. The first was published in 1999. Keep an eye out and biographical sketches will appear in your newspaper.

MAGAZINES

Biography magazine is devoted entirely to writing that comes from research into people's lives, and there are a variety of formats used to craft this research into engaging features throughout the magazine. Most of the major news magazines will have features from time to time that clearly have been written from biographical research, and children's magazines will have them sometimes, too.

PICTURE BOOKS

There are lots of picture book biographies to choose from out there. I would look especially for the ones not written by full-time biographers. I believe writers who don't usually write in this genre but choose to do it because of their fascination with a person, come to the writing with different intentions. It seems to me that these writers are truly drawn to the idea of the person they're writing about more than the genre itself. Here's a starter stack of picture book biographies.

Celia Cruz, Queen of Salsa	Veronica Chambers
Handel Who Knew What He Liked	M.T. Anderson
Little Stevie Wonder	Quincy Troupe
Mother to Tigers	George Ella Lyon
Talkin' About Bessie: The True Story of	Nikki Grimes
Aviator Elizabeth Coleman	

COLLECTIONS

There are lots of collections of short biographical sketches, but some of them are not very engaging to read. The texts in them sound more like encyclopedia entries. Professional biographers usually write these to be placed in school libraries so children can do research on famous people. That's not what you're looking for. Following the same advice for picture book selection, look for writers who came to the genre because of a true fascination with the people they are researching. When this is the case, the writers will work harder to make you think the people are fascinating, too. Here's a starter stack.

The Blues Singers: Ten Who Rocked the World	Julius Lester
The Book of Rock Stars: 24 Musical Icons That Shine Through History	Kathleen Krull
Ladies First: Women Athletes Who Made a Difference	Ken Rappoport
Lives of the Athletes: Thrills, Spills (and What the Neighbors Thought)	Kathleen Krull
Margaret, Frank and Andy: Three Writers' Stories	Cynthia Rylant

EXCERPTS

I find the idea of using an excerpt from a chapter-length biography in this study problematic. Such an excerpt would almost certainly have a very narrow window of time it covers in the person's life, and the challenge of short biography is to cover more time in less space.

INTERNET

Check out www.biography.com as a great start.

STUDY POSSIBILITY
Editorials, Commentary, and All Things Op-ed

When Leonard Pitts won the Pulitzer prize for *commentary* in 2004, it caused me to learn something new about the label—*editorial*—that I'd been using for his writing. I learned that technically, the label *editorial* refers quite specifically to the official opinion of the newspaper itself on an issue. All the other writing by columnists on the op-ed pages is referred to as *commentary* and it is the work of this writing to comment on what's going on in the world of politics, culture, and society. In other words, anything that's current and happening and people are talking about might be the subject of commentary. There is also a rich tradition of sports commentary about what's happening in the sports world, but it's typically found in the sports section, not on the op-ed page.

In contrast to editorials, which are most often published without bylines as they are meant to represent the position of the paper itself (not one person's thoughts or opinions), commentary is often printed with the writer's photograph beside it so readers can see exactly who it is that is expressing the opinion in the writing.

In a study of writing on the op-ed page (lumping editorials and commentary together), you'll see writers doing a range of work. Some pieces will communicate the clear positioning we typically think of in an editorial, stating a strong opinion up front and working hard to convince readers of the validity of that opinion. Other pieces will be much more essay like, taking readers on a journey of thought that *ends* with the important idea rather than starting with it, the intention seeming less about *convincing* than it is about *provoking*. As you might imagine, editorials tend to do more of the clear positioning work, though recently the editorial in our local paper was a thoughtful, reflective piece about the passing of two icons over that weekend, Richard Pryor and Eugene McCarthy, so this doesn't always hold true. You'll see that range of work in both editorials and commentary by individual columnists.

NEWSPAPERS

Newspapers are the most obvious place to find this kind of writing, and most large papers have at least two pages to the op-ed section most every day and one or more pieces of sports commentary each day, too. Follow columnists you like by accessing them through newspaper archives on the Internet, and look for examples that would be high interest for the students you teach. I recently cut one out that's about the ongoing wrangle over whether to say "Merry Christmas" or "Happy Holidays" to patrons in public business spaces. *USA Today* (access it online) has great (and short!) op-ed writing on issues from all around the country. Here's a short list of newspaper columnists I look for regularly.

Susan Ager	*Detroit Free Press*
Mitch Albom (mostly sports)	*Detroit Free Press*
Mike Lopresti (sports)	Gannett News Service
Kathleen Parker	Tribune Media Services
Leonard Pitts	*The Miami Herald*

MAGAZINES

Depending on the topics the writers have chosen, certainly some of the writing published on the back pages of magazines under the label *essay* could fit into this stack of texts. If the writer is commenting on something that is current and happening, then the work of the essay is the work of commentary. For the most part, I classify most of Rick Reilly's columns on the back page of *Sports Illustrated* each week as commentary as he is often taking on something everyone is talking about in the world of sports and giving readers his take on it.

COLLECTIONS

Kick Ass: Selected Columns of Carl Hiaasen	Carl Hiaasen
The Life of Reilly: The Best of Sports Illustrated's *Rick Reilly*	Rick Reilly
Loud and Clear	Anna Quindlen
(*Just as with* Thinking Out Loud, *some essays are more personal in this collection, but many others are good examples of the work of commentary.*)	
Paradise Screwed: Selected Columns of Carl Hiaasen	Carl Hiaasen

INTERNET

I have recently discovered that amazon.com actually sells downloads of works of commentary from popular columnists such as Kathleen Parker, Mitch Albom, Leonard Pitts, and others. While this certainly represents another way to access commentary, I find it easier to simply check into the archives of their respective papers or news services periodically and see what they've published.

STUDY POSSIBILITY
ABC Texts

The cover of the December 5, 2005 issue of *Time* says, "The Year in Medicine from A to Z." Seeing only this title, I had clear expectations about what I would find when I opened to this article, and sure enough, the long, lead piece is written in an alphabet structure beginning with "acupuncture" and ending with "zinc."

The alphabet text is the only text structure I ever suggest as a study by itself and the reason I do is because it is an icon in terms of its recognition in the world of readers. Many people have a very deep, old connection to alphabet books, and while the structure can do the work of many genres, the ABC text is really almost a genre unto itself.

One of the reasons I feel alphabet texts can stand alone as a study is because there is so much room for students to make different decisions in terms of how their texts will be crafted, even when everyone is writing an alphabet text. Writers use these texts to fulfill a wide variety of different genre intentions, from memoir to short story to lead feature article in a major news magazine, so students can decide what kind of meaning work they'd like their alphabet texts to accomplish. In addition to the genre and topic decisions, how the letters of the alphabet are used in the written text varies widely and students will have to figure this out as well.

PICTURE BOOKS

M Is for Music	Kathleen Krull
P Is for Putt: A Golf Alphabet	Brad Herzog
The Racecar Alphabet	Brian Flora

EXCERPTS

D Is for Dahl: A Gloriumptious A–Z Guide to the World of Roald Dahl	Wendy Cooling
(*very interesting, chapter book–length ABC book*)	

STUDY POSSIBILITY
Reviews

All kinds of marketable things in the world are reviewed in writing: books, movies, music, plays, restaurants, and all sorts of products from video games to refrigerators to lawn mowers. Reviews are written to give helpful advice to consumers about the content and/or quality of something that's being marketed. Reviews aren't the highest literary art form, perhaps, but they're a common, useful kind of writing in the world. And a good review does ask that the writer convey clear, informed judgments or descriptions of something and back these up with specific detail to support them.

If you'd like to study reviews, you'll need to decide whether you want to look at them in general and consider a variety of kinds. In this case students would then decide which kind to write as well as what they would review. Or you might study just one type of review and have everyone write that kind, choosing their own book, movie, restaurant, or whatever you've studied to review.

And here's the good news. Gathering reviews is a no-brainer. They're very easy to find. One note on gathering: while there are some reviews that are collected into volumes, particularly those for products and restaurants, they tend to be less engaging to read than those published in newspapers and magazines. This is likely because the collections are used as reference tools and readers go to them with a built-in desire to read them. Reviews published as features in the media must work harder to make readers stop and read them, and so they are usually much more carefully crafted in terms of working to engage the reader.

NEWSPAPERS

Practically all newspapers of any size and heft carry reviews of all kinds. Often, newspaper reviews are weekly features rather than daily, with different kinds of things reviewed on different days. Children's sections of newspapers certainly review products of interest to children, but you find these in the adult sections as well. For example, it's the holiday season as I'm writing this, so we are getting three or four reviews of new toys in the paper weekly. I just added two to my

"*Shrek 2:* Movie Review"
Chris Vognar

Dallas Morning News, May 21, 2004

L ike its predecessor, *Shrek 2* is both sweet and low-down. That's an odd combination in Hollywood, but it works like a charm for this big green franchise.

Even more than the first one, *Shrek 2* is the ultimate fractured fairy tale. It makes fun of the conventions at every turn, but it also makes them hip, relevant and often literal (much of the action takes place in the kingdom of Far, Far Away). This second helping of ogre fires off zinger after zinger and digs deep into its bag of irreverent pop culture references (everything from Joan Rivers to *From Here to Eternity*). And it maintains a high level of smart cuteness, working the "beauty isn't just skin deep" theme that helped make *Shrek* such a winner.

Where most of *Shrek* unfolded in the great wide open of a mock hero's quest, this one starts off as a domestic saga. Shrek (still the voice of Mike Myers) and Fiona (still Cameron Diaz) have settled in the swamp, their love undiminished. Donkey (Eddie Murphy) remains in tow. But soon it's time to meet Fiona's royal folks (fine voice performances from John Cleese and Julie Andrews), who would rather have a human daughter and son-in-law than a pair of ogres.

As if that weren't enough stress, a materialistic Fairy Godmother (Jennifer Saunders of *Absolutely Fabulous* fame) and her shallow son, Prince Charming (Rupert Everett), are scheming to turn Fiona back into a human so she can become Mrs. Charming.

Ms. Saunders's plump, busty Fairy Godmother is one of the film's best conceits; she lords over her potion mega corporation like a ruthless, two-faced CEO. But the most inspired new character is the passive-aggressive Puss-in-Boots, voiced by a wickedly self-parodying Antonio Banderas.

Hired by the weak-willed king to off his daughter's big, green husband, Puss turns out to be, well, something of a pussycat. He snarls and claws at his foes, but uses his big, soft kitty-cat eyes when they're more appropriate to the task at hand. He's also a gleeful send-up of chivalry and, in typical *Shrek* fashion, ends up being quite chivalrous.

Shrek 2 is fast and goofy, more frenetic than its predecessor and prone to short lulls when the gags and poop jokes go flat. But it's also loaded with grace notes and details that make fallen jokes forgivable. Many of these grace notes are struck on the soundtrack, a savvy mix of scene-appropriate pop cuts from the likes of Tom Waits, Nick Cave and the Bad Seeds, and Butterfly Boucher, doing a knock-out cover of David Bowie's "Changes." Then there's the road to Far, Far Away, a mix of medieval décor and conspicuous brand names. The barrage of product placements goes overboard, but they add a great deal of texture and color to the CGI sets.

Shrek 2's creative team, which includes three directors and four screenwriters, knows its way around the pop culture landscape. A partial list of targets includes O.J. Simpson, *Cops*, *Spider-Man*, *Mission Impossible* and Bob Barker. The references would be a lot more superfluous if they weren't integrated so well into the movie's overall scheme.

But *Shrek 2*'s deft balancing act is its real charm. On one level, the movie is silly, slick pop art. But the packaging helps guide some valuable lessons without overt moralizing. Love who you want to love, go beyond superficial appearances, and always try to be yourself. These are lessons worthy of a modern fairy tale, one that tears away at old ideas of "happily ever after" and creates new ones of its own.

---

notebook today, one for a "Finding Nemo" video game for preschoolers, and one for a remote controlled super car that climbs walls (how cool is that?).

MAGAZINES

Magazines are another container rich with reviews, and depending on the kind of magazine and its readership, different kinds of things are reviewed in different ways. For those of you who teach middle school, NCTE's journal *Voices from the*

Middle regularly publishes book reviews written by students, and *Stone Soup* often has them as well.

INTERNET

In addition to the archives of magazines and newspapers, there are a few sites I go to regularly to build my collections of reviews. For book reviews, I actually use amazon.com quite often. If you pull up a book title and scroll down to the very bottom of the page, Amazon includes usually three to four different reviews of the book from sources like Kirkus and the American Library Association. These are fairly concise reviews, perfect for second and third graders studying them for the first time.

At www.bookloons.com you can find hundreds of book reviews. The site is updated often and it also includes lots of "list" articles where short reviews are combined under some theme.

The other site I use often is www.rottentomatoes.com. On this site you can type in the name of any movie and it will give you links to newspapers all over the country that have reviewed it. Anytime a new movie for children comes out, I go on and find several good reviews of it to add to my collection. The site also connects you to reviews of video games. I probably wouldn't study reviews of video games as a class study (especially since I have trouble reading them), but I like knowing where to find them because students might be interested in writing them as back-up work.

Book Review

"Review of audio for *Because of Winn Dixie*"
Lori Craft

School Library Journal

Gr 4–6. In this audio version of Kate DiCamillo's Newbery Honor book (Candlewick, 2000), ten-year-old Opal Buloni's life is changed for the better when she takes in a stray dog she finds running wild in a grocery store. With Winn-Dixie (named after the store she found him in) by her side, Opal starts to make friends in the small town of Naomi, Florida where she has recently moved. More importantly, she is able to come to terms with her feelings about her mother who abandoned her years earlier. Performed by Tony award-winning actress Cherry Jones, this is one of the few audio books that actually transcends the book itself. The story is presented through Opal's first person point of view, and Cherry Jones becomes southern-twanged Opal, sharing the story of her first summer in Naomi. Jones' seamless performance is honest and believable, and she pulls listeners in like a master storyteller. This great production of an award-winning book definitely belongs in every library audio collection.

"Book review of *Because of Winn Dixie*"
Emilie Coulter

Amazon.com

Because of Winn-Dixie, a big, ugly, happy dog, 10-year-old Opal learns 10 things about her long-gone mother from her preacher father. Because of Winn-Dixie, Opal makes new friends among the somewhat unusual residents of her new hometown, Naomi, Florida. Because of Winn-Dixie, Opal begins to find her place in the world and let go of some of the sadness left by her mother's abandonment seven years earlier.

With her newly adopted, goofy pooch at her side, Opal explores her bittersweet world and learns to listen to other people's lives. This warm and winning book hosts an unforgettable cast of characters, including a librarian who fought off a bear with a copy of *War and Peace*, an ex-con pet-store clerk who plays sweet music to his animal charges, and the neighborhood "witch," a nearly blind woman who sees with her heart. Part Frankie (*The Member of the Wedding*), part Scout (*To Kill a Mockingbird*), Opal brings her own unique and wonderful voice to a story of friendship, loneliness, and acceptance. Opal's down-home charm and dead-on honesty will earn her friends and fans far beyond the confines of Naomi, Florida. (Ages 9 and older)

STUDY POSSIBILITY
News Reporting

There are two kinds of news reporting in most newspapers. The short pieces of news that come from the wire services and usually don't have bylines are not the kinds of news I would study in a writing workshop. They are voiceless, just-the-facts-m'am pieces of writing.

The other news reporting is where writers have "covered" a story, asked questions, interviewed people who were there, found out important background information about what happened, and basically tried to get as many facts as they can to write an interesting, engaging news story. This is what I would study if I were going to study news reporting in the writing workshop, and of course, examples of this kind of writing will be very, very easy to find.

The real teaching challenge in a study of news reporting is making a commitment to help students choose a newsworthy topic of interest to them and then truly cover it as a news story. They can't do that sitting in a classroom, and so you'll have to think through the logistics of getting them out into the neighborhood to find some news to cover. And a personal pet peeve (but that's all it is), I don't think students should be writing news stories about things that happened in history. That's not news, it's history, and in the world outside school news reporting is writing about things that are happening now, things that are truly *news*. By the way, that's what separates this kind of writing in a newspaper or magazine from other feature articles: the current-event-status of the topic the reporter is covering.

NEWSPAPERS

I guess it goes without saying that this is where you find this kind of writing. But one point I'd like to make is that children's sections of newspapers often have some good "beginner" kinds of news reporting about topics of high interest to children and are sometimes written by children themselves.

News magazines (for adults) certainly have news reporting in them that is typically longer and more in-depth than what you find in many newspapers. Studying articles of this sort would probably be most appropriate for more advanced writers in high school. However, news magazines for children and teens such as *Time for Kids* and *Junior Scholastic* also have articles based on news reporting.

STUDY POSSIBILITY
Photo Essay

A photo essay serves the same intentions as an essay, but the journey of thought moves through a series of text and photographs. To truly be a photo essay, the text should be more than just captions, and the photographs should add significant meaning to the text. The two basically carry equal weight in developing the journey of thought. Of course, herein lies the gray area: what does "more than just captions" mean and how do you determine equal weight? What I'm looking for is a composition where the photographs really seem to matter. In other words, they couldn't have been added on after the text was written. It needs to feel like the photographs helped *generate* the text itself and were a crucial part of the composing. I know, still gray area, but hopefully helpful to your thinking.

I could put lots of "coffee table books" in my stack of photo essays, though I have to make sure the text is doing a lot of the meaning work, and the series of photos really does take the reader on a journey of thinking about the topic. In some beautiful books of this type the text is really just captioning the photos—they don't work together in any way.

NEWSPAPERS

At the end of the year, many newspapers will often include a photo essay and title it something like, "The year in pictures." Sometimes you'll also find photo essays in newspapers after a major event of some historical significance: the events of 9/11, Hurricane Katrina, the end of a President's term in office, the Boston Red Sox winning the World Series . . . (I in no way put these events together to equate them or trivialize them—they are simply the kinds of events that often prompt photo essays).

MAGAZINES

Basically the same thing is true for magazines as for newspapers. Newsmagazines especially will use photo essays to revisit significant events or periods of time.

10,000 Days of Thunder: A History of the Vietnam War	Philip Caputo
A Cool Drink of Water	Barbara Kerley
Kindsight	Robert Zukerman
Priceless: The Vanishing Beauty of a Fragile Planet	Bradley Trevor Greive (Photos by: Mitsuaki Iwago)
Remember: The Journey to School Integration	Toni Morrison

Without the distance and reflection of memoir, without the journey of thought inherent in personal essay, lots of writers simply take the truth and fabric of everyday life and craft it into literature. Readers enjoy reading "slice-of-life" pieces because they identify with the uniquely human need to share life and the spirit of life with others.

Some of the slice-of-life writing in my stack is more narrative driven in mode, the text moving through events in time, the writer telling a good story that really happened (once or many times) so others might enjoy the vicarious experience of it. In schools, we often use the label *personal narrative* for this kind of writing, but that label is problematic because the rest of the reading world outside school rarely uses it. The other picture books and news and magazine features in my stack of slice-of-life writing don't move through events in time. They're about topics of interest in people's everyday lives: family, friends, work, love, loss, and so on, but they're not stories per se.

Usually written from a first-person stance, the intention in slice-of-life writing seems to be simply to share these stories and bits of life with others who might be interested because, well, they live too! There is some gray area in the slice-of-life distinction, particularly concerning when something leans more toward personal essay than slice-of-life, but most of the time the distinction is fairly easy to make. With picture book examples, of which there are many, I just look for anything that sounds like a writer taking a slice-of-life stance, not worrying about whether the first-person stance is from their own experience or not. The choice to write about an everyday life topic in a personal way is what I'm looking for.

NEWSPAPERS

Most newspapers have columnists who write slice-of-life pieces for the family or living sections of the paper. Susan Reinhardt is a columnist in my local paper, *The Asheville Citizen-Times*, who does this kind of writing. A recent addition to my notebook was a humorous piece by Reinhardt about attending a Christmas

"Murphy the Dog: A Gift Who Kept on Giving"
Craig Wilson

USA Today, March 23, 2005

Our dog Murphy died last week, on her bed in the corner of the dining room just before noon on a cool but sunny late winter's day. The kind of day she loved most.

She was 14, plus a few months. A good long life.

We knew the end was near, but we weren't ready. No one ever is. How could you be?

As she lay dying, I wrapped her in an old afghan, sat down on the floor next to her and waited. And when her labored breathing finally came to an end and her cloudy eyes stared off in the distance, I had a good cry. Just Murphy and me.

Dog people will understand. Those who say, "It was just a dog. Get over it," will not.

But I'm not writing to those people today. I'm writing to those who know what joy a dog can bring. And Murphy brought us great joy. I don't think there was a day she didn't make me laugh.

My partner, Jack, always said she was an angel sent to us from above. I'm not sure "angel" is the right word, and our neighbors would surely agree with that. But I understand. She was a gift, as all dogs are.

Yes, she was just a dog. But she was our dog. And we loved her. Quirks and all.

Murphy was a soft-coated wheaten terrier, a feisty lot, and she more than lived up to her Irish clan's reputation. She had her definite likes and dislikes, from the mailman (pure evil) to fashion (keep it simple).

She never tolerated poorly dressed people. She could spot them a block away. A sinister-looking hat. A too-long coat. Furry boots. All of that sent her into a barking frenzy, exposing fashion victims for what they were.

Hundreds of times I crossed the street, never knowing what to say. "Sorry, my dog doesn't like your outfit" never seemed quite right.

For years, we spent each morning in the woods of D.C.'s Rock Creek Park, exploring. And that included the creek. Murphy took to water like her ancestors took to Guinness.

She'd wade out until she was just covered, then wag her tiny tail so furiously that a fountain of spray would appear at her rear, an act people came from far and wide to see.

And back home, tired at the end of the day, she'd claim my seat the moment I stood up. I then moved on to another perch. It just seemed the natural thing to do.

Her dying in the dining room seemed right. She spent so much time there, sitting by my chair, waiting for whatever would "drop" her way. She preferred white meat and warm buttered rolls, but she wasn't choosy. She accepted all gifts from above.

But in the end, she would give the ultimate gift: Dying at home on her terms. No vet. No needle. No final trip in the car with her in my arms.

Where Murphy once raced through the woods and into the creek, our new pup, Maggie, will follow come summer.

With any luck, there will be another 14 years of sunrise strolls, dropped rolls, lost seats.

And, over time, Maggie will grow to know us as well as Murphy once did, and love us just the same. Quirks and all.

Because that's what dogs do.

---

cookie exchange party with other women in her neighborhood. Craig Wilson is a regular slice-of-life columnist for *USA Today* whose work I really like. I check his archived columns regularly.

MAGAZINES

Magazines of all kinds, but especially women's magazines, often have feature pieces that fulfill the intentions of slice-of-life writing. These can show up in features and columns with all sorts of labels, so you want to be on the lookout for a writer taking that first-person, slice-of-life stance. Local magazines often have a fair amount of slice-of-writing in them as the readership closely identifies with stories of life in the area.

PICTURE BOOKS (MORE NARRATIVE DRIVEN)

Beekeepers	Linda Oatman High
Camping	Nancy Hundal
Car Wash	Sandra Steen and Susan Steen
Come On, Rain!	Karen Hesse
Puddles	Jonathan London

PICTURE BOOKS (NONNARRATIVE)

Big Sister, Little Sister	LeUyen Pham
In My New Yellow Shirt	Eileen Spinelli
Loki & Alex	Charles R. Smith, Jr.
One of Three	Angela Johnson
When You Visit Grandma & Grandpa	Anne Bowen

COLLECTIONS

In My Momma's Kitchen   Jerdine Nolen
(*a picture book, but written as separate vignettes*)
The Fun of It: Stories from The Talk   Lillian Ross, editor
    of the Town
(*a collection of pieces from the popular column in* The New Yorker)
Guys Write for Guys Read   Jon Scieszka, editor
(*a few selections I would categorize as slice-of-life*)

"Baby, It's Cold"
Steve Bender

Southern Living, January 2005

When my wife, Judy, tells me she was born and raised in Birmingham, I don't need to see her birth certificate to know that it's true. All I need to do is record the times she tells me that she's cold.

She's cold in the morning. She's cold at night. She's cold on Mondays, Wednesdays, and Fridays. She's cold at church. She's cold in the mall. And in winter, her feet are the coldest objects in our solar system outside of the British Royal Family.

Like Judy, many Southerners express discomfort at temperatures that people from other places around the world consider positively balmy. If the famed 19th-century explorer Henry Morton Stanley had been from the South, his first words upon meeting David Livingstone in the jungles of Tanzania would have been, "Dr. Livingstone, I presume you'll turn down the AC. This rain forest is freezing."

I don't know the physical reasons for this. Maybe warm-weather Southerners have no hemoglobin. Maybe they have only one artery in their bodies. Maybe they can't tell when they're dead. What I do know is that if global warming proves to be nothing but a theory, a lot of Southerners will be gravely disappointed.

Not me. I grew up in Maryland (aka the Upper South). I know what real cold is. Real cold is when you go to start your car in sub-zero January, and the battery files a lawsuit. Real cold is when you jockey in the morning to be the last person in the bathroom. (Those icicles are sharp.)

I'll never forget the work conference I attended some years ago on the Alabama Gulf Coast. It was May at Gulf Shores, and I engaged in an act so unspeakably weird that it rendered my colleagues as well as other bystanders speechless: I went swimming.

As soon as my body hit the 75-degree water, a collective gasp from the incredulous crowd sucked in sufficient air to form a low-pressure system. "Is he loony?" they all wondered aloud. "Doesn't he have the sense to know that you don't go swimming in May when it's cold?"

Judy doesn't swim in May. She doesn't swim in June either. In fact, she won't put an ankle in the water until it's warm enough to cook a three-minute egg.

It's no wonder Southerners cringe at the thought of leaving home and moving north. We're not talking about moving to Fargo, North Dakota. We're talking about people who shiver at the thought of relocating to Tulsa. It's just too cold.

Sometime in the not-too-distant future, humankind will visit other worlds. Momentum at NASA favors an outpost on Mars, but Southerners should push for one on Venus instead. Mars, after all, is freezing most of the time, while the Venusian surface maintains a steady 890 degrees.

Judy says that's just about right.

STUDY POSSIBILITY
Topical Writing

I have no idea exactly what to call this kind of writing; *topical* is a bit of a default label for it. But I can make a big, tall stack of it from my picture books. In these books, writers take a place, a person, an object, a season or time, an animal—some *thing* that can be described and they write a full, rich description of it that stands alone. The intention in the writing seems almost to pay tribute to the topic, or to help the reader see it in a new way, a closer way. It's different from feature article writing because the factual, informative intentions aren't there. The writer really has just tried to describe the topic from a variety of different angles.

Descriptive writing would seem to be the logical label for this kind of writing, but that's not something you can ask for in the bookstore and I don't think it's the operational label writers have when they're envisioning this kind of text. Depending on how much work there is to help you see the topic through new eyes, the books might be called *descriptive essays*. *Scarecrow* (1998) by Cynthia Rylant seems almost essaylike in this way.

Outside the container of picture books, I believe the texts that most closely match this kind of writing are descriptions of places in travel magazines, and perhaps, descriptions of food in cookbooks or culinary magazines. I believe this would be an interesting study possibility all the way through high school (using picture books to anchor the study) because the mode of the writing, description, is used in so many other kinds of writing and learning to write it well will serve many varied intentions.

PICTURE BOOKS

There's a list of these kinds of books in Chapter 4. Here are five more about a wide range of topics.

Appalachia: Voices of Sleeping Birds	Cynthia Rylant
(a classic and longer example, very essaylike)	
Canoe Days	Gary Paulsen
Long Night Moon	Cynthia Rylant
Rock of Ages	Tonya Bolden
Under New York	Linda Oatman High

STUDY POSSIBILITY
Survey of Different Kinds of Writing in the World

If students are fairly new to the work of a writing workshop, it might be a good idea to simply study the different kinds of published writing that exist in the world, the purposes they serve, the intentions they fulfill for the people writing them, and the kinds of topics they address. This can be a great study to launch a workshop because one thing you want students to do is get up and going with some independent projects that can become their over time, back-up work (see Chapter 11 for a discussion of this).

You might have students look at any or all of the kinds of writing suggested in these resource sections, plus the multitudes of others not covered here because they don't seem to me to make much sense for whole-class study. This might include things like notes inside CD covers, scripts for plays, mysteries, cookbooks, advice columns, science fiction, advertising and catalogue copy—basically anything written for an audience. Let students help you gather all kinds of writing and then work together to stack them by genre. As part of the inquiry, you might also have students sort all the writing inside a magazine, a newspaper, or a stack of picture books.

The goal of this study would be first to simply help students understand the concept of genre and what this means to them as writers. Studies of specific genres seem to make more sense in the context of genre conceptually—that there are different kinds of writing in the world written for a variety of purposes. The second goal of a study like this is to help students plan for kinds of writing they would like to do during the year when the genre they choose is optional in showing the work of a unit of study.

STUDY POSSIBILITY
Multigenre Writing

Sometimes writers combine several different kinds of writing in the creation of a single text, creating a sort of writing collage on a given topic. Based on the topic, these multigenre texts can do the combined work of memoir, poetry, feature article, essay, recipe—basically any kind of writing—in a single text. Because of the layout and illustrative possibilities in picture books, multigenre texts are actually easy to find in this container.

PICTURE BOOKS

Diamond Life (about baseball) and *Rimshots* (about basketball)	Charles R. Smith, Jr.
Discover the Seasons	Diane Iverson
Double Dutch: A Celebration of Jump Rope, Rhyme, and Sisterhood	Veronica Chambers
From Slave Ship to Freedom Road	Julius Lester
Katja's Book of Mushrooms	Katya Arnold and Sam Swope

STUDY POSSIBILITY
How Writers Use Punctuation as a Crafting Tool

"Santa arrived here Saturday. And there was no room for him in the inn.
    Not the Holiday Inn. Not the Pfister. Not the Hyatt. Not the Wyndham.
Not the Hilton. All full. Sorry, big guy, but you should have called ahead."

I clipped the feature article where this was the lead from the November 19, 2000 *Milwaukee Journal Sentinel* when I was attending NCTE. Crocker Stephenson, the writer, made some interesting punctuation decisions here and throughout the article, and I wanted to add it to my collection to support studies of writers who do this.

At every grade level, kindergarten through college, I think this is an interesting, important study in a writing workshop. The nuances of punctuation and how it can be used in so many ways to make writing interesting and to communicate a writer's voice are just endlessly fascinating. This is not a study of marks; it's a study of the interesting decisions writers make about punctuation as they craft their texts. And I don't believe there is any prerequisite punctuation knowledge students need to have to engage in this study either. "It is what it is," as my husband likes to say, and what punctuation is is a tool invented by humans to help us get words down on paper so they sound and mean the way we want them to sound and mean when we're not there to speak them. Think about how different this passage would sound and mean if the writer hadn't made the punctuation (and paragraphing) decisions he made.

The youngest writers might anchor this study in picture books with lots of interesting punctuation decisions in them, but older writers can anchor lots of their study in excerpts from novels, feature articles, essays, memoirs, and basically any kind of writing. Excerpts from several pieces I've shown in this book could go in a study of how writers use punctuation in interesting ways to craft their texts: the Leonard Pitts piece in Chapter 7, for example, or the Nancy Gibbs essay from *Time* (on page 210) could both be studied in this unit. Basically you and your students need to be on the lookout any time you're reading for writers who are "showing off" with punctuation, making clearly deliberate, interesting decisions about how the text is going down on the page, and save these for this study.

The goal of a study like this is to deepen students' understandings about punctuation and its potentials. To show what they've learned in a study like this, students can choose a topic and genre for a piece of writing they'd like to do, craft the piece with some interesting punctuation decisions, and then articulate why they made the decisions they made.

Punctuation decisions are found wherever people are writing, and lots of them are interesting if you pay attention to them, so I don't need to go through the various containers for this study. You may remember, however, that in Chapter 1 there is a list of ten picture books Lisa Cleaveland used for this study in her first-grade class.

STUDY POSSIBILITY
How Illustrations and Graphics Enhance Meaning

While this study is such an important study for the youngest writers who need illustrations to carry lots of meaning in their writing, I'd like to suggest that this is an interesting study even for middle and high school students. In the world where these students will grow to be competent writers, composition isn't just about written text anymore. Composition includes possibilities for how a writer might make meaning using graphics, font, layout, audio, video, photography, and so on. The possibilities are endless, and composing to support work in many adult professions will require that writers understand them.

The goal of this study would be for students to see more possibilities for using graphics and illustrations to enhance meaning, and to become more thoughtful in their decision making when composing with both text and graphics. The curriculum for the study will come from looking at texts where writing and some other form of graphics work together to create meaning for the reader. Across grade levels, picture books are an obvious choice to anchor this study, and while you might study any picture book, I'd suggest you weight your stack heavily with books where the writer and illustrator is the same person. Your students will make decisions as both writer and illustrator, so they can see evidence of this process in these books.

Outside of picture books, magazines, especially, are a good source for this study. Many articles in children's magazines use photographs and illustrations in close conjunction to do lots of the meaning work. With older students and more adult magazines, look for articles where the illustrations, photographs, and other graphics really carry meaning that is not in the written text. You can find texts like this in some newspapers too. *USA Today* actually does a lot with charts, inset graphics, and other illustrations in a fair number of its feature articles.

Websites are the newest kind of composition where a variety of different symbol systems come together to make meaning. A website with written text only would be laughed off the world wide web in a hurry! Older students might anchor this study in really looking at how meaning is composed in different ways on a variety of websites.

STUDY POSSIBILITY
How Writers Make Paragraphing Decisions

The convention of dividing long text into manageable "chunks" known as *paragraphs* took hold as printing presses began mass producing books for general audiences. The wisdom behind this convention was that readers could digest longer texts more easily if they were broken into smaller sections, and this wisdom still informs paragraphing decisions today. Outside of school, that is.

Perhaps more than any other convention of written texts, the curriculum in schools around paragraphs is full of myths. There is no such thing as "how to write a paragraph" or a requisite number of sentences a paragraph should have. The idea that students should learn to write a well-written paragraph before they advance to longer texts is ludicrous. If it's only one paragraph, it doesn't need to be one; you need at least two paragraphs for either one of them to make any sense as a paragraph! Paragraphing is about breaking long text up in sensible ways, and writers who are crafting long texts aren't thinking at the single paragraph level.

The goal of this study is to help students make better decisions about how they are chunking long texts into paragraphs, and your curriculum will come from studying how writers have made paragraphing decisions in a variety of texts. While it would be easy to say that any kind of text would serve this study as long as it has writing that has been divided into paragraphs, you can't just say that. Newspaper columns, for example, and many of the columns in magazines as well, because they are narrow, make breaks in texts far more often than if the text ran the full width of paper as it does in a book. Where the breaks come and how frequent they are is closely tied to the format in which the text is published. Remember, the goal is to break it up in ways that make sense and keep it from getting too long for the reader's eyes.

One decision you'll have to make, then, is whether you want to study paragraph breaks in a variety of published formats, or stay focused on one format such as books or news columns. Paragraph breaks in books, clearly, most closely match the breaks students need to make in the most traditional school sense of writing. Single chapters of books can serve this study well, as well as articles and essays that have been collected and published in books. One piece of advice: I would not equate page breaks in picture books with paragraph breaks. There is a different line of thinking that leads to decisions about where page breaks should come in picture books.

Another decision you'll have to make is whether you want to study paragraph decisions in both fiction and nonfiction kinds of texts, or whether you want to separate those. Clearly there are some different kinds of decisions made about paragraph breaks in a novel versus an essay.

To show their learning in this study, you might ask students to finish a piece of writing (topic and genre of their choosing) and then articulate why they made the decisions they made about where the paragraph breaks should go.

STUDY POSSIBILITY
How Writers Craft Texts in Interesting Ways

To anchor a general study into the craft of writing, you'll want to gather some texts where writers have taken an obvious, deliberate stance to crafting their texts in interesting ways. This is a good study to undertake when students have no experience with what it means to read like writers. The study will teach them to notice how things are written and to consider the evidence of writers' decision making in crafting texts. This reading-like-writers habit of mind is really essential to all other product studies of any kind.

A general study might also make sense for students who have lots of experience reading like writers if careful consideration is given to choosing anchor texts that will both broaden (seeing new possibilities) and deepen (seeing familiar possibilities in new contexts) students' vision of what's possible when crafting.

Select texts in a variety of genres (craft crosses genre), and look for a whole gamut of interesting crafting possibilities:

- approach
- structure
- ways with words, sentences, and ideas
- punctuation
- formatting and illustrating

Your goal is to become articulate about some of the crafting techniques writers use to make their writing wonderful to read. To show their learning in the study, students might choose a topic and write a piece in any genre, highlighting the specific techniques they've used to craft their finished writing.

Texts to anchor this study could truly come from any of the containers we've considered throughout the book. A few of the whole-text examples shown in *Study Driven* would make great additions to a stack of texts for a general craft study: for example, "Murphy the Dog: A Gift Who Kept on Giving" by Craig Wilson and shown in an earlier section, is very deliberately crafted. Excerpts from chapter books are especially good additions to craft studies in the upper grades, so have your students be on the lookout for passages you might use for this purpose as they're reading. So many picture books could go into this study, but here's a starter stack of just five of my favorites.

PICTURE BOOKS

The Barn Owls	Tony Johnston
Dreamplace	George Ella Lyon
Homerun	Robert Burleigh
Hello Harvest Moon	Ralph Fletcher
Welcome, Brown Bird	Mary Lyn Ray

STUDY POSSIBILITY
How to Craft Using Obvious Text Structures

Sometimes writers will use a very obvious text structure to organize either a whole text or a section of text. In May of 2002, for example, I clipped a Richard Benedetto column from the op-ed page titled, "For Bush, It Was a Week That Went Downhill in a Hurry." The roughly seven hundred-word commentary is organized so it moves predictably through the days of the week. Or there's the Rick Reilly column I clipped from the December 13, 2004 issue of *Sports Illustrated* about Barry Bonds' denial of steroid use. The first sentence reads, "I believe Barry Bonds." And then every sentence at the beginning of every single paragraph after that begins with the repeated phrase, "I believe. . . . " The obvious text structures organizing these two pieces are part of what make them interesting to read.

Much of the time the organization of text (meaning how all the parts work together) is very subtle and readers hardly notice as they move from one idea to the next, so seamless is the transition. But sometimes, as in these two examples, writers make the structure that's organizing the text very obvious. A study of structures like this is a fine way to both heighten students' awareness of organization and to broaden their repertoire of crafting possibilities to include structure as another tool they might use to make their writing interesting.

Other than an alphabetical structure, which I believe is suitable for study all by itself, I would recommend that your study be of a *variety* of text structure possibilities, not a study of a single text structure. This is because the structures themselves aren't the point of the study; the point is that structure is one way a writer can craft a text. If students aren't shown a variety of text structures, then there is no decision making left to them when it comes time to show the work of the study in a finished piece of writing. Students need to choose a text structure that will work best for the writing they'd like to do from a variety of text structures they've seen in the study.

You can find writers using obvious text structures to organize the writing in all kinds of containers. Writers of chapter-length books or very long essays, articles, speeches, and so on, often use a structural device to organize a few sentences or paragraphs (not the whole text), so excerpts of longer texts work well in this study. You and your students will want to be on the lookout for these as you're reading so you can photocopy excerpts for this study.

Here are two picture book possibilities each for a variety of text structure possibilities you'll want to look for in all containers and in all genres of writing. Most of this list is taken from *About the Authors: Writing Workshop with Our Youngest Writers* (Ray 2004).

BEGINNINGS AND ENDINGS THAT MATCH

The Trip Back Home	Janet S. Wong
The Relatives Came	Cynthia Rylant

A REPEATED PHRASE THAT TIES VIGNETTES TOGETHER OR IS A TRANSITIONAL DEVICE

In My New Yellow Shirt	Eileen Spinelli
Mother Are Like That	Carol Carrick

A SERIES OF QUESTIONS AND ANSWERS

Do You Know What I'll Do?	Charlotte Zolotow
Winter Lullaby	Barbara Seuling

A SINGLE QUESTION WITH A SERIES OF ANSWERS

Daughter, Have I Told You?	Rachel Coyne
I Want to Be	Thylias Moss

A TEXT THAT MOVES CLEARLY THROUGH A TIME PERIOD—A DAY, A WEEK, MONTHS, SEASONS

A South African Night	Rachel Isadora
What a Wonderful Day to Be a Cow	Carolyn Lesser

A TEXT THAT MOVES PREDICTABLY BACK AND FORTH BETWEEN TWO KINDS OF CONTENT

Before I Was Your Mother	Kathryn Lasky
The Two Mrs. Gibsons	Toyomi Igus

A TEXT THAT MOVES THROUGH A SERIES OF PLACES, PEOPLE, ANIMALS

So Much	Trish Cooke
Rain	Manya Stojic

A TEXT THAT MOVES THROUGH A *PHYSICAL* PLACE (TAKES THE READER ON A TOUR)

Let's Go Home	Cynthia Rylant
My New York	Kathy Jakobsen

A TEXT THAT MOVES THROUGH A SERIES OF COLORS

All the Colors of the Earth	Sheila Hamanaka
Chidi Only Likes Blue	Ifeoma Onyefulu

A TEXT THAT MOVES THROUGH A SERIES OF NUMBERS (COUNTING BOOKS)

Gathering: A Northwoods Counting Book	Betsy Bowen
One Smiling Grandma	Ann Marie Linden

A "TWO-SIDED TEXT" WITH A TURNING POINT IN THE MIDDLE

And Then the Sun Came Out . . .	Crescent Dragonwagon
Summerbath/Winterbath	Eileen Spinelli

The Work of Author's Notes in Texts

At the end of Kristine O'Connell George's poetry collection *Hummingbird Nest: A Journal of Poems* (2004) there is a two-and-half-page author's note that tells all about how the collection of poems came to be. No doubt you will be mining author's notes like this for what they can teach your students about the process of writing. In these notes—found in all kinds of texts, but most frequently in picture books—writers often tell about where they got their ideas for the book, and sometimes they share important information about the research and work that led to the writing. These notes can teach students a lot about the process behind writing.

What I'd like to suggest here, however, is not a process study but a genre study of author's notes where students look at a variety of books that have notes in them and then study both how they are written and all the different reasons why writers sometimes include them. You'll also look at the kinds of information in the notes, how it is presented, and where it is placed in relation to the main text. I should be clear that I'm not talking about the notes in an "About the Author"; I'm talking about notes written by the author to explain something about what reader's have read in the main text.

To show their work in this study, students could choose their own topics and genres and finish pieces of writing, and then write author's notes to go with them. They might also explain in an assessment how they decided what "work" they wanted their notes to do in relation to their main texts.

Articles in newspapers and magazines occasionally have author's notes published with them, so you'll want to be on the lookout for these as you read. Again, picture book texts are a very common short-text container for author's notes, and the study can span grade levels simply by using more sophisticated picture book texts in the upper grades. And remember, students finished pieces of writing don't have to be illustrated as picture books just because these texts have anchored the study.

PICTURE BOOKS

Flying over Brooklyn	Myron Uhlberg
Hoop Kings and *Hoop Queens*	Charles R. Smith, Jr.
John's Secret Dreams: The Life of John Lennon	Doreen Rappaport
Rock of Ages: A Tribute to the Black Church	Tonya Bolding
Visiting Day	Jacqueline Woodson

STUDY POSSIBILITY
How Writers Decide on Titles

Certainly a close look at titles could be a substudy for a day or two in any genre study, but I'd also like to suggest that you and your students might look at titles across genres as a study all by itself. As a writer, I know how important titles are to the finished work. The title of a piece of writing is actually a very important marketing tool, and both writers and publishers take them seriously. In syndication, feature articles and pieces of commentary are given different titles in different newspapers based on what would most likely appeal to readers of that newspaper.

Many students don't think much about their titles, and they actually *label* the writing more than they *title* it. But titling something actually involves rather complex thinking where writers have to consider what's important in a piece of writing and how to get some essence of that importance across. They also have to think about what might appeal to readers, which leads to deeper thinking about audience and the kinds of people who might read the writing.

This study is meant to help students become more thoughtful about what the title of something should be, and to develop a repertoire of possibilities for how titles might be generated. To show their work in the study, students might choose topics and finish pieces of writing in genres of their choosing. In an assessment, they would explain how they decided on their titles and how the work of the study supported their decisions.

Almost any text in any container will do for this study, but here are five picture books and five chapter books where I believe writers and their publishers have made interesting title decisions.

PICTURE BOOKS

Come On, Rain!	Karen Hesse
If a Bus Could Talk	Faith Ringgold
Ish	Peter H. Reynolds
Players in Pigtails	Shana Corey
Show Way	Jacqueline Woodson

CHAPTER BOOKS

But I'll Be Back Again	Cynthia Rylant
Bronx Masquerade	Nikki Grimes
Margaret, Frank, and Andy	Cynthia Rylant
My Life in Dog Years	Gary Paulsen
Witness	Karen Hesse

Appendix A

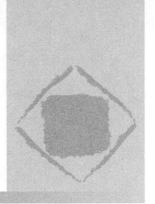

Books with Lots of Information About the Instructional Framework
Known as *Writing Workshop*

About the Authors: Writing Workshop with Our Youngest Writers
Katie Wood Ray with Lisa B. Cleaveland

The Art of Teaching Writing, 2nd edition
Lucy Calkins

Independent Writing: One Teacher—Thirty-Two Needs Topics, and Plans
Colleen Cruz

In the Company of Children
Joanne Hindley

In the Middle: New Understandings About Writing, Reading, and Learning
Nancie Atwell

The No-Nonsense Guide to Teaching Writing Strategies, Structures, and Solutions
Judy Davis and Sharon Hill

Writing Essentials: Raising Expectations and Results While Simplifying Teaching
Regie Routman

Writing: Teachers and Children at Work
Donald Graves

Writing Through Childhood: Rethinking Process and Product
Shelley Harwayne

Writing Workshop: The Essential Guide
Ralph Fletcher and JoAnn Portalupi

The Writing Workshop: Working Through the Hard Parts
(and They're All Hard Parts)
Katie Wood Ray with Lester Laminack

Works Cited

Professional Literature

Anderson, C. 2000. *How's It Going? A Practical Guide to Conferring with Student Writers*. Portsmouth, NH: Heinemann.

Angelillo, J. 2005. *Making Revision Matter*. New York: Scholastic.

Atwell, N. 1998. *In the Middle: New Understandings About Writing, Reading and Learning*. Portsmouth, NH: Heinemann.

Barnes, D. 1992. *From Communication to Curriculum, 2d ed.* Portsmouth, NH: Heinemann.

Berghoff, B., C.B. Borgmann, and C. Parr. 2003. "Cycles of Inquiry with the Arts." *Language Arts* 80: 353–62.

Bomer, R. 1995. *Time for Meaning: Crafting Literate Lives in Middle and High School*. Portsmouth, NH: Heinemann.

Buckner, A. 2005. *Notebook Know-How: Strategies for a Writer's Notebook*. Portland, ME: Stenhouse.

Calkins, L. 1994. *The Art of Teaching Writing*. Portsmouth, NH: Heinemann.

Calkins, L., with S. Harwayne. 1990. *Living Between the Lines*. Portsmouth, NH: Heinemann.

Cambourne, B. 1988. *The Whole Story: Natural Learning and the Acquisition of Literacy in the Classroom*. New York: Scholastic.

Campbell, J., and C. Collison. 2002. *Authors by Request: An Inside Look at Your Favorite Writers*. Hillsboro, OR: Beyond Words Publishing.

Copeland, J., and V. Copeland. 1994. *Speaking of Poets* 2. Urbana, IL: NCTE.

Dewey, J. 1938. *Experience and Education*. New York: Collier.

Dorn, L., and C. Soffos. 2001. *Scaffolding Young Writers: A Writers' Workshop Approach*. Portland, ME: Stenhouse.

Eisner, E. 2003. "The Arts and the Creation of Mind." *Language Arts* 80: 340–44.

Fletcher, R. 1993. *What a Writer Needs*. Portsmouth, NH: Heinemann.

———. 1996a. *A Writer's Notebook: Unlocking the Writer Within You*. New York: Harper Trophy.

———. 1996b. *Breathing In, Breathing Out: Keeping a Writer's Notebook*. Portsmouth, NH: Heinemann.

———. 2000. *How Writers Work*. New York: Harper Trophy.

Fox, M. 1993. *Radical Reflections: Passionate Opinions on Teaching, Learning and Living*. New York: Harcourt, Brace & Co.

Gere, A.R., L. Christenbury, and K. Sassi. 2005. *Writing on Demand: Best Practices for Strategies and Success*. Portsmouth, NH: Heinemann.

Graves, D. 1989. *Discover Your Own Literacy*. Portsmouth, NH: Heinemann.

———. 2001. *The Energy to Teach*. Portsmouth, NH: Heinemann.

Gutkind, L. 1997. *The Art of Creative Nonfiction: Writing and Selling the Literature of Reality*. New York: John Wiley & Sons, Inc.

Harste, J., V. Woodward, and C. Burke. 1984. *Language Stories and Literacy Lessons*. Portsmouth, NH: Heinemann.

Harste, J. 1992. "Inquiry Based Instruction." *Primary Voices K–6*: 2–5.

Heard, G. 2002. *The Revision Toolbox*. Portsmouth, NH: Heinemann.

Janeczko, P., ed. 2002. *Seeing the Blue Between: Advice and Inspiration for Young Poets*. Cambridge, MA: Candlewick.

Johnston, P. 2004. *Choice Words: How Our Language Affects Children's Learning*. Portland, ME: Stenhouse.

Keene, E. September 14, 2005. Workshop at Lovett Lower School. Atlanta, GA.

Kress, G. 1999. "Genre and the Changing Contexts for English Language Arts." *Language Arts* 76: 461–69.

Lattimer, H. 2003. *Thinking Through Genre: Units of Study in Reading-Writing Workshops 4–12*. Portland, ME: Stenhouse.

Marcus, L. 2000. *Author Talk*. New York: Simon & Schuster.

McClure, A., and J. Kristo. 1996. *Books That Invite Talk, Wonder, and Play*. Urbana, IL: NCTE.

Nia, I.T. 1999. "Units of Study in the Writing Workshop." *Primary Voices K–6*, 8 (1): 3–9.

Performance Standards. 1997. National Center on Education and the Economy and the University of Pittsburgh. Washington, DC: New Standards.

Ray, K. 1999. *Wondrous Words: Writers and Writing in the Elementary Classroom*. Urbana, IL: NCTE.

———. 2002. *What You Know by Heart: How to Develop Curriculum for Your Writing Workshop*. Portsmouth, NH: Heinemann.

Ray, K., with Laminack, L. 2001. *The Writing Workshop: Working Through the Hard Parts (and They're All Hard Parts)*. Urbana, IL: NCTE.

Ray, K., with Cleaveland, L. 2004. *About the Authors: Writing Workshop with Our Youngest Writers*. Portsmouth, NH: Heinemann.

Romano, T. 2004. *Crafting Authentic Voice*. Portsmouth, NH: Heinemann.

Rosenblatt, L. 1978. *The Reader, the Text, the Poem: The Transactional Theory of the Literary Work*. Carbondale, IL: Southern Illinois University Press.

———. 2005. "From *Literature as Exploration* and *The Reader, the Text, the Poem*." *Voices from the Middle* 12 (3): 25–30.

Routman, R. 2005. *Writing Essentials: Raising Expectations and Results While Simplifying Teaching*. Portsmouth, NH: Heinemann.

Schuster, E. 2004. "On the Necessity for Subversion." *English Journal* 94: 101–5.

Short, K., and C. Burke. 1991. *Creating Curriculum: Teachers and Students as a Community of Learners*. Portsmouth, NH: Heinemann.

Short, K., J. Schroeder, J. Laird, G. Kauffman, M. Ferguson, and K.M. Crawford. 1996. *Learning Together Through Inquiry: From Columbus to Integrated Curriculum*. Portland, ME: Stenhouse.

Short, K., and J. Harste, with C. Burke. 1996. *Creating Classrooms for Authors and Inquirers*. Portsmouth, NH: Heinemann.

Smith, F. 1988. *Joining the Literacy Club: Further Essays into Education*. Portsmouth, NH: Heinemann.

Watson, D., C. Burke, and J. Harste. 1989. *Inquiring Voices*. New York: Scholastic.

Whitin, D., and P. Whitin. 1997. *Inquiry at the Window: Pursuing the Wonders of Learners*. Portsmouth, NH: Heinemann.

Wiggins, G., and J. McTighe. 2001. *Understanding by Design*. Upper Saddle River, NJ: Merrill Prentice Hall.

Zinsser, W. 2001. *On Writing Well: 25th Anniversary Edition*. New York: Quill, A Harper Resource Book.

Trade Literature

Anderson, M.T. 2001. *Handel Who Knew What He Liked*. Cambridge, MA: Candlewick.

Appelt, K. 2004. *My Father's Summers—A Daughter's Memoir*. New York: Henry Holt and Company.

Asch, F. 1995. *Water*. New York: Scholastic.

Beil, K.M. 1999. *Fire in Their Eyes: Wildfires and the People Who Fight Them*. New York: Harcourt Brace & Company.

Burleigh, R. 1991. *Flight*. New York: The Putnam & Grosset Group.

Carle, E. 1997. *Flora and Tiger: 19 Very Short Stories from My Life*. New York: Philomel Books.

Chambers, V. 2005. *Celia Cruz, Queen of Salsa*. New York: Dial Books for Young Readers.

Cisneros, S. 1989. *The House on Mango Street*. New York: Vintage Books.

Collier, B. 2000. *Uptown*. New York: Henry Holt and Company.

Coman, C. 2000. *Many Stones*. Asheville, NC: Frontstreet.

Cronin, D. 2000. *Click, Clack, Moo, Cows That Type*. New York: Simon & Schuster.

Davies, N. 2003. *Surprising Sharks*. Cambridge, MA: Candlewick.

dePaola, T. 1999. *26 Fairmont Avenue*. New York: G.P. Putnam's Sons.

DiCamillo, K. 2003. *The Tale of Despereaux*. Cambridge, MA: Candlewick.

Doyle, M. 2002. *Cow*. New York: Margaret K. McElderry Books.

Ehrlich, A. 2003. *Rachel: The Story of Rachel Carson*. San Diego: Silver Whistle.

Ehrlich, A., ed. 1996. *When I Was Your Age, Vol. 1, Original Stories About Growing Up*. Cambridge, MA: Candlewick.

———. 1999. *When I Was Your Age, Vol. 2, Original Stories About Growing Up*. Cambridge, MA: Candlewick.

Erdrich, L. 2002. *The Range Eternal*. New York: Hyperion Books for Children.

Eugenides, J. 2002. *Middlesex*. New York: Picador.

Flake, S. 2004. *Who Am I Without Him?: Short Stories About Girls and the Boys in Their Lives*. New York: Hyperion.

Fletcher, R. 2005. *Marshfield Dreams*. New York: Henry Holt and Company.

Fox, M. 1997. *Whoever You Are*. New York: Harcourt Brace & Company.

Frazee, M. 2003. *Roller Coaster*. New York: Harcourt.

French, J. 2002. *Diary of a Wombat*. New York: Clarion Books.

Gantos, J. 1998. *Joey Pigza Swallowed the Key*. New York: Farrar, Straus and Giroux.

George, K.O. 2005. *Fold Me a Poem*. New York: Harcourt.

———. 2004. *Hummingbird Nest: A Journal of Poems*. Orlando: Harcourt.

Giovanni, N., ed. 1994. *Grand Mothers: Poems, Reminiscences, and Short Stories About the Keepers of Our Traditions*. New York: Henry Holt and Company.

———. 1999. *Grand Fathers: Reminiscences, Poems, Recipes, and Photos of the Keepers of Our Traditions*. New York: Henry Holt and Company.

Greenfield, E., and L.J. Little. 1979. *Childtimes: A Three-Generation Memoir*. New York: Harper-Trophy.

Hiassen, C. 2001. *Paradise Screwed: Selected Columns of Carl Hiaasen*. New York: Berkley Books.

Hundal, N. 2002. *Camping*. Allston, MA: Fitzhenry & Whiteside.

Johnson, A. 1998. *Gone from Home: Short Takes*. New York: Laurel-Leaf Books.

———. 1998. *The Other Side: Shorter Poems*. New York: Orchard Books.

Johnston, T. 2000. *The Barn Owls*. Watertown, MA: Charlesbridge.

Kalman, M. 2004. "Doctors and Dentists." In *The Milestones Project*. R. and M. Steckel, eds. Berkeley: CA: Tricycle Press.

Kincaid, J. 2001. *Talk Stories*. New York: Farrar, Straus and Giroux.

Kingsolver, B. 2002. *Small Wonder: Essays*. New York: Harper Collins.

Krull, K. 2003. *The Book of Rock Stars: 24 Musical Icons That Shine Through History*. New York: Hyperion Books for Children.

Laminack, L. 2004. *Saturdays and Teacakes*. Atlanta: Peachtree.

Lamott, A. 1999. *Traveling Mercies: Some Thoughts on Faith*. New York: Anchor Books.

Lester, J. 2005. *Let's Talk About Race*. New York: Amistad.

London, J. 1997. *Puddles*. New York. Viking.

———. 1998. *Dream Weaver*. New York: Silver Whistle.

———.1999. *Baby Whale's Journey*. San Francisco: Chronicle Books.

———. 2000. *Panther: Shadow of the Swamp*. Cambridge: Candlewick.

MacLachlan, P. 1993. *Baby*. New York: Dell.

McCaughrean, G. 2002. *My Grandmother's Clock*. New York: Clarion Books.

Medina, T. 2002. *Love to Langston*. New York: Lee & Low Books.

Mercado, N.E., ed. 2004. *Tripping over the Lunch Lady and Other School Stories*. New York: Dial Books.

Miller, D. 2000. *I Rant, Therefore I Am*. New York: Doubleday.

Minshull, E. 2002. *Eaglet's World*. Morton Grove, IL: Albert Whitman & Co.

Morrison, T. 2004. *Remember: The Journey to School Integration*. Boston: Houghton Mifflin Company.

Myers, W.D. 2004. *Here in Harlem: Poems in Many Voices*. New York: Holiday House.

Nelson, M. 2001. *Carver: A Life in Poems*. Asheville, NC: Frontstreet.

———. 2004. *Fortune's Bones: The Manumission Requiem*. Asheville, NC: Frontstreet.

———. 2005. *A Wreath for Emmett Till*. Boston: Houghton Mifflin Company.

Nikola-Lisa, W. 1991. *Night Is Coming*. New York: Dutton.

Nye, N.S. 1996. *Never in a Hurry: Essays on People and Places*. Columbia, SC: University of South Carolina Press.

Park, B. 1998. *Psssst! It's Me . . . the Bogeyman*. New York: Antheneum Books for Young Readers.

Paulsen, G. 1992. *Clabbered Dirt, Sweet Grass*. New York: Harcourt Brace & Company.

Pitts, L. 1999. *Becoming Dad: Black Men and the Journey to Fatherhood*. Atlanta: Longstreet.

———. 2003. "Players Foul Out When They Forget That Team and Sport Belong to Fans." *Asheville Citizen-Times*, November 2, 2003, section A10.

Prosek, J. 2004. *A Good Day's Fishing*. New York: Simon & Schuster.

Quindlen, A. 1993. *Thinking Out Loud: On the Personal, the Political, the Public and the Private*. New York: Fawcett Columbine.

Raschka, C. 1993. *Yo! Yes?* New York: Orchard Books.

Ray, M.L. 1996. *Mud*. New York: Harcourt Brace & Co.

Reilly, R. 2000. *The Life of Reilly: The Best of* Sports Illustrated's *Rick Reilly*. New York: Total Sports Illustrated.

Rosoff, M. 2004. *How I Live Now*. New York: Wendy Lamb Books.

Ryckman, L. 2005. "Prepare to Bare," *Asheville Citizen-Times*, June 28, 2005, D–1.

Ryder, J. 1996. *Earthdance*. New York: Henry Holt.

Rylant, C. 1982. *When I Was Young in the Mountains*. New York: Dutton.

———. 1984. *Waiting to Waltz: A Childhood*. New York: Simon & Schuster.

———. 1985. *Every Living Thing*. New York: Aladdin Books.

———. 1991. *Appalachia: The Voices of Sleeping Birds*. New York: Harcourt Brace Jovanovich.

———. 1992. *Missing May*. New York: Dell.

———. 1994. *Something Permanent*. New York: Harcourt Brace & Company.

————. 1996. *The Whales*. New York: The Blue Sky Press.

————. 1998. *Scarecrow*. New York: Harcourt Brace & Company.

————. 2000. *In November*. New York: Harcourt.

————. 2000. *The Wonderful Happens*. New York: Simon & Schuster.

————. 2001. *The Great Gracie Chase*. New York: The Blue Sky Press.

————. 2002. *Christmas in the Country*. New York: Blue Sky Press.

————. 2003. *God Went to Beauty School*. New York: Harper Tempest.

Sachar, L. 1998. *Holes*. New York: Frances Foster Books.

Scieszka, J., ed. 2005. *Guys Write for Guys Read*. New York: Viking.

Smith, Jr., C.R. 2003. *Hoop Queens*. Cambridge, MA: Candlewick.

————. 2004. *Hoop Kings*. Cambridge, MA: Candlewick.

Smith, D.J. 2002. *If the World Were a Village: A Book About the World's People*. Tonawanda, NY: Kids Can Press.

Smith, G. 2000. *Beyond the Game: The Collected Sportswriting of Gary Smith*. New York: Atlantic Monthly Press.

Soto, G. 1985. *Living Up the Street*. New York: Laurel Leaf Books.

Spinelli, J. 2000. *Stargirl*. New York: Alfred A. Knopf.

————. 2002. *Loser*. New York: Joanna Cotler Books.

Steckel, R., and M. Steckel, eds. 2004. *The Milestones Project: Celebrating Childhood Around the World*. Berkeley, CA: Tricycle Press.

Swinburne, S.R. 1999. *Coyote: North America's Dog*. New York: Boyds Mills Press.

Thomas, J.C., ed. 2003. *Linda Brown, You Are Not Alone: The Brown v. Board of Education Decision*. New York: Jump at the Sun.

Torricelli, R. 1999. *In Our Own Words: Extraordinary Speeches of the American Century*. New York: Washington Square Press.

Velasquez, E. 2001. *Grandma's Records*. New York: Walker & Company.

Wallace, K. 1998. *Gentle Giant Octopus*. Cambridge, MA: Candlewick.

Weatherford, C.B. 2002. *Remember the Bridge: Poems of a People*. New York: Philomel Books.

White, E.B. 1952. *Charlotte's Web*. New York: Harper Collins.

Woodson, J. 2005. *Show Way*. New York: G.P. Putnam's Sons.

Wulffson, D. 2000. *Toys! Amazing Stories Behind Some Great Inventions*. New York: Henry Holt & Company.

————. 2001. *The Kid Who Invented the Trampoline: More Surprising Stories About Inventions*. New York: Dutton Children's Books.

Yolen, J. 2003. *Hoptoad*. New York. Harcourt.

Index

class publications, 160
Cleaveland, Lisa, 9–15, 19, 20, 22–23, 25, 27–29, 30, 51, 56, 76, 109–10, 111, 141, 151, 164, 256
Click magazine, 222
"Close Encounters" (Berry), 150
close study, 19, 111, 128–37
    immersion and, 129
    possibilities for, 157–58
    process studies and, 168
    purpose of, 140
    returning to individual texts for, 133–34
    time allotted for, 128–29
    touchstone texts for, 133–35
    ways of working, 129
    working from whole-class lists of student noticings, 129–32
    working with a single question in mind, 134–36
    of writing process, 170–76
Coates, Ta-Nehisi Paul, 96
Cobblestone, 200
coffee table books, 245
collections
    biographical sketches, 233–34
    essays, 213
    family stories, 204
    feature stories, 217
    historical narrative, 202
    interview-based feature articles, 228
    memoir, 193–94
    practical how-to writing, 221
    as resources, 191
    short stories, 196–97
    slice-of-life writing, 249
    as study texts, 71
Collier, Brian, 55
Collison, Cathy, 228
colons, 14f, 27–28
color, text structure based on, 264
columnists, 235–37. *See also* commentary; editorials
Coman, Carolyn, 34
commas, 14f
commentary. *See also* essays
    characteristics of, 26
    defined, 235
    examples of, 3, 4f
    functions of, 5f
    reading, 4–5
    simplifying, for students, 27
    student involvement in, 6–7
    study possibilities, 235–37
    for teachers' writing collections, 75
    text selection for, 66–67
commentary study example, 3–8, 90
    approximation in, 91

assessment of, 7f
    genre study and, 51
    guiding questions for, 6
    planning, 6
    student interest in, 6
    student writing examples, 8f
    text selection for, 3, 96, 102–3
conferring, 29, 165
content, texts moving between types of, 263
content expertise, 29
cookbooks, 251
Coulter, Emilie, 242f
counting books, 38–42, 264
    student example, 39t–42f
    writing techniques, 38
Cow (Doyle), 145–46
Coyote: North America's Dog (Swinburne), 72
Craft, Lori, 241f
craft magazines, 68
Craft Pauses. *See also* writing craft
    deliberate overuse of words, 21
    description, 106
    engaging the reader, 178
    leads, 52
    memoir endings, 150
    phrasing, 163
    present tense, 138–39
    purpose of, xiii, 143
    referring to details, 123
    repetition, 63, 93–94
    show, don't tell, 34
    voice, 77
"creative nonfiction," 56
Creech, Sharon, 172
Cricket, 69, 196
culinary magazines, 251
"Culture Comes to Pearl Street" (Hiers), 195f
curriculum, 140–49
    myth, 177
    noticings and, 141–43
    part-to-whole framework, 31
    studies and, xii, 84–90
    "uncovering," 19
    whole-part-whole framework, 31
    writing instruction and, 185
    writing performance standards, 86–87
curriculum translation, 85–90, 88

Dallas Morning News, 240f
Davies, Nicola, 90–91, 178
dePaola, Tomie, 72
descriptive writing
    in fiction excerpts, 72
    function of, 54
    as mode, 58

noticing, 77, 106
    real-world writing *vs.,* 53
    study possibilities, 251–52
details, noticing, in writing, 123
Detroit Free Press, 67, 228
Dewey, John, 25
DiCamillo, Katie, 149
Dig, 69
directions, writing, 87–88
discipline, 32
discipline-based inquiry, 25
discussion
    about noticings, 142
    about writing process, 165, 169
    idea development and, 157
    time needed for, 180–81
"Disney World" (student writing), 103–4
"Does Your Pet Come with Papers? Pet Resumes Newest Trend in Lease Negotiations" (Lesel), 226f
Dorn, L., 54
Doyle, Malachy, 145, 146
drafting, 158
Dream Weaver (London), 146

Eagle's World (Minshull), 12f
Earthdance (Ryder), 146
eastoftheweb.com, 73, 198
editorials
    defined, 235
    selection of, 66–67
    study possibilities, 235–37
Ehrlich, Amy, 52, 71
Eisner, Elliot, 30
ellipsis
    student comments about, 14f
    study of, 9–15
    thinking about, 22–23
    uses of, 9–10
    writing craft and, 101
empathy, of teachers, 184
endings, to memoirs, 150
end-of-year photo essays, 67
Erdrich, Louise, 144, 150
Esperanza Rising (Ryan), 204
essays. *See also* commentary
    defined, 209
    five-paragraph, 26, 27
    journeylike, 209
    length of, 65
    in magazines, 236
    picture books and, 70
    studies of, 78
    study possibilities, 209–14
    writing craft and, 101
Eugenides, Jeffrey, 93
evaluation, 160–61. *See also* assessment; testing

historical narrative
  historical fiction *vs.*, 201
  study possibilities, 201–2
Holes, 183
Hoop Kings (Smith), 47
Hoop Queens (Smith), 47
Hoptoad (Yolen), 13f
House on Mango Street (Cisneros), 35, 38
How I Live Now (Rosoff), 58
how-to writing
  article types, 75
  informative, 222–23
  as narrative procedures, 87, 88
  practical, 220–21, 224
How Writers Work (Fletcher), 171
Hummingbird Nest: A Journal of Poems
  (George), 265
humor, as writing craft, 102
Hundal, Nancy, 163

idea development
  discussion and, 157
  for feature articles, 121f
  in writer's notebooks, 156–57
If the World Were a Village (Smith), 70
illustration
  study possibilities, 257
  writing *vs.*, 74
immersion, 19, 30, 111, 124–28
  close study and, 129
  possibilities for, 125–28, 156–57
  process studies and, 168
  reading aloud during, 126–27
  writing process and, 168–70
Independent, The (newspaper), 21
independent reading, 124
independent work time
  close study, 157–58
  reading immersion, 156–57
  writing under the influence, 159–60
independent writing
  activities during, 113
  back-up work, 155
  planning for, 81–83
  Student Questionnaire for, 82f
  time for, 151
informative how-to writing, 222–23
In November (Rylant), 55
"In Order of Importance" (Reilly), 99
In Our Own Words (Torricelli), 71
inquiry. *See also* studies
  about punctuation decisions, 146–49
  context for, 113
  discipline-bases, 25
  immersion stage, 19, 30, 124–28
  noticings about memoir, 143–44
  noticings about picture books,
    145–46
  as predictable teaching, 110–13

sense of urgency in, 6
text selection for, 95–105
in writing instruction, 19–20, 22
inquiry stance, 19
  characteristics of, 32–33
  rationale for, 23
  reading and, 36
  reading like writers and, 25
  real-world writing and, 26–27
  value of, 27
"inside voice," of characters, 34
instructional expertise, 29
instructional framework
  menu of possibilities, 112
  part-to-whole, 31
  recursive nature of, 112
  for studies, 19–20, 110–13
  whole-part-whole, 31
instructions, writing, 87–88
intention, 46–51
  in biographical sketches, 232
  genre studies and, 190–91
  in historical fiction, 199
  in picture books, 70–71
  representativeness of, 99
  teacher's role in, 46
  tension in, 47, 51
  in topical writing, 251
  vision and, 47
interests of students
  studies based on, 83–84
  text selection and, 96–98
International Reading Association, 85
Internet. *See also* web sites
  advice writing, 225
  biographical sketches on, 234
  essays on, 213
  feature stories on, 218
  graphics on, 257
  informative how-to writing on, 223
  interview-based feature articles on,
    229
  list articles on, 231
  reviews on, 241
  short story sites, 198
  study texts from, 72–73
interview-based feature articles, 227–29
interviews
  finding study texts, 67
  transcripts of, 227
I Rant, Therefore I Am (Miller), 71

Jack & Jill, 196
Joey Pigza Swallowed the Key (Gantos), 93
Johnson, Angela, 71, 100
Johnston, Peter, 22
Johnston, Tony, 55
journal articles, length of, 65
Junior Scholastic, 244

Kalman, Maira, 144
Keene, Ellin, 179
Keeter, Nicole, 193
Kincaid, Jamaica, 21
kindergarten
  approximation in, 90
  counting book writing in, 38–42
  travel guide writing in, 42–46
  vision for writing in, 38–46
  writing under the influence in, 151
Kingsolver, Barbara, 71
Kirkus review, 134
knowledge base, of teachers, 27–29
Kooser, Ted, 124

Ladies Home Journal, 68–69
Ladybug, 196
Lamott, Anne, 101, 169
language, revising, 173–74
language studies, 78
leads
  engaging the reader with, 178
  noticing, 52
Learning Research and Development
  Center, University of Pittsburgh,
  85
length guidelines
  for real-world writing, 65
  for study texts, 65–66
Lesel, Helene, 226f
lesson-delivery stance, 24, 26
lessons, studies *vs.*, xi–xii
Lester, Julius, 78
Let's Talk About Race (Lester), 78
Levin, Alan, 138
Life of Reilly, The (Reilly), 71
Linda Brown, You Are Not Alone
  (Thomas), 71
list articles, 230–31
literary nonfiction, 56, 91
  noticings from, 141–43
  study possibilities, 215–19
literature review, 116
Little, Lessie Jones, 93
Living up the Street (Soto), 144
"loaded invitations," 22–23
local history, finding study texts on, 67
London, Jonathan, 85, 90–91, 146
Lopresti, Mike, 148, 149
Loser (Spinelli), 101
Love to Langston (Medina), 47
Ludwig-Vanderwater, Amy, 54

MacLachlan, Patricia, 134
magazines
  advice writing in, 224
  author's notes in, 265
  biographical sketches in, 232, 233
  children's, 69

Smith, Charles R., Jr., 47, 110
Smith, David J., 70
Smith, Debora L., 216f
Smith, Frank, 122
Smith, Gary, 68, 71
Smith, Jennifer, 45f
Smith, Michael N., 216f
Soffos, C., 54
"So I Ain't No Good Girl" (Flake),
    148
Something Permanent (Rylant), 78
Soto, Gary, 144
"Southern Journal" column, in *Southern
    Living*, 211
Southern Living, 68, 74, 88, 193, 195f,
    211, 220, 250f
specialty magazines, 68
spelling instruction, 182
Spider, 69
Spinelli, Jerry, 72, 101
Sports Illustrated, 3, 68, 236
sports writing, 71
standards
    time issues and, 179, 184–86
    writing performance, 86–87
Stargirl (Spinelli), 72
starter stacks, 191. *See also* study texts;
        text selection
    ABC texts, 238
    advice writing, 225
    author's notes, 266
    editorials and commentary, 236
    essays, 211, 213
    family stories, 203–4
    feature articles based on interviews,
        228
    feature stories, 217
    historical fiction, 200
    historical narrative, 201, 202
    informative how-to writing, 223
    list articles, 231
    memoir, 193–94
    multigenre writing, 254
    photo essays, 246
    picture books, 233–34
    poetry, 206–8
    practical how-to writing, 221
    realistic short stories, 197
    slice-of-life writing, 249
    text structure, 263–64
    titles, 267–68
    topical writing, 252
    writer's craft, 261
Steckel, Michele, 63
Steckel, Richard, 63
Steffans, Emily, 3–8, 19, 20, 22–23, 25,
        51, 90, 91, 96, 97–98
Stephenson, Crocker, 255
sticky notes, note-taking on, 127

Stone Soup, 69, 196, 240
story-level revision, 174–75
strategy-based teaching, 171
student publications
    class publications, 160
    formal, 159, 160
    published, 240
Student Questionnaire, for independent
        writing, 82f
studies. *See also* genre study; inquiry
    assessments and, 84–90
    based on students' needs and
        interests, 83–84
    challenging, 90–92
    connections between, 133
    curriculum guidelines and, 84–90
    deciding what to study, 78–92
    downtime between, 182
    evaluating student work during,
        160–61
    expectations for, 117
    fifth-grade commentary example,
        3–8
    first-grade punctuation example,
        9–15
    framework for, 19–20, 22
    gathering real-world writing for, 19,
        25–26
    goals for, 79–80
    immersion stage, 124–28
    instructional framework for, 110–13
    length of texts for, 65–66
    menu of items for, 111
    parent notification of, 117
    planning, 79–81, 92
    possibilities for introducing, 115–17
    preparing for, 111, 114–22
    of process, 83
    of product, 83
    punctuation example, 119f–120f
    purpose for, 79–81
    requirements for, 117
    sharing resources with others, 116
    student roles in, 23
    teacher learning from, 28
    text selection for, 65, 95–105
    types of, 78–79
    value of, xi–xii, 22–23
    when to start writing, 151–52
    whole class, 83–92
    working definitions for, 115
    writing under the influence of, 19,
        111, 151–62, 159–60
study texts. *See also* gathering texts; real-
        world writing; starter stacks; text
        selection
    collections, 71
    excerpts, 72
    feature articles, 67

historical essays, 67
Internet sites, 72–73
interviews, 67
length of, 65–66
local history, 67
magazines, 68–69
memoir, 67
newspapers, 66–67
picture books, 69–71
writing collections for teachers,
        74–76
Suellentrop, Chris, 214f
Sullivan, Andrew, 123
"Superdome's Past Glory Hard to
        Imagine Now" (Lopresti), 148
Surprising Sharks (Davies), 178
Swinburne, Stephen R., 72

Tale of Despereaux, The (DiCamillo),
        149
teachers
    empathy with authors, 32
    empathy with students, 184
    helping students developing
        intentions as writers, 46
    knowledge base of, 27–29
    as learners, 28
    modeling by, 31–32
    writing experiences of, 169
Teaching Behind About the Authors, *The*,
        151
teaching stances, 23–24. *See also* inquiry
        stance
    modeling and, 31–32
tension, in intention, 47, 51
testing, 179, 184–86. *See also*
        assessment; evaluation
*text*books, 140
text selection, 95–105. *See also* gathering
        texts; starter stacks; study texts
    access possibilities, 113–14
    collecting writing examples, 64–65
    collections, 71
    criteria for, 95–104
    essay collections, 71
    excerpts, 72
    genre representation and, 99–100
    Internet selections, 72–73
    length, 65–66
    magazines, 68–69
    for memoir studies, 143–44
    newspaper articles, 66–67
    previewing, 115
    readability, 98–99
    real-text qualities, 96
    short story collections, 71
    sports writing collections, 71
    starting a writing collection, 74–76
    student interest and, 96–98

by students, 116
for studies, 65
for teaching writing, 47, 64–76
variety in, 64
writing craft and, 100–104
text structure. *See also* organization
alphabetical, 262
study possibilities, 262–64
variety in, 262
themes, establishing in leads, 52
"thinking ellipsis," 14f
Thinking Out Loud (Quindlen), 71
Time for Kids, 62, 69, 90, 228, 244
Time for Meaning (Bomer), 70, 186
time issues, 179–86
deepening writing instruction, 182–84
priorities for writing instruction, 180–82
standards and testing and, 179, 184–86
Time magazine, 68, 101, 123, 210f, 211, 228, 255
time periods, text structure based on, 263
titles, study possibilities, 267–68
topical writing
defined, 251
study possibilities, 251–52
topics charts, 157
touchstone texts, 133–35. *See also* study texts; text selection
Toys! Amazing Stories Behind Some Great Inventions (Wulffson), 71
transactional mode, 54
Travel and Leisure, 68
travel articles/guides, 42–46, 45–46
student examples, 43t–44f, 45f
Traveling Mercies (Lamott), 101
travel magazines, 251
Tripping over the Lunch Lady and Other School Stories (Mercado), 71
"Truth Behind the New Movie *Shark Tale,* The" (Mason), 219f
26 Fairmont Avenue (dePaola), 72
"two-sided" text structure, 264

"uncovering curriculum," 19
Understanding by Design (Wiggins and McTighe), 29
units of study, 24
on writing process, 165
Uptown (Collier), 55
USA Today, 66–67, 138, 222, 236, 248, 257

Velasquez, Eric, 144
video game instructions, 88
vignettes, 35, 78

vision, 35–51
expository writing and, 62
genre types and, 56–57, 59–60
intention and, 47
for memoirs, 74
in presentation, 73–74
reading and, 36–38
revision and, 29–30, 172, 173
for writing, 35–36, 38–46
vocabulary instruction, 182
Vognar, Chris, 240f
voice, 77, 163
Voices from the Middle (NCTE), 240

Waiting to Waltz: A Childhood (Rylant), 100, 175
Wallace, Karen, 141
War Poems for Dr. Green (student writing), 47, 48f–49f
Water (Asch), 55
Watson, Dorothy, 6
Weatherford, Carole Boston, 78
web sites. *See also* Internet
finding study texts on, 67
as genre, 73
publishing student writing on, 73
text selection from, 73
We Had a Picnic This Sunday Past (Woodson), 205
What You Know By Heart: How to Develop Curriculum for Your Writing Workshop (Ray), 57
"When Grace Arrives Unannounced" (Sullivan), 123
When I Was Your Age: Original Stories About Growing Up (Ehrlich), 71, 144
Whoever You Are (Fox), 78
whole class studies, 83–92
based on curriculum guidelines and assessments, 84–90
based on students' needs and interests, 83–84
on process of writing, 83
on products of writing, 83
whole-part-whole framework, 31
whole-school writing instruction, 182–84
Wiggins, G., 29
Wilfrid Gordon McDonald Partridge (Fox), 197
Wilson, Craig, 67, 248, 248f, 260
wire service stories, 243
women's magazines, 248
Wonderful Happens, The (Rylant), 13f
Woodson, Jacqueline, 163, 169, 205
words, deliberate overuse of, 21
Wreath for Emmett Till, A (Nelson), 78
writers, reading like, 24–25

writer's notebooks
back-up work in, 154–55
close study and, 158
evaluation of, 160
idea development in, 156–57
note-taking in, 127
process studies and, 169
writing
about writing, 170
back-up work, 154–56
counting books, 38–42
illustration *vs.,* 74
intention in, 46–51
learning from, 81
pre-draft, 152
quality of, 155, 160–62
quantity of, 155, 176
reading and, 37, 98, 121–22, 124
reading levels and, 98
selecting texts for, 47, 64–76
student examples, 115
time needed for, 179–86
travel guides, 42–46
understanding similar types of, 35
vision for, 35–36, 38–46
"What have you read that is like what you are trying to write?", 35–36, 53, 57, 59, 81, 83
writing conferences, 29, 165
writing craft. *See also* Craft Pauses
Craft Pauses and, 143
evaluation of, 161
present tense as, 138–39
punctuation and, 119f–120f
study possibilities, 260–61
text selection and, 100–104
writing instruction
framework for, 110–13
goals of, 160
grounded teaching, 25–27
immersion in, 19, 30
inquiry in, 19–20
possibilities for, 181–82
predictability in, 110
priorities for, 180–81
structuring for surprise, 110
student understanding of, 109–10
text selection for, 95–105
whole-school efforts, 182–84
writing mentors, 168–69, 184
writing performance standards, 86–87
writing process. *See also* process studies
author quotes about, 171–76
discussion about, 169
evaluation of, 160–62
interviewing authors about, 169
language of, 168, 171
process studies, 164–77
units of study on, 165